A Woman's Work

Also by Dorothy Jane Mills

Historical Fiction
The Sceptre (Patrician Publications, 1999)
The Labyrinth (Patrician Publications, 2003)

Education
Word Recognition: The Why and the How, with Patrick Groff (Charles C. Thomas, 1987)
Toad Charts, Paper Faces, and Other Ideas for Visual Comprehension (Scott, Foresman, 1988)

Essays
Fear Not to Sow Because of the Birds: Essays on Country Living and Natural Farming from Walnut Acres, with Paul Keene (Globe Pequot Press, 1988)

Vegetarian Cooking
Meatless Meat: A Book of Meat Substitutes (Patrician Publications, 2001)

Children's Books
Ann Likes Red (Pitman and Grosset, 1965; Purple House Press, 2001)
Ballerina Bess (Pitman and Grosset, 1965; Patrician Publications, 2002)
The Tent (Pitman and Grosset, 1965; Patrician Publications, 2003)
Big Beds and Little Beds (Pitman and Grosset, 1965; Patrician Publications, 2003)
The Sandwich (Pitman and Grosset, 1965; Patrician Publications, 2004)
Brad and Nell (Pitman and Grosset, 1965)
The Rabbit (Pitman and Grosset, 1965)
Stop Pretending (Pitman and Grosset, 1965)
The Pond (Pitman and Grosset, 1965)
Bill and the Fish (Pitman and Grosset, 1965)
The Crate Train (Pitman and Grosset, 1965)
The Pine Park Team (Ginn and Company, 1974)

By Harold Seymour with Dorothy Jane Mills

Baseball: The People's Game (Oxford University Press, 1990)
Baseball: The Golden Age (Oxford University Press, 1971)
Baseball: The Early Years (Oxford University Press, 1960)

A Woman's Work

Writing Baseball History with Harold Seymour

DOROTHY JANE MILLS
(Dorothy Z. Seymour)

foreword by Steve Gietschier

McFarland & Company, Inc., Publishers
Jefferson, North Carolina, and London

LIBRARY OF CONGRESS CATALOGUING-IN-PUBLICATION DATA

Mills, Dorothy Jane
    A woman's work : writing baseball history with Harold Seymour / Dorothy Jane Mills (Dorothy Z. Seymour) ; foreword by Steve Gietschier.
        p.   cm.
    Includes bibliographical references and index.

    ISBN 0-7864-1848-6 (softcover : 50# alkaline paper)

    1. Mills, Dorothy Jane. 2. Baseball historians — United States — Biography. 3. Women historians — United States — Biography. 4. Seymour, Harold, 1910–[1992] 5. Baseball — Research. I. Title.
GV865.M515A3   2004
796.357'092 — dc22   2004001524

British Library cataloguing data are available

©2004 Dorothy Jane Mills. All rights reserved

No part of this book may be reproduced or transmitted in any form or by any means, electronic or mechanical, including photocopying or recording, or by any information storage and retrieval system, without permission in writing from the publisher.

On the cover: The author with the three Seymour books and the first Seymour Medal ever awarded (Peter Blashil, *The Province*, Vancouver, B.C., 1996)

Manufactured in the United States of America

McFarland & Company, Inc., Publishers
  Box 611, Jefferson, North Carolina 28640
  www.mcfarlandpub.com

Acknowledgments

The staff of the Seymour Collection at the Carl A. Kroch Library of Cornell University has several times graciously assisted me in my research for this book. The collection is one that I gathered myself, over a lifetime of research and writing. In 1992, after the death of Harold Seymour, my late husband and colleague, I contributed this entire collection to the university, according to the terms of his will.

Reviewing our fifty-year collection of correspondence and some of the other manuscript material in the collection ten years after donating it to the library helped me recall, for my two web sites and then for this book, many of the events connected with my work on Seymour's dissertation and his three-volume series of books for Oxford University Press.

This book also uses some material from my web sites, especially from the baseball history site *www.HaroldSeymour.com*, which I wrote in 2001 and opened in 2002. I am grateful to Ralph Wallace of Chicago for his donated services in designing and mounting this site and *www.Dorothy-JaneMills.com* as well.

I also thank the Society for American Baseball Research (SABR) for the many attentions to me over the years since our association, especially since the creation of the Seymour Medal in 1996. Director John Zajc always responds promptly to any query. Members of both SABR and of the North American Society for Sport History (NASSH) have also generously contributed book reviews to the Seymour web site in order to make it into a more useful tool for researchers. My work on the Seymour web site helped propel me into the development of this book.

An even more direct inspiration for this book is an article that Ethan

Casey, CEO and Editor-in-Chief of the online journal *Blue Ear*, requested that I prepare. He asked me to write about my contribution to the Seymour books. SABR printed the resulting article, "A Woman's Work," in pamphlet form. Later, I was asked to expand on the article by writing a book about my experiences.

I also acknowledge with thanks the cooperation of those who furnished photographs for the illustrations of this book or who replied to research queries. That includes the staff of the New York office of Oxford University Press; the staff of the Carl A. Kroch Library of Cornell University, Ithaca, New York; William C. Barrow, Special Collections Librarian of Cleveland State University, who researched the Cleveland Memory Project and the Cleveland Digital Library; Vern Morrison, librarian at Cleveland State University; Tim Wiles, Director of Research for the National Baseball Hall of Fame Library in Cooperstown, New York; Steve Gietschier, Senior Managing Editor of Research for *The Sporting News,* St. Louis, Missouri; Ralph Wallace, President of College Sporting News and publisher of I-AA.org Magazine and TOTK.com Sports, of Skokie, Illinois; Barry K. Evans of Chicago; Ethan Casey, CEO and Editor-in-Chief of *BlueEar.com: A Global Journal of Our Time,* Surrey, England; Mary Ellen Kollar, Head of Social Sciences for the Cleveland Public Library, and her associate Ann Marie Wieland; Glenda Thornton, Library Director of Cleveland State University; Ken Burns of Florentine Films, Walpole, New Hampshire; Kate Bird, Librarian of *The Province*, Vancouver, British Columbia; Justine Siegal of Toronto; Jill Morgan, president of Purple House Press in Cynthiana, Kentucky; Diane Asséo Griliches, who granted permission to use one of her library photos; Jack Zerby, who snapped photos of me at the women's championship baseball game in Fort Myers in 2002; Professor David Zang of Towson University; and my husband, Roy Mills, who took several of the photographs used in this book.

I am grateful to the late Harold Seymour for having had the idea of writing about baseball as a part of American history, for courageously pursuing the first doctorate on the subject, and for asking me to help him in his work. Doing so not only sent me on an exciting lifetime adventure in baseball history but also helped me become a better writer and researcher. Seymour once told me that through my work on baseball history I had developed my historical research abilities to at least the level of a master's degree. More important, my work in this field opened to me the world of historical writing, which I later put to use in writing historical fiction on subjects close to my heart.

I'm grateful as well to Steve Gietschier for agreeing to write a foreword for this book. Steve is the only researcher who has examined the complete files of the Seymour Collection at Cornell University, so he is in the best possible position to understand the work I have done with Harold Seymour. I greatly appreciate Steve's keenly perceptive analysis of my work and my relationship with Seymour, as well as his well-expressed remarks about both.

Finally, I am deeply thankful to my husband, Roy E. Mills, who since we met in 1993 has steadily supported my work on this and other books, especially by his critical readings but by his kindness as well in making sure that I had the time to work at my writing.

Contents

Acknowledgments — v
Foreword by Steven P. Gietschier — 1
Preface — 3

1. The Starting Lineup — 5
2. Taking the Field — 20
3. Getting to First Base — 34
4. Delivering the Pitch — 52
5. Right Off the Bat — 69
6. A Whole New Ball Game — 84
7. The Knuckleball — 92
8. Two Strong Innings — 107
9. Curve Ball — 121
10. Relief Pitcher — 136
11. Cleanup Hitter — 153
12. The Change-Up — 165
13. Who's on First? — 182
14. Throw Like a Girl — 199
15. Extra Innings — 212

Bibliographical Note — 225
Index — 233

Foreword
by Steven P. Gietschier

The book you are holding in your hands is more precious than the memoir it purports to be. It is an extraordinarily personal essay, bearing witness in sometimes painful detail to remarkable achievement tarnished by haughty injustice. If Hemingway was right when he characterized courage as grace under pressure, then my friend Dorothy Mills is as courageous as they come. It might not be proper in some circles to call a woman a lady, but Dorothy is very much a lady. Betraying not a whit of bitterness at what she endured over many years, she writes with tact and restraint, disguising just how notable her story is.

Harold Seymour's standing as the dean of serious baseball historians remains secure. It was he, we cannot forget, who persuaded his graduate committee in the history department at Cornell University to accept a dissertation with baseball as its subject. It was he, too, who resolutely pursued his dream and got the dissertation finished, and he who turned a chance meeting with a representative from Oxford University Press into a book contract that led to publication of the enduring classic *Baseball: The Early Years*. And it was he who persevered in his chosen field to produce two more books, *Baseball: The Golden Age* and *Baseball: The People's Game*, to complete an unusual trilogy that forms the foundation of every serious baseball library.

How these events transpired, often against the odds, is well worth telling, and Dorothy does it with finesse and style. Graduate students in sport history and many other fields will be either amazed or dismayed at the number of research trips and hours spent cranking through microfilm before the dissertation and the books could be produced. Instructive, too, is her explanation of how to generate note cards properly and how to transform them into outlines and first drafts of chapters. The Harold and Dorothy Seymour Collection, now at Cornell's Kroch Library, inhabits some 71 boxes and is imposing testimony to the effort this magnificent project entailed.

What the collection also reveals, though, are note cards written in two different hands, one of them decidedly feminine. I have spent a good deal of time with these boxes, and they emphatically confirm the contributions Dorothy made to her husband's work. And that, in fact, is the crux of this book. Starting as what we might call a research assistant, she gradually assumed expanded duties, doing the research, taking the notes, organizing the materials, writing the outlines, editing the drafts, and eventually composing the text herself. Even at the dissertation stage, the extent of her contribution to the work probably exceeded the bounds of academic propriety. By the time *The People's Game* was finished, she had become a more accomplished historian than he. Throughout this process, though, Seymour himself denied the extent of her role and categorically refused to grant her work anything close to the recognition it deserved. He eventually grew reclusive and depressed, but his jealous behavior was in place long before.

When Dorothy first decided to set the record straight in a short essay she wrote for an online magazine, the baseball literary community was astounded. No one who had read the Seymour books had any reason to suspect that they were anything but the work of one person, a man whom many revered. Now we have before us an extended explanation of how these books really came to be. The astonishment remains, and it is burnished by a great deal of sympathy. Some may call Dorothy Mills a victim or a survivor or a feminist heroine, but these descriptors seem to me hackneyed and inadequate. Perhaps it is better to admire the depth and breadth of what she was able to achieve and to marvel at her ability to write about it with such simple dignity.

Steve Gietschier
Senior Managing Editor, Research
The Sporting News

Preface

When I was selected for inclusion in the 2003 edition of *Who's Who in America,* I assumed that I'd been chosen because of my work in the field of baseball history, and I submitted full information about my work in that field to the company that publishes this famous series of reference volumes. But when I received the description of my life written by the *Who's Who* editor, I discovered that it failed to even mention baseball! So I corrected it, stating firmly that I am the unattributed co-author of the first history of baseball by a historian.

I consider my work as the first woman to write baseball history to be one of my most important contributions to knowledge and to the advancement of respect for women's abilities. Although I worked in this field for most of my life, the world of baseball was unaware of my contributions. The opportunity eventually arose to disclose my heavy participation in preparing Seymour's dissertation and the three-volume history of baseball that followed in the years 1960–1990 under the name of Dr. Harold Seymour.

My article revealing this contribution, "A Woman's Work," surprised many. They wondered how I came to devote a lifetime to what was then the new field of baseball history and why I kept my contribution to this work in the background. This book explains how it all happened.

Dorothy Jane Mills
Naples, Florida, February 2004

1

The Starting Lineup

As I turned the corner of the street that led to my home near the end of Pythias Avenue, I heard, blaring from almost every radio on the street, the voices of Jack Graney and C.M. "Pinky" Hunter giving the play-by-play account of the Cleveland Indians' baseball game on station WHK. It would have been easy to keep constant track of what was happening in the game simply by listening as I walked past all the neighbors' houses.

That is, if I had been interested in baseball.

But sports failed to capture my attention. The doings of the Cleveland baseball team, or any other sports team, remained outside my interest, occupied as it was by the thrill of attending college.

The child of first-generation blue-collar Americans, I had astounded my parents by announcing that I yearned for higher education. By saving the money I earned working during my high school years, and with contributions from my parents, I became the first in our entire extended Zander family to get to college.

I was studying English, the love of my life, and beginning to realize that history, too, was opening new vistas of knowledge for me. But I had no inkling, that warm September day in 1946, that the three subjects of English, history, and baseball would eventually conjoin in a new field that would fill my entire life.

I couldn't afford living away from home to study, so I had to attend locally. Like other ambitious children of blue-collar workers, I commuted by streetcar to Fenn College, now Cleveland State University, in downtown Cleveland. Fenn's modest cost was something our family could manage. There I enthusiastically pursued everything related to the English language: studying its history and its grammar as well as its famous authors and the literature they produced, and engaging in writing of all kinds. I doted on reading, particularly historical novels like those of Thomas Mann and Upton Sinclair; they broadened my knowledge of life as well as my understanding of the power of ideas when developed and expressed by skillful writers.

Thrilled at the opportunity of attending college and studying English, I'm hugging my textbooks as I stand at the entrance to Fenn Tower, the main building of Fenn College, now Cleveland State University. Fenn College was also where I met Harold Seymour and began helping him with his work on baseball history. (Photograph by Lou Moore of the *Cleveland Press*, in Cleveland Press Collection, Cleveland State University Library, courtesy of Bill Barrow, Special Collections Librarian, and Dr. Glenda Thornton, Library Director.)

I was one of the lucky people for whom a lifetime goal surfaced early. Journalism was my goal, one I believed attainable. By the time I entered third grade I already knew what I wanted to do in life: work with words. In school and out, I wrote essays, poetry, newspaper articles, book reviews, fiction, and even the class play, a comedy peopled by titled aristocrats — never dreaming that some day I would actually meet and interview titled Europeans. "What do you want to do when you get to high school?" asked my sixth-grade teacher one day on the playground at Memorial School. "Get onto the high school paper," I responded immediately.

So in high school, journalism became my

specialty. I learned everything I could about applying my skill in writing to the style used in newspapers and to the production of the weekly high school newspaper, the *Collinwood Spotlight*. I even made friends with Linotype operators by proofing the newspaper right at the printing establishment and taking the opportunity of asking them to explain their work. One operator cast my name in ALLCAPS onto a slug that he gave me; I still keep it on my desk as a memento of fifty years ago. While I was writing for and editing the high school paper, one of my stories was picked up by a local metropolitan paper, the *Cleveland News*, and I felt pride when the writer, in his story, referred to me as "Reporter Zander."

Editing came easily to me: I started editing friends' work while still a senior in high school. I filled several editorial positions on the high school and college newspapers as well as writing for the high school and college magazines. As a sophomore at Fenn I earned money in the evening by tutoring adults in English; my English professor, Randolph Randall, recommended my services. My name appeared often on the Dean's List, and letters from college administrators complimented me on my "many valuable contributions to the life of the college in the field of extracurricular activities." Fenn twice granted me an Activity Award to aid in covering my tuition. These honors surprised me, because I was only doing what I passionately desired to do. Acting as Managing Editor of *The Cauldron*, the Fenn College paper, gave me the chance to exercise skills I had been developing since childhood.

I enjoyed my work as managing editor for the Fenn College newspaper, *The Cauldron*, as shown in this picture snapped in 1946, 1947 or 1948. (Author's collection.)

My father was a printer who was particularly proud of his spelling and proofreading abilities. When I visited his shop he demonstrated flatbed printing, in which the metal type is locked into a frame and inked; the paper is applied to the inked letters as the bed of the press moves. I noticed that my father hovered constantly over the small press he operated, adjusting a control or peering into the machine to check inking as he coaxed the machine to produce the excellent work he demanded of it. I grew to love the scent of printer's ink.

The college operated with a work-plus-study plan. During some semesters, students worked full-time at jobs related to their career goals. This plan also gave them a chance to earn some needed money and thus pay for their tuition. For my first job, the college obtained a position for me at the *Cleveland News,* where I acted as "copy boy"; when a writer called "Boy!" I jumped up and reported for duty, running errands, sending completed copy up the vacuum tube to the printer's floor, delivering mail and typed materials, picking up photos from a room that smelled of developing chemicals, and fetching coffee from a nearby shop and Cokes from machines in the lunchroom.

At the *News* I envied the men (all of them were men) who worked as editors on the copy desk, where they checked the stories for typos and other errors — especially the man on "the slot," the opening in the U-shaped table around which the copy editors worked. That man, Gus Utter, directed the work and assigned the headlines to be written. It occurred to me that I was performing similar work on the Fenn newspaper and that I might some day aspire to Mr. Utter's position.

Whenever I got the chance, I paused behind the station of a man (all of them were men, too) who operated a Linotype machine, watching with admiration as the operator, who controlled a huge keyboard by which he directed the machine to select each letter he typed, set it in a line of hot metal, then place each line of type in a long metal tray called a galley. A compositor then inked the galleys to prepare proofs that I felt honored to carry to the editors for checking. Those were the days when galley proofs were really made from galleys; nowadays they are produced electronically in the form of pages instead of long columns resembling ancient boats.

At the *News* I discovered that I was one of the select few who could already identify ETAOIN SHRDLU. That was not the name of an ethnic Clevelander but just the letters on one level of the linotype operator's keyboard. If the operator made an error, he completed the line of type by running his finger over that level, producing the esoteric-looking code name that some people were sure referred to an Eastern European who worked in the pressroom. Others thought Etaoin was the gremlin who caused the error, especially since sometimes the line with "his name" was accidentally included in a story.

One day I found a typo in the banner headline of Page One, although I didn't discover it until Page One had been composed, made into a curved metal plate, and inserted into the huge printing machine. The printing of the first edition was already under way when I pointed out the error to Gus Utter, who picked up the phone to give the time-honored cry: "Stop the presses!" Whereupon the thundering sound of printing stopped throbbing through the building, and embarrassed newsmen directed the printer how to correct Page One.

As I began my sophomore year in September of 1947, the *Cleveland News* publicized Fenn's work-study program with a story featuring four of the 300 students who were benefiting from it: a fellow studying engineering, another who was a psychology major, a young woman specializing in sociology, and me. The reporter described me, in the style of the day, as "Miss Dorothy Zander ... majoring in English with an eye to journalism as a career," adding that I had "spent the summer as a copy girl [a term obviously invented for the story] at the *News*," quoting me as declaring I had obtained "a lot of groundwork in the business. Books on journalism mean a lot more when you have observed the operations of a metropolitan daily." The accom-

Hal Lebovitz, one of the sports writers I knew when I worked as a copy boy at the *Cleveland News* in 1947. When Hal or any of the other writers called "Boy!" I reported for duty. (Photograph by Betsy Molnar of Cleveland.)

panying photo made me seem less clear-witted than do these words: it showed me chewing on a pencil.

Doris O'Donnell of the *Cleveland News* became my role model. She had made it to the exalted level of news reporter despite the usual relegation of women to lifestyle reporting no matter what their particular interests were. Men dominated the newsroom and kept the sports department for themselves. But after my college paper published a story about my appointment as managing editor, a couple of sports department writers, Hal Lebovitz and Howard Preston, took an interest in me and began to give me some routine assignments for writing "sports shorts"—one-paragraph announcements of coming or recent minor events. So despite my unathletic background, my first published stories for a city audience were sports stories.

Each day at the *News* I greeted—and was acknowledged in a deep voice by—the veteran sports columnist Ed Bang, who walked through the newsroom peering through his trademark black-rimmed glasses and leaving behind a miasma of liniment. I didn't realize at the time that Bang, in coming to the *News* in 1907, had succeeded the famous writer Grantland Rice, about whom I would read much later. I caught glimpses of Ed McAuley, whose sports comments rivaled in popularity those of Gordon Cobbledick in the morning paper, the *Cleveland Plain Dealer*, and those of Franklin "Whitey" Lewis, whose columns my Dad read every evening in the *Cleveland Press*.

Once a reporter on my college paper discovered and revealed that Case Institute of Technology had forced Fenn's withdrawal from a track meet, so I gave Hal Lebovitz the story. When he wrote it up, a writer on the other afternoon paper, the *Cleveland Press*, phoned him to mourn being "scooped." (Fifty-five years later, both Hal and I would be interviewed and featured in stories published by the magazine of our alma mater, Case-Western Reserve University.) Follow-up stories in the *News* about the track meet controversy revealed that the problem behind the dispute lay in Fenn's possible subsidization of its athletes. This is a topic I would not revisit until forty years later, when I began working on the history of early college baseball for some chapters in the third book I helped Harold Seymour write: *Baseball: The People's Game*.

In Cleveland of the 1940s, even without enjoying baseball I could hardly help becoming aware of the flamboyant owner of the Indians, Bill Veeck, who appeared to have an enormous amount of fun just being a fan among other fans. His lighthearted promotions like "Joe Early Night," as played up in the newspaper we subscribed to at home, the *Cleveland Press*, made for jolly hometown celebrations that Clevelanders talked about. Everyone knew the names of the players. I recognized Hank Greenberg when he and his wife showed up at a celebration of ethnic food-tasting in front of the Cleveland Art Museum. Like many others, I knew the name of the Indians' popular groundskeeper, Emil Bossard.

But even if I had become a Cleveland journalist, I could not have aspired to report on the Cleveland Indians. My experience at the *Cleveland News* made me aware that most women writers who wanted to pursue journalism, no matter what their particular interests, were relegated to the lifestyle section of the paper. At the *News*, women covered not hard news or sports but features like food, movies, and the theatre, or the page listing births, weddings, and deaths. Doris O'Donnell, as a general news reporter with a regular beat, represented an anomaly. Realizing this gave me pause, but it did not quench my desire to become a journalist. If Doris could do it, why couldn't I?

My other major job during my college years led me into a different branch of publishing. In November of 1947 I was assigned to the position of proofreader in the advertising department at Halle Brothers Company, a well-known Cleveland department store operated by a prominent local family. There I read and corrected proofs of ads that would appear in the three Cleveland newspapers. In the Halle system, the ad writers and the artists, as well as the art director and the advertising manager, all had a chance to make their corrections on the proofs, and the proofreader recorded them, located errors, and saw that all corrections were made before publication in the following day's newspapers and in a dozen other periodicals.

At Halle's I learned more about typography and graphic design as well as production. The advertising manager occasionally assigned me some copywriting and rewriting — higher-level tasks that I could handle easily. But before leaving Halle's I also wrote a report criticizing the department's inefficient production system, which caused much waste of time and duplication of effort, carrying with it a strong potential for error.

When I returned to Halle's as a proofreader the following summer, the advertising manager again assigned me some copywriting jobs and directed me to start copy markup work, which required deciding upon type sizes and fonts for the ad copy as well as placing the type appropriately. But the art director frequently borrowed my services, drafting me away from this fascinating work to model clothing for the artists. There I had to stand perfectly still for twenty minutes or a half-hour, sometimes on one leg or holding one arm high in the air.

At least through performing these physical contortions I got the opportunity of meeting interesting and skillful graphic artists, some of them Europeans. And during this second stint at Halle's I discovered that the department head, Anne Sinnen, had implemented my suggestions for improving the efficiency of the production system. Through Miss Sinnen I also met one of the best typographers in the country, Arno Bohme, as well as his partner Harry Blinkmann. From them I received a tour through the B & B typography house, a company known locally as the Cadillac of typesetters. Because of these two specialists in display advertising, I learned to appreciate the beauty of well-designed type faces, the felicitous arrangement of type, and the importance of proper spacing. Beyond that, Arno Bohme had been in the German Army and told me of his exploits; Harry Blinkmann, discovering my Germanic background, engaged me in a long conversation on German dialects. So from these fascinating persons I received not only instruction in presenting type felicitously, I gained some insights into German history that would help me fifty years later while writing my historical novels about Austria, *The Sceptre* and *The Labyrinth*.

My overarching thrill in these days remained my introduction to college. How exciting it was to learn on an adult level!—to be responsible for one's own education by pursuing every intellectual interest, meeting students from other parts of the country (many were older men and women attending on the G.I. Bill) and even a few from Europe and South America, as well as receiving mental stimulation from the intriguing faculty members I was connecting with. These instructors, I discovered with delight, lived mostly for the life of the mind. In addition to teaching us what they knew about their specialties, they were constantly learning themselves. I admired them immensely.

Foremost in my mind among these faculty members, aside from the excellent English faculty, was a history professor through whom I became interested for the first time in American history and who changed and deepened my understanding of European history. This man was Professor Harold Seymour, transplanted from New York City and a demand-

1—The Starting Lineup

ing but stimulating instructor. I discovered that the study of history was broadening my view of life and of the world.

While acting as secretarial assistant to Professor Randall, Chairman of the English Department, I learned that Professor Seymour, too, was looking for assistance, so I applied. By then Seymour had learned of my abilities in English and gave me his lectures to type; I found myself explaining to him how I could reorganize and edit them while I was typing.

Soon he was telling me about his doctoral dissertation. He had fulfilled the course and residence requirements for the doctorate at Cornell University and must now write a dissertation. This piece of work, I learned, had to be an original and unique contribution to knowledge, based on extensive research and complete with scholarly support in the form of footnotes and bibliography. I realized, from my introduction to the writing of college term papers, that preparing a dissertation must be a formidable task. Even finding an appropriate topic to develop would be challenging.

What topic had this history professor chosen for his dissertation? Baseball.

Baseball has a history? Well (I thought to myself), I guess everything has a history. But baseball? All I could think of was those radio broadcasts of the Indians' games and the reports in the Cleveland newspapers. Was there more to it than that? I soon found out.

Not only did baseball have a history, this professor was digging it out. He had spent countless hours in the New York Public Library unearthing material about the earliest known practitioners of baseball in this country and how they played. He had discovered the relationship of baseball to earlier games played in England. Most important, he had convinced his own professors at Cornell that the topic he wanted to pursue, early baseball history, was a topic worthy of scholarly study.

The members of Seymour's doctoral committee knew little about baseball. The committee chairman, Paul W. Gates, a specialist in American land policy, thought his students should follow in the field of their mentor, but when Seymour tried to pursue this precept he found himself too bored with the material to work on it.

Seymour then suggested to Gates that he study an alternative topic: a history of the D.A.R. (Daughters of the American Revolution), the group that had, in 1939, rejected Marian Anderson as a singer in Constitution Hall in Washington because Anderson was a black woman. With Seymour's liberal leanings, this dissertation could have turned out to be a damning document, one that the D.A.R. would certainly protest; Gates told Seymour several times during the 1950s that his work, although excellent, was "too contentious." Acceptance of this controversial topic as a subject for his doctoral thesis would have prevented Seymour from turning to baseball as a theme. (In 2002 Steve Gietschier of *The Sporting News* wrote me, "Where would baseball history be if Paul Gates had approved this thesis?") But Gates rejected the idea. It was then that Seymour turned to his true love, baseball, as a possible topic.

Why did the committee of historians overseeing Seymour's work become so forward-looking as to accept baseball history as a topic for a dissertation? Perhaps because two of them had athletic interests. Professor Frederick Marcham had once been a wrestler. Professor Julian Bretz once stopped Seymour in the hall and told him, "You know, when I was very young I saw Cap Anson play. And I've explained to Professor Gates that he shouldn't expect every one of his graduate students to write on something in his own field of interest." Marcham's explanation must have had an effect on Gates, or else the two men remembered the situation differently, because after Seymour's passing, Gates wrote me, "I was aware that to do such a project [write on baseball history] would raise considerable difficulty. Fortunately, most of my department were interested in athletics, and they agreed to allow the subject." Thus both Gates and Marcham later recalled themselves as occupying an instrumental position through which they could influence others to forward a project that turned out to be both innovative and successful. Memories are like that. It's one reason historians must view nostalgic and autobiographical writing with caution. (This book excepted, of course!)

Harold Seymour at a cottage near Monroe, New York, where we worked together during the summer of 1959 on the footnotes prepared for, but not published in, *Baseball: The Early Years*. (Author's collection.)

1—The Starting Lineup

Harold Seymour, born in Manhattan but reared in Brooklyn, grew up a devoted Dodger fan. He had played ball since early childhood and organized and managed sandlot teams of younger boys who loved the game as much as he did. They played on corner lots and then on fields like the Parade Grounds of Prospect Park, where hundreds of teams of the twenties and thirties gathered and competed for honors. On the Parade Grounds the teenaged Harold became known as Cy Seymour, after a famous professional ball player, James Bentley "Cy" Seymour, who was no relation. Whenever Harold was asked if he was related to the player, he would reply, "Sure. He's my uncle."

When Harold Seymour and his boyhood pals discovered Ebbets Field, a baseball stadium within walking distance of their homes, where the professionals played, they used every artifice to gain admission and see their heroes perform. And when Seymour was chosen to be batboy for the Dodgers, he became a local hero himself.

At the same time, he grew convinced that higher education lay in his future, and through a local minister he gained admission to Brothers College of Drew University in New Jersey, despite his poor record in high school where, in his final year, with help from a tutor hired by his mother, he passed the Regents' Exams only by cramming, thus making up for having loafed through his earlier classes, spending his energies on high-school baseball instead. At Drew he starred in baseball and ran the college's baseball club.

Thinking he might become a physician, Seymour soon found that the required afternoon science labs would interfere with baseball, so he changed his major to history and added courses in education, planning to become a history teacher/baseball coach. Unexpectedly becoming fascinated by history, he realized he wanted advanced training and took a master's degree at Cornell.

Before finding a college teaching position, he accepted a post teaching junior high-school history in Norwich, New York, having been assured that he would also coach baseball. But when he arrived to begin work he found that he would instead be coaching wrestling—about which he knew nothing! He enlisted the help of the star wrestler, learned how to coach and inspire the fellows, traveled to competitions with them, and produced a winning team.

After Seymour's passing I discovered that he had affected the lives of a number of boys, not only as a result of coaching ball teams but also by interesting them in history and by encouraging them to try for a college education — even helping them to obtain scholarships. One student, Ed Flanagan, wrote me later that Seymour, in his high-school teaching, "used baseball analogies and baseball names with abandon," thus "sparking the interest and pleasure" of many students. After school he also hit fly balls to the boys.

Seymour decided he needed the doctorate in his field. When I met him at Fenn College, he had already fulfilled Cornell's residence requirements. Proudly, he revealed to me that he had convinced his doctoral committee of the historical value of the unique topic he had selected to study. No historian had ever studied and written on baseball history.

He explained this to me at Fenn, where he had obtained his first teaching position after World War II; before then, he had taught at Presbyterian College in South Carolina, but he left teaching to help in his father's marine contracting business on the New York waterfront, where the company serviced war supply ships. Returning to teaching, he came to Fenn, with a small downtown campus and no baseball team for him to coach.

I found myself intrigued by this professor's unusual background. He showed his increasing trust in me by telling me colorful stories about his teaching R.O.T.C. students at Presbyterian College — for example, what happened the day an umpire failed to show up for the College's game against a hated rival, upon which Seymour was asked to take his place. At a tense moment in the action, when Seymour ruled against a home-team player, the P.C. manager approached and strongly protested the decision. Seymour replied in no uncertain terms, and probably in Brooklynese, that the manager was out of order, so the furious protestor retreated in a great huff. The next day in class, one of Seymour's students inquired about this conversation: What did the manager say, and what was Seymour's reply? "Well," explained Seymour, "he told me what a fine umpire I was, and I told him what an excellent manager he was." His students greeted this interpretation of the event with considerable hilarity.

Seymour owned a small plastic umpire's indicator, one that I eventually contributed to the Seymour Collection at Cornell University. It's doubtless the same device he was using the day he made his decision against Presbyterian College's team. This college is also the place he encountered, and encouraged, a student named Lou Brissie, who later became a big-league pitcher.

Seymour entertained me with stories about his war work on the New York waterfront, where he had taken over his father's business and had to deal with tough longshoremen and their union. He also suggested I start a Fenn College Liberal Club, with him as advisor. More important, he began explaining the work he needed to do on his dissertation. As we talked over his work in his office, I realized that Seymour and I were becoming not only colleagues but also friends.

We were both interested in education and in writing. At the suggestion of Dagmar Kunz, the editor of Fenn College's magazine, *Topper* (a student who, like me, became a writer), Seymour and I wrote related articles, his entitled "The Perspective of History" and mine called "Are We Learning to Think?" Perhaps significantly, my remarks in this piece, written before I even imagined how important research would become to my life, recommended "investigative efforts" to unearth information related to what one is learning. I was to spend much of my life engaged excitedly in such investigative efforts.

After a while Seymour revealed to me that his marriage had for a long time not been working as he expected. I was flattered by his attentions and charmed by his manner, and by the end of my second year at Fenn, when he began divorce proceedings, we were dating — but secretly, so that the administration would remain unaware of our relationship. As soon as his divorce was final and my junior year of college was over, we married, and I transferred to Mather College of Western Reserve University, since in those days being both student and faculty wife at Fenn would have proved awkward.

How I might address this man who began as my mentor and eventually became my husband was at first a dilemma. Only his mother and first wife had called him Harold; "Hal" and "Cy," his baseball names, seemed to me excessively casual for a person with his dignity. I settled finally on the usage common among academic colleagues: they last-named each other. He became "Seymour" to me.

It was during our courtship that my life took a major shift, for Seymour gradually convinced me that a career in journalism was too precarious, especially for a woman, and that teaching offered a more solid employment base and a more respectable profession than newspaper work ever could. Reluctantly, I gave up my plans to enter journalism, thinking that Seymour, as an experienced man of thirty-nine (I was twenty when we married), must know better than I did about such matters. In future years, however, I often regretted permitting myself to be led into a field that was not my first choice.

One of the important reasons Seymour wanted me to enter education is that if we were both teaching, we would have summers together to work on his dissertation and the projects to follow. And those summers together would prove crucial for our work, not only for planning, organizing, and writing together but also for the research trips we would engage in. So my entering teaching was a step that moved the baseball work forward immensely.

But not immediately, for in order to receive my degree in education at Western Reserve within a year, I needed to attend some summer classes and fulfill other requirements of the college that differed from Fenn's. And another obstacle suddenly loomed: Seymour was fired from his teaching position at Fenn. The college administration, in an effort to stave off financial difficulties, had decided to lop off all those instructors most recently hired. Seymour was one of them. His position at Fenn may have suffered by his publication of an article in the *Journal of Higher Education* called "A Communist in the Classroom," in which, with my editorial help, he described having invited both a local communist and a local capitalist to speak to his Contemporary History class, preparing the students in advance so that they could challenge the ideas of both. A magazine called *Best Articles and Stories* reprinted the piece. Seymour had also suggested to the faculty a course in sport history, but they gave him no encouragement for the idea.

At this point I could contribute nothing to our income because I still had a year of study ahead of me to complete my undergraduate degree at Mather. And Seymour was giving financial support for his two children to his ex-wife (she did not remarry until later). So instead of applying to other colleges and universities all over the country for a teaching position, as he would ordinarily do in such circumstances, Seymour scrambled around for something else in the Cleveland area. He found it in the Cleveland Better Business Bureau, where he soon moved up from investigator to vice president.

Now it was Seymour who had to work summers! I helped by writing material for his new job. Together we produced a periodical called *The Facts*, a newsletter warning members of recent business scams. I even

1—The Starting Lineup

drew the cartoon-like illustrations for this publication, receiving no credit or pay; requesting recognition or remuneration never occurred to me. In those days, wives helped husbands with their work.

I also wrote the dialogue for a new Better Business Bureau radio program, "Buyer Beware," which I based on information circulated nationally among the Bureaus. We both took part in this program, giving tips on how to avoid being cheated in business. Programs usually opened with introductions like, "My wife Dorothy and I will talk about gyp schemes and shady practices," and then went on to reveal and warn the public of current business scams. The program was aired on WDOK every Saturday noon. At that time I was a much better writer than Seymour was and could easily adapt to the styles of the newsletter and the radio script. His writing tended to the pedantic and even turgid, influenced as it had been by heavy exposure to stuffy scholarly articles, boring books, and dull dissertations.

At the same time we plunged into work on what would become "The Rise of Major League Baseball to 1891," the first-ever dissertation on baseball history. I was a member of the two-person starting lineup.

2

Taking the Field

The dissertation on baseball history that we were preparing soon became central to our lives. In our two-room apartment on the third floor of an old house (housing was scarce in Cleveland just after World War II), we began sorting and organizing materials in order to find out what we had so far on each topic and what was still needed — where the research holes were — and what the organization of the work might be. We did this by spreading materials on the bed that occupied most of the space in the "living room."

My studies proceeded at the same time. I had already begun working toward my master's degree at Western Reserve University when I started teaching in the Cleveland Public Schools in the fall of 1950. My assignment was to teach kindergarten at the Dunham Elementary School, so I took the Payne Avenue streetcar to East 66th Street. As I alighted from the trolley for the first time I realized that in approaching the school I had to skirt a boarded-up area. On inquiring about it, I learned that what I was to pass each day on my way to the school was an old baseball park, where the Cleveland major-league team used to play.

Years later, I found out that people with near-mythical names and reputations had experienced triumphal moments there. Frank DeHaas Robison, who also owned the Payne Avenue streetcar line, built this baseball park, known as League Park, and opened it for his Cleveland team in 1891. At League Park, Addie Joss pitched a perfect game in 1908; Bill Wambsganss made his astounding unassisted triple play in 1920; Babe Ruth hit his 500th home run in 1929; Bob Feller pitched his first professional game in 1936; the Cleveland Buckeyes won the Negro American League's pennant in 1947; Tris Speaker, Eddie Collins, Walter Johnson, and Ty Cobb all played there. Just a couple of years before my arrival at Dunham School, League Park had lost its famous big-league tenants to the new Cleveland Stadium. But I knew none of this at the time.

In the 1970s, when I lived in Ireland — especially when I took walks in the quiet gorse-bordered lanes at twilight — I often got the feeling of being watched by the ghosts of ancient people who lived there long ago. I wonder now if the ghosts of famous baseball players observed my passage at League Park, somehow leaving an impression on my psyche as I walked by this old baseball park daily in 1950–51. If I were spiritually inclined, I might say that perhaps they influenced me in some unknown manner to gain an appreciation for their exploits.

While teaching in the Cleveland School System, I was broadening my knowledge of history by taking graduate courses with Professor Donald Grove Barnes of Western Reserve. His obvious fascination with history and control of his subject came through during his lectures. With his toothy grin, his sharp wit, and his nonchalant appearance before us in heavy English tweeds even on the hottest of summer days, Barnes presented a unique persona. I think of him as an oversized elf in English tailoring, almost dancing with excitement over what he could tell us (or try to pry out of us) about the events of history and what historical research could reveal to us. From him I grasped the importance of discovering the key details that steered events in the direction they seemed to move.

When Seymour began receiving a salary from the Better Business Bureau, we searched for better living conditions and found a one-bedroom apartment in a new building in the west-side suburb of Lakewood. Because the apartment had no separate workroom, we used a second-hand desk in the living room and the table in the dining area for our work. He wrote in longhand; I organized, critiqued, edited, and revised.

Because Seymour did not type, the onerous job of typing the dissertation, in the form of an original with several carbon copies, fell to me. Three of those copies were to be bound. In those days before personal computers, the typing of the manuscript proved tedious, especially since it turned out to be so long that when bound by Cornell it became two fat volumes. In addition, footnotes had to be typed at the bottom of each page. I found it difficult to judge exactly how much space to leave for, say, six or eight footnotes, some of which might require several lines each. On one page, for example, the footnotes — five of them — took up half the page. Many pages required several retypings before they looked right.

Since we were both working outside the home full-time, he for the Bureau and I for the Cleveland School System, that meant research and writing every evening as well as most of our weekend hours. On many evenings I felt too exhausted to engage in the work, but I did it anyway. I learned to keep going by changing to another task when I became too tired to continue performing the one I was engaged in.

We spent Saturdays in the Cleveland Public Library, where we were unearthing unexpected treasures, particularly in the Charles Willard Mears collection, which included clippings, manuscripts, guides, scrapbooks, newspapers, photographs, and telegrams as well as helpful books. When I left the Cleveland School System for that of Parma Heights, I took advantage of the change to remain away from teaching for a semester in order to spend full time researching. I became so well known to the librarians of the Cleveland Public Library that they invited me to join them each midday in the staff lunchroom.

In the CPL's valuable old baseball guidebooks I found clues to unexpected events like early official discrimination against black players, games in which women took part, organizational meetings of amateur groups, and the extracurricular activities of major leaguers. I spent many hours studying early newspapers like the *Cleveland Leader*, copies so old that they sometimes crumbled into little yellowed fragments when I tried, ever so delicately, to turn each fragile page. When I rose from my chair in the library, tiny flecks that didn't adhere to my clothes fell to the floor in a little shower. The disintegration of historic newspapers continues to be a problem for libraries, which often lack the funds needed to preserve them as well as the space to store them.

The librarian in charge of the library's John G. White Collection, Francis Sommer, told us about a cardboard box of material on a seldom-visited mezzanine that proved to include priceless legal documents. We were delighted to examine the contents, for when studied, the materials helped us interpret the workings of the early baseball associations.

Besides the old *Leader* I used the *Cleveland Plain Dealer*. We were already subscribing to current issues of the *Cleveland Press* and *The Sporting News*, the famous St. Louis sporting periodical, so we kept up with current developments in baseball that way.

Librarian Francis Sommer seated at his desk in the John G. White Room of the Cleveland Public Library, the first important library in which I worked, starting with the 1940s, on research related to the Seymour dissertation and the three Seymour books. The mezzanine shown in the photograph is where Sommer produced for us the carton of miscellaneous baseball material that furnished new information about the early history of baseball. The wooden card catalog is one I used freqently. (Photograph courtesy of the Cleveland Public Library.)

At that time, with my meager experience of the scholarly world, I failed to realize that the amount of assistance I was giving Seymour with his dissertation was inappropriate. I was taking over not only the editing of each draft but also the research and organization of the material before it was even written. Moreover, I had begun outlining the notes in such a complete way that he could write directly from my outlines, often copying the very words and phrases I had used in preparing the material for him.

In those days the common joke among faculty members taking their Ph.D. degrees was that the wives of these academics were getting their

P.H.T. degrees. The initials P.H.T. stood for "Putting Hubby Through." Wives helped by working full time at jobs outside the home in order to support the family, by typing their husbands' writing, and by performing clerical tasks as needed. My P.H.T. was a little different. I was actually involved in obtaining and organizing the information needed for the writing of the dissertation as well as in preparing it.

The question of whether the arrangement we had fallen into was a legitimate one never dawned upon me. At the time I didn't perceive that my work life was developing largely along the nineteenth-century conception of a wife's role as "helpmate." My mind focussed instead on the engrossing material I collected and fitted into the pattern. I knew only that I was contributing heavily to a wonderfully unique historical project, and I was finding the work intellectually satisfying.

Using my help so substantially never concerned Seymour. He felt that because of having chosen such an unusual subject, he had to produce an extraordinary dissertation in order to prove that the subject was worthy of study on a doctoral level, and he was glad to have my skilled assistance in doing it. We worked well together, and as I came to have a firm grasp of the historical method, I steadily increased my contribution to the project.

Despite the excellence of the Cleveland Public Library's holdings, research trips also proved necessary. A few months after our marriage in 1949, we made our initial trip to St. Louis to perform research in *The Sporting News*, baseball's trade paper. This publication had long been operated by the Spink family.

J.G. Taylor Spink, nephew of the newspaper's founder, had made *The Sporting News* into "the bible of baseball," and we knew that research into this source was indispensable. The problem with studying back issues of *The Sporting News* is that in those days Spink would not sell microfilmed copies of the paper, so anyone who wanted to study them had to come to the newspaper office and use the film and the microfilm readers there. We may have been the first serious researchers ever to do so.

In his response to our letter of request, Taylor suggested that on arrival we ask for his son, C.C. Johnson Spink, but we were welcomed instead by another staff member, who enabled us to work steadily at the microfilm machines for three days in a row, so we met neither Johnson nor Taylor.

When I walked into that newspaper office, I felt all eyes upon me. There were, of course, no other women present. This was a sports publication, after all: few women wrote sports in those days, and none did at *The Sporting News.* Moreover, in those days most women wore hats and white gloves to all occasions outside the home, business or social, so I entered the newsroom in an elegant summer suit with matching accessories, while rough-looking men in tieless shirts turned from their typewriters to gaze at me in surprise. Some nearly knocked over their paper cups of stale coffee; others almost lost cigars from their open mouths. After my first glance, I paid no attention to them as I seated myself at the microfilm reader and was soon absorbed in taking notes. I was used to newspaper offices.

J.G. Taylor Spink, editor of *The Sporting News*, trade paper of baseball, in a typical pose — on the telephone. Taylor and his writers were surprised when I walked into his all-male newsroom in 1949. (Photograph courtesy of *The Sporting News*.)

When we returned home we received a letter from Taylor Spink to "Prof. Seymour" regretting "that you did not make your identity known when you were in our office" because "I recall you very well, especially your attractive wife. To be perfectly honest with you, I wondered why a man who had such a nice-looking wife was hauling her around to a baseball publication office to check some records." Taylor obviously didn't grasp exactly what we were doing there. Nor did it cross his mind that I might enjoy research; I believe he assumed instead that I had been browbeaten into accompanying a husband who wanted to "check some records."

We squeezed in a lot more research trips. In September of 1950 we traveled to Cincinnati in order to perform research in the collection relating to the Cincinnati Baseball Club that was archived by the Historical and Philosophical Society at the University of Cincinnati. The Cincinnati Red Stockings, as the first known professional team, required considerable attention in the dissertation.

To get permission for our visit, Seymour wrote, and I typed, "Mrs. Seymour and I will appreciate the opportunity of examining the collection" and asked if we could work on Sunday, too. In the collection we discovered a copy of the American Association's player contract and also studied the *Cincinnati Enquirer*. We went back again in July of 1952 to work on *Porter's Spirit of the Times*.

During the Christmas holidays of 1950 we made our first visit to Cooperstown to begin research at the library of the Hall of Fame, which at that time consisted of a small room above the Hall itself. We wrote J.A.R. "Bob" Quinn, then director of the library, to ask for permission to visit for research, and Quinn, a retired sports writer, acquiesced, although I believe from comments he made that he didn't really understand what we were doing there. But then, why would he? It was entirely new work we were engaging in.

The first important collection received by the Hall of Fame's library was the Mills Papers, from Abraham G. Mills (no relation to this author). Mills, an early chairman of the National Commission, was responsible for entrenching the Doubleday Myth. Eventually, the library also housed the valuable papers of August "Garry" Herrmann, a later Commission chairman, although accessioning the latter collection came too late for use in the first Seymour volume.

We were back in Cooperstown again in the summer of 1953, this time with the assent of the new library director, former baseball journalist Ernie Lanigan, who had succeeded Quinn. We returned to the library again in 1956, arriving Christmas night in order to perform research during the school holiday period.

In 1954 I traveled to Cincinnati alone, over the weekend of June 21–23, to use more files of the *Enquirer*. My tiny plane landed on the Kentucky side of the river, and I took a taxi to a very modern hotel within walking distance of the library, where, when I touched a button, the bed crawled out of the wall. I made friends with the young female librarian and enjoyed the weekend.

Staff members of these libraries, historical societies, and newspaper offices weren't as startled at my appearance in their midst as were the reporters at *The Sporting News*. After all, women had long dominated the field of library science. Only the sports writers who then supervised the library of the Hall of Fame seemed surprised at my presence and my participation in the research; I believe they thought originally that I had come for a social visit. They soon saw otherwise, and they quickly got used to me when they saw that I was interested in nothing but my work.

Heads of some historical societies were not always willing to let us use their material, however. In at least one case it took considerable persuasion for a director to permit us, as researchers, to even look at the society's holdings. This person seemed to want to keep the institution's archives out of public view permanently and entirely, thus preserving them from any contact with the hands of those for whom they were being saved. This was taking one's responsibility for protection of the archives a bit too far, and luckily we finally convinced the protector that we were responsible scholars who would refrain from damaging or stealing the society's materials.

In the summer of 1954 we also conducted research at the library of the city of Chicago, where we wanted to use the *Tribune* for the 1870s through the nineties. The librarian responded favorably to our request that two microfilm machines, not one, be available; the letter we wrote under Seymour's name said, "My wife and I will both be working on this, and we prefer to work individually because so much more can be accomplished this way." Being able to work on separate machines simultaneously meant double the amount of work done.

We returned to St. Louis in the summer of 1955, not only to work at *The Sporting News* offices again but also to visit the city library as well as the Missouri Historical Society. There we studied the *St. Louis Globe-Democrat* and *The St. Louis Republican* as well as the Society's collection of manuscripts and clippings. We needed the local viewpoint on that colorful challenge to the major leagues, the Union Association of the 1880s, often nicknamed "the Onions."

The *Globe-Democrat* was not unfamiliar to me. I had used quotations from it, and told a story about it, while writing a footnoted paper for my undergraduate course in American history at Fenn College (taught by Professor Seymour) about William Randolph Hearst's almost single-handed creation of the Spanish-American War of 1898. For this paper I utilized my interest in newspaper work by studying the role of newspapers in an important and pivotal historical incident. Seymour admired the paper and suggested I submit it to the Fenn College magazine, *Topper;* it was published in May of 1948, at the end of my sophomore year (and the fiftieth anniversary of the War), under the title "I'll Furnish the War; The Story of Yellow Journalism."

During the 1950s Seymour spoke for the first time on baseball history, at the invitation of his friend Dr. Frank Lankard, Dean of Baldwin-Wallace College in Berea, Ohio. Dr. Lankard had been Dean at Drew University when Seymour was a student and ballplayer on the college team. In fact, it was Lankard who had in the spring of 1931 received a telegram in Latin from the team's coach, Sherman Plato Young, Drew's professor of Latin, on the occasion of the team's first win of the season — which was also the last game of the season — an away game against New Haven College. In the telegram Young triumphantly announced, in the words once written by Caesar: "*Veni. Vidi. Vici.*" (I came. I saw. I conquered.) The speech Seymour delivered at Baldwin-Wallace College at Dr. Lankard's request, "Baseball: Mirror of American Life," was one he subsequently used several times in various versions, since it explained the way he saw baseball: reflecting American life as well as affecting it. Not until 1990, with the publication of the third volume of the Seymour baseball history, *Baseball: The People's Game,* would that view of baseball find its fullest expression in print.

In the fifties we also made several research trips to New York to perform research in that outstanding reference library, the New York Public, at East 42nd Street and Fifth Avenue, where Seymour had already found material in the 1940s, before I met him. He had used the library's valuable Spalding Collection, containing the Harry Wright materials (Harry being the first professional baseball manager) as well as the materials relating to the New York Knickerbockers, the first-known organized team of the 1840s. We were following up on the revelation of Robert W. Henderson, a librarian at the NYPL, in a 1940 article asserting that baseball could not have been invented in the United States by General Abner Doubleday, as had long been assumed, and we found more information that buttressed this fact. Henderson's book, *Ball, Bat, and Bishop,* displayed evidence that many ball games probably related to American baseball were played in England and the United States before 1829. We added to that research, too.

The NYPL contains untold treasures. Every visit is exciting. I still tell everyone it's my second home. When I first began using this famous library, its huge catalog consisted of an entire room full of wooden file drawers; just leafing through one of the drawers labeled "Baseball" created an entertaining hour. To examine a drawer, a patron removed it from the wall case, carried it to a nearby high and narrow table, and sat at a high chair, like the ones used in bars. If someone else was using a file drawer needed by a patron, that researcher was out of luck. If that happened to me, I attacked the research from another angle so that I could use another drawer. Sometimes a patron returned a drawer to the wrong hole in the wall, whereupon it was "lost" (out of commission) until a librarian discovered the problem.

Then in the 1970s the library threw away all the catalog cards, after photocopying them in the form of fat, heavy volumes stored in the same catalog room on shelves installed where the catalog drawers used to be housed. Presentation of the catalog in the form of heavy, hard-to-lift books at least preserved copies of the fascinating original catalog cards, many of which bore the original annotations of librarians. Now, as in most large-city libraries, patrons use an electronic catalog, so librarians all over the country are trashing those informative old catalog cards. I preferred the original cards, because I liked reading the individual notes inscribed in typical "librarian backhand" by anonymous cataloguers commenting on the various editions of a book, perhaps telling who edited each version, or explaining how it changed publishers, or directing patrons to the library divisions that each carried a copy of the book. The librarians' commentary, which sometimes approached chattiness, provided a valuable historical record of its own.

The NYPL's book-use system differs from any I've seen, even in libraries abroad. After using a catalog to find a book, patrons submit a three-by-five request form for each book they want to use, writing on it the author's name, the title, and the book's number or class designation. These forms are handed to one of the librarians at a desk located between two large reading rooms. At the desk, a patron is handed a ticket with a number, such as 352, and whether this number is odd or even decides which reading room the patron uses for waiting to have his or her book delivered.

Waiting is supposed to take place on a permanently-installed wooden bench with an uncomfortable straight back. The bench, well polished by many bottoms over the years, is big enough for only three or four patrons, so most people waiting for a book to be delivered just stand behind or next to it. The bench is erected in front of an electric sign, where a number lights up when a book or books assigned that number become available. Library pages — the people who actually locate the books — working deep within the bowels of the library, search the

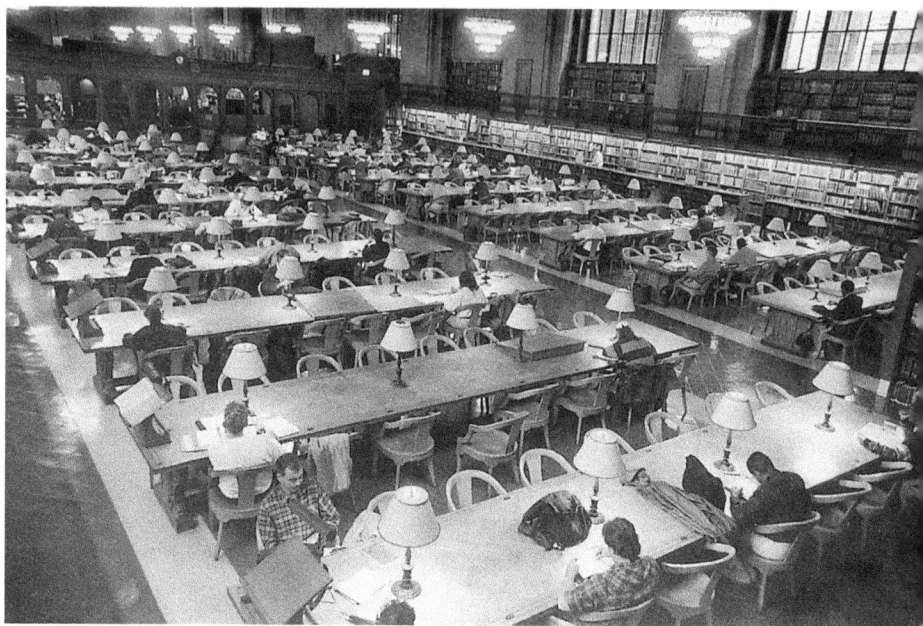

The reading room of the New York Public Library, my favorite of all great libraries, where I spent many hours of satisfying research for the Seymour dissertation and the three Seymour books. (Photograph by Diane Asséo Griliches from her booklet of postcards *For the Love of Libraries* [Rohnert Park, CA: Pomegranate Press, 1998], which originally appeared in her book *Library: The Drama Within* [University of New Mexico Press, 1996].)

stacks and send up books on lifts. As soon as my number lights up, I can approach the desk, present my ticket, and claim my treasure: the book or books I want to use.

When the librarians and pages become very busy, they limit the number of books a patron can order. And sometimes the area around the electric signs becomes crowded with standees waiting for what seems like ages for a book to surface. Occasionally an order form is returned with the regretful annotation "LOST" or "UNAVAILABLE" or "IN STORAGE." Usually, however, patrons leave carrying their trophies triumphantly and searching for an empty chair at one of the heavy tables in the huge reading room.

This reading room is one of my favorite places in the world. In *For the Love of Libraries* by photographer Diane Griliches, she presents a fine photo of this room — or, rather, one of the two rooms separated by the two-sided booth where patrons pick up their ordered books. In her photo, people work calmly at stations very familiar to me: a couple of dozen long library tables each bearing four permanently-installed reading lamps. She describes the atmosphere of the room as one of "quiet intensity," a "commodious space" that has "nurtured generations of writers and scholars." It's a place of discovery, a sort of public graduate school where those learning on their own can find the knowledge that speaks to them.

At the NYPL I soon learned that this library was also the repository of important sporting newspapers like the *New York Clipper,* and I used everything available in this set for the early years of baseball. I read partial files of other early New York papers like the *Herald,* the *Mercury,* the *World,* and of course the *New York Times*—a newspaper I would depend on much later, in working on a different project, for its broad coverage of American and European life of the 1930s. Library pages furnished me with periodical volumes so large (sometimes two feet square) that I found them difficult to carry to a table. Other volumes, tied with cotton ribbons and bows to keep them together, or slipped into heavy tagboard envelopes, seemed close to the end of their usability, and I opened the pages gingerly.

I enjoyed examining the files of such curious old papers as *The Base Ball Tribune, The National Chronicle,* and the *New England Base Ballist.* Printers prepared these early papers with type no larger than eight points and inserted hardly any space between lines, so after reading a few pages, I had to rest my eyes by looking around at the other readers or by checking something else, perhaps a book printed in twelve-point type. The New York Public, as subsequent scholars discovered, also owned such important early sources as Henry Chadwick's *The American Game of Base Ball* (1888), Francis C. Richter's *History and Records of Baseball* (1914), Charles Peverelly's *American Sports and Pastimes* (1866), George Moreland's *Balldom* (1914), Harry Palmer's *Athletic Sports in America* (1889), and important early baseball guides like De Witt's and Spalding's. We of course examined volumes like Robert Smith's 1947 book on baseball, Alfred H. Spink's *The National Game* (1910), Adrian "Cap" Anson's *A Ball Player's Career* (1900), Gustaf Axelson's *"Commy"* (1919), and Bucky Harris's *Playing the Game: From Mine Boy to Manager* (1925). All these sources contributed their authors' own personal views as well as information about early baseball in America, and some of them, their historical value more appreciated now, are even being republished. The NYPL also owns vital journals like *Baseball Magazine* as well as early boys' books containing striking illustrations of baseball being played long before 1839, when Doubleday supposedly invented the game.

At the NYPL we also used the manuscript room, where rare items may be examined by scholars who obtain special permission and who sign a solemn promise not to bring pens into the room, since inadvertent ink marks could deface irreplaceable materials. I learned to carry in my purse several sharpened pencils with good erasers. Nowadays, of course, laptops are permitted in collections of rare items.

The other kind of library I enjoy is the kind that permits students to go directly into the stacks, like Cornell's Olin Library, the Cleveland State University Library, part of the Cleveland Public Library, and the University of Victoria Library in Victoria, British Columbia, Canada. In this kind of library I can scan an entire shelf and locate books related to the one I am searching for, sources that I didn't realize existed and ones that might offer even more information on my subject than the book I am looking for. Besides, I can either sit at a tiny desk between the stacks to examine these books or, in some libraries, just sink to the floor with an armful of books and wallow in them, as booklovers like me enjoy doing.

In the fifties, besides researching in libraries and historical societies, we produced Seymour's article on Harry Wright, called "Baseball's First Professional Manager," for the *Ohio Historical Society Journal*. Wright is an important baseball figure who is only now attracting the attention he deserves from researchers.

In August of 1955 Seymour received a letter from Boyd Shafer of the American Historical Association, who stated that a scholar named David Q. Voigt had attempted to record his declaration of the topic of the history of American baseball for a Ph.D. dissertation. Boyd stated that he had informed Voigt that Seymour, having already registered that topic, owned the priority. We heard the following month from Voigt, asking for Seymour's plan for his dissertation — was he going ahead with it? Seymour replied that not only did he plan to go ahead, his thesis was "virtually complete" and "rather catholic in scope." Voigt had in mind possibly splitting the field between them, but Seymour would have none of it. We were, in fact, fully launched and deeply involved in producing what would prove to be something entirely unique: a history of baseball based firmly upon the historical sources.

By diligent work, we planned, organized, shaped, wrote, and rewrote the seventeen heavily-footnoted chapters that made up the final version of "The Rise of Major-League Baseball to 1891." The Seymour team was taking the field.

3

Getting to First Base

We opened the dissertation by asserting that baseball's importance in American society could be compared with the importance of the Olympic games in Greek history. Then we presented a section explaining why baseball could not have been created in Cooperstown, New York, in 1839, as long assumed by many who wrote baseball books and articles. This chapter, called "Baseball Beginnings," demonstrated that Albert G. Spalding's declaration of an American origin for baseball was spurious, for baseball had been played in England in the 1700s and had been enjoyed by Americans at least as early as the time of the Revolutionary War. Searches of old autobiographies and early children's books showed us examples of Americans playing baseball and its related games long before it was supposedly created by General Abner Doubleday.

To refute the claims for Doubleday, claims he never made himself, we described his life, which may or may not have included baseball (he said that as a youth he liked poetry, art, reading, math, and topographical work), and then we showed how it happened that the New York State legislature spent $10,000 to promote the hundredth anniversary of baseball's creation in Cooperstown — a creation event that probably never occurred.

To open this chapter Seymour insisted on a sentence declaring that baseball in America was less a sport than it was a business: a factual statement, but one that had to be supported. The support, in the form of a long footnote citing multiple sources, took up most of the page. I argued against opening with such a formidable footnote, which could prove to be a stumbling block to readers, but he countered that transposing the information out of this informative footnote into the text moved us too far off the subject, so I gave in.

In the second chapter we introduced the "nursery stage of baseball," which "revealed in microcosm the talent of Americans for private association." The chapter explained the contribution of the New York Knickerbockers to the development of American baseball by using descriptions by early writers about the American tendency to form clubs, a tendency noticeable as early as the 1830s. The Knickerbockers, described by an 1866 writer as "gentlemen," at first enjoyed playing among themselves. With a large club membership, they could, as other social clubs did, arrange their own matches internally.

The records of the Knickerbocker Club housed in the New York Public Library proved invaluable for describing how they ran their club, played their games, chose their equipment, settled upon rules, and celebrated wins at jolly social affairs. I enjoyed learning of their banquets at Madame Fijux's and discovering, in reading their records, that they might sometimes try to play when "inebriated" or that they had to be restrained from using "profane or improper language" during games. Even the Knickerbockers were human.

The work we had done in early guidebooks and early newspapers as well as the scrapbooks of Henry Chadwick, an early baseball writer, helped us describe the entrance of workingmen's clubs into the game. Baseball could not long be monopolized by white-collar workers; others wanted to play as well. We found references to many such teams, some of whose exploits were described in the records. How interesting, I thought, it would be if these clubs, too, kept records of their affairs. Finding those records took many years and other researchers' work, but gradually some information on other clubs of the era were found. We ourselves located, in the NYPL, the constitution and by-laws of the Mohican Club, a group that considered itself "elegant and aristocratic," its members scorning to play on sites where "rowdies and loafers" congregated. There we also found the papers of the Eagles, the Takewambaits, and the Excelsiors in the NYPL, and those of the Socials in the Cleveland Public Library.

At this point in the explication, a very long footnote again interrupts the story. We had collected much information about baseball terminology, and in describing the way early teams played, the use of the word "hitter" sent Seymour into a long discussion of baseball terms that included references to the work of H.L. Mencken, the language scholar Mitford Mathews, and others who had commented on the phenomenon. My background in linguistics had inspired me to collect such references. Also mentioned is a 1949 article from my favorite magazine (to which I still subscribe), *The New Yorker*: "The Cliché Expert Testifies on Baseball," which I found, and kept for our files, during the summer of the year we were married. Now scholarly articles about baseball slang appear regularly in publications of the American Dialect Society.

For the third chapter, in which we described the development of "the New York game" as opposed to "the Massachusetts game," I drew two diagrams, one relating to each style of play, describing the baseball field used in each, along with a few of the more important rules used in each style. These diagrams are taken mostly from a little 1859 book in the New York Public Library called *The Base Ball Player's Pocket Companion*. Fifty years later I would read with regret about this little book's disappearance from the library.

To describe early play by the teams of this era, our work in *Porter's Spirit of the Times* and the *New York Clipper* proved indispensable. In this section, Seymour's detailed knowledge of the way baseball was played in the twentieth century enabled him to compare the games of a hundred years earlier with the modern style of play. The richness of the sources we used made it possible to present baseball of the 1850s and 1860s in colorful detail. I enjoyed selecting quotes describing a game, for example, as "a spirited and manly contest" and as a place where ladies might survey the players for "the qualities of what might make a serviceable future husband." One significant trend of the 1850s lay in the increasingly negative comments by spectators, whose "hooting" and "yelling" sometimes included "loudly expressed dissent" concerning the umpire's decisions. To fans of today, a comment by a reporter of 1859 who said some spectators seemed to think games were "got up" for "their special entertainment" seems humorously prophetic.

For the fourth chapter we presented baseball during the Civil War. With figures we collected from sources like *Beadle's* and *De Witt's* baseball guides as well as the *New York Clipper* and the *Ball Players' Chronicle*, I drew a chart showing the number of clubs at yearly conventions of the amateur association, a chart demonstrating that although the number declined at the start of the War, it began a steep rise in 1865. Meanwhile, baseball had already spread over much of the country.

3 — Getting to First Base

We also proved, by consulting regimental histories, that the Civil War did not bring baseball to the South through prison camps, as had been thought; baseball was played there before the War. By checking histories of the Civil War like Bell I. Wiley's *Johnny Reb* and *Billy Yank*, we were able to show that soldiers of both the North and the South played ball during the conflict whenever they had the chance.

Some historical societies were beginning to publish articles about local baseball as it developed very early in their own areas. In this way we discovered information about early baseball in the American Midwest.

I found evidence in a DeWitt Guide that by 1867 blacks had already formed clubs like those of the whites and that some "white clubs" might include a black player or two. The minutes of an 1867 convention of the National Association of Base Ball Players proved that the Association banned black clubs from its membership, so these black clubs were at that time already prominent enough to be recognized as clubs of a type that whites had to take into account: should members of the National Association play such clubs or not? The answer they decided upon was "no."

It was surprising to find that so many state, regional, and even national associations of baseball players and clubs had formed and set up rules as early as 1870, and that amateurism was already being undermined with surreptitious payment of some players and early attempts to collect admission to baseball grounds. These developments occurred as expenses for club travel increased and as trophies were offered for winners of tournaments. By that time, some players had decided to go into baseball as a livelihood instead of an avocation.

And then — earlier than others had thought — came the entrance of chicanery, in the form of a politician's offer to a player to break his written contract. Betting and intentional loss of a game followed, with the first player expulsion for cheating. No, not in 1919. In 1865.

In the following chapter, the fifth, we documented the way professionalism gradually took over the amateur game. As before, nearly every sentence brandished its footnote, some more than one. Sources like the *New York Clipper*, the *New England Base Ballist*, and the *American Chronicle*, which I had studied, helped substantiate our points. This story led to the presentation of the first-known fully professional team, the Cincinnati Red Stockings, led by Harry Wright. Harry's account books in the New York Public Library became the basis for the explication, supplemented by early newspaper stories and the descriptions in early guidebooks. Later sources, like Harry Ellard's *Base Ball in Cincinnati: A History* (1907), provided additional information, as did Lee Allen's work in his book about the Cincinnati Reds (1948) and information he furnished in a letter to us.

The success of Harry's team inspired the formation of other professional clubs, and the result was the association of professionals formed in New York in 1871. We were lucky enough to find the proceedings of this convention in both the New York and the Cleveland Public libraries. The early professional era also spawned the "muffin" clubs, who supposedly knew baseball theory but were "somewhat weak in the practical part of it," thus affording hilarious entertainment for fans.

What seemed to be required next, from the notes we had collected, was a careful description of the way professionalism changed the game, both in playing style and in the presentation of contests to fans. Our statements here were supported mainly by our notes from early guides and newspapers as well as convention proceedings, constitutions, the scrapbooks of the early sports writer Henry Chadwick, Harry Wright's correspondence and account books, some information from the early books on baseball, and even baseball songs of the 1860s.

Contributing color to the story were descriptions of the times Harry and his team played some rollicking exhibition games of cricket and the day his club held a festive champagne celebration on shipboard while trying to keep their merrymaking at a low sound level so as not to disturb the female passengers on board.

We then launched into the story of the creation of the National League, as a natural outgrowth of professionalism in the game. Americans seem to want to make a business out of every idea; baseball was no exception. As I think about this now, from the perspective of nearly fifty years later, I compare and contrast the American business-spawning tendency in sport with developments in Canadian curling, which, despite large and enthusiastic audiences, has remained determinedly amateur. Are Americans more financially acquisitive than other societies?

Curling's popularity in Canada stems partly from its broad base among participants young and old, male and female, but the top practitioners do not "turn professional"; they keep their day jobs or professions. Skilled American players in baseball, football, or basketball, by contrast, seem to desire to "go the whole hog," to devote all their time to their play, even if their careers can last only a few years, while they are at the top of their physical condition. So after their professional sport careers are over they must then figure out another way to make a living. The American tendency to make a career out of a game is displayed right from the time of these early moments in American baseball, when so many men who found they could play the game well discarded all else to devote themselves to it. "All or nothing" appears to be an American trait, that of many who aspire to membership on an extreme team.

While discussing the creation of the National League, we were able to bring in the contributions to baseball of the newspapers and of early sporting goods manufacturers like Peck and Snyder as well as Albert Spalding's own company, founded with his brother. Spalding's company thrived by means of vigorous advertising and Albert's close connection with baseball.

The professionals' baseball association had been riddled with problems caused by cheating on the part of both players and their backers. Our description of the new plan of Chicagoan William Hulbert for what seemed like competition on a more businesslike basis than the earlier association came from sources like the *Chicago Tribune,* the *New York Clipper, Sporting News, Spirit of the Times,* the *Cleveland Leader,* the early guides, Chadwick's and Wright's records, *Baseball Magazine,* A.G. Spalding's book (*America's National Game*), Spalding's scrapbooks in the New York Public Library, and the constitution of the new league as published in *Spalding's Guide for 1880.* Before this, nobody had documented the formation of the new National League in this way or revealed negative reactions to it.

The new league selected its member clubs carefully for the size of their markets and the skill of their players. Its "mercenary motives" were much maligned by clubs that had been left out of this tight cabal, but the *Chicago Tribune,* which became the league's mouthpiece, explained that the decisions made by the new governing group were merely businesslike. From now on, only one club in each city would operate as league members; the other clubs were cast aside, to go it on their own. Newspaper reporters saw the new league as it really was: a monopoly. Everyone who has read American history knows that the late nineteenth century was a time when businesses in every important field formed such monopolies. To the so-called robber barons of big business, monopoly wasn't a board game; it was a method of increasing wealth by cornering the market. Big baseball was no exception.

Then it was time for us to document, in the eighth chapter, "Establishing a Business," the way the new league operated: its problems and successes, its measures to deal with the gambling and game-fixing that had been part of the previous association's life, its financial reverses and its problems in player relations (which revealed the flaws in its setup), its efforts at price-fixing (undermined by its own members), and the disagreements over playing Sunday ball and over whether beer should be sold in the parks. The Cincinnati Club, of course — as explained by the *Enquirer*— could hardly exist without beer sales, because, the reporter asserted defensively, "we drink beer in Cincinnati as freely as you used to drink milk, and it is not a mark of disgrace, either." A delicious remark, I decided, and quoted it. Cincinnati was ousted from the league, it so happened, not for breaking a rule against beer-selling, for there was none, but for engaging in beer-selling, a practice that the other members of the league planned to ban in the future. Monopolies can do things like that.

In deciding to ban beer and Sunday ball, the monopoly was of course trying to reverse a trend in American life that would not be countered, but in the 1890s that truism wasn't yet clear.

We had learned through the early newspapers that other groups rivaling the National League sprang up almost immediately, so we presented information on them. One group, the International Association of Professional Baseball Players, lasted only a couple of seasons. We were able to document its challenge through its constitutions, found in the Cleveland Public Library. Then another group formed, so Spalding of the National offered a sort of associate membership rather than the real thing. But the new group's founder, L.C. Waite of St. Louis, responded only with scorn, which surfaced in the *Tribune* as vituperation: Spalding's "walk-into-my-parlor epistle" and his "heads-I-win-tails-you-lose" plan were merely devised to keep out clubs in League cities, Waite retorted. No doubt. Nevertheless, some independent clubs actually joined this associate membership, soon called the League Alliance, but the National abolished it within a few years, thus bearing out Waite's astute analysis.

Another of these "minor" leagues, the Northwestern, which formed in 1879, became important only later, when it would join the first great inter-league agreement to govern professional baseball.

3 — Getting to First Base

All my newspaper work, as well as our research in various libraries, came to fruition in these chapters detailing the early development of baseball as a business. Nobody had ever uncovered these details and revealed all the dog-eat-dog machinations of the baseball club owners that typified American business as a whole in the late nineteenth century.

A huge concern of the National League was labor relations, so we devoted two chapters to the way all this worked out. First was the League's movement to toss out a crooked player, dismissed and banned in December of 1877. We found the minutes of the League's meeting attached to its constitution for the year to follow. We also noticed, in Harry Wright's letters, that this first banned player complained to Harry about his expulsion. Because I had organized our notes carefully by topic, the way scholars do, we were able to quickly link this player's letter to the dispute in question.

The National League's other problems, we found, could be classified as finding ways to regulate players more closely, to establish and enforce territorial rights, to exclude other clubs from the membership, and to cut labor costs. Establishing salary limits went a long way toward keeping labor costs down. Restricting competition for players worked even better: clubs could reserve certain players to themselves, and other clubs were not to offer to hire them the following season.

This "gentlemen's agreement" was the beginning of the famous "reserve clause," adopted in September of 1879, as proven by a secret agreement bound with the constitution of the league. Gradually, the League moved to extend the list of each club's number of reserved players until practically the entire list of players on the club became reserved (bound to its club permanently, or as long as the club wanted them). Because it proved useful beyond the imagination of its earliest creators, the reserve system would last, not for the thousand years once predicted for the Nazi Reich, but for almost a hundred, which in the United States is a very long time.

The players' contracts, we realized, at first didn't even mention the reserve; until 1887 this restriction came into it by reference only. We also discovered the owners' abuses of the reserve system: to penalize holdouts, or to hold onto unpaid players. One example came directly from the papers of Abraham G. Mills. The Mills Correspondence is a valuable manuscript collection owned by the Hall of Fame Library in Cooperstown. Mills headed the National League as well as the Commission that governed organized baseball.

What is "organized baseball"? It's the clubs and their leagues that have banded together to make one interrelated business and to shut out other clubs and leagues. Organized baseball is organized in order to effect a monopoly, which is buttressed by the reserve system. That system permitted players to be sold and traded "like livestock," as John Montgomery Ward put it in *Lippincott's Magazine* in 1886. I discerned the various uses of the reserve by analyzing and organizing information on the cases we had collected in which players complained or on which the media reported. The reserve turned out to be much more useful in controlling players than originally intended.

To try to figure out what level of salaries players were receiving, we studied the fragmentary evidence, especially the contracts of the Cincinnati club found in the Historical and Philosophical Society of Ohio, which we had examined at the University of Cincinnati. There we also found proof that the owners cheated on the rule by offering some players extra money "under the table." I delighted in finding an admission by A.G. Mills, in his Correspondence, that advances on salaries, too, would in some cases have to be made "or the poor devil will starve." Perhaps publishers pay advances on book royalties for the same reason.

Despite owners' attempts to keep a lid on player salaries, they gradually rose. To give some idea of the rise in the level of average salaries, we put together the data we had collected for the years 1881 through 1899, and from these figures I drew a bar chart showing the increase in averages over these years: from about $1,243 to $2,670. We illustrated our remarks about salaries with examples from individual cases we had collected.

To continue our discussion of labor relations, we brought in evidence of other legislation passed by the owners to buttress their control of the players, like blacklisting and classifying them by ability and personal conduct into various levels for the purpose of determining their salaries. *The Reach Guide* revealed the classification plan as well as the adoption of salary limits, and newspapers like *Sporting Life, New York Times, Sporting News, Chicago Tribune, Cleveland Leader,* and the *Official Base Ball Record* all commented on the new rules — and on their almost immediate violation by some owners. More proof of violations came from player letters found in the correspondence of the Cincinnati Baseball Club.

Evidence of fines and suspensions for player misconduct came from the Wright Correspondence, the *New York Mercury*, and the Mills Correspondence, as well as the guides and newspapers cited earlier. Player behavior was doubtless no better than it is today; some players displayed little self-control. Probably the first player strike, as we characterized it, came in 1889 when a St. Louis player, William "Yank" Robinson, was fined after cursing a gatekeeper for preventing an errand boy from bringing him a clean uniform when he had been ordered to change. Cursing had been frowned upon since the days of the old Knickerbockers. But Robinson objected to being fined for his outburst, and his teammates backed him. A strike was threatened, and only later was the matter smoothed over. I found this story in the *St. Louis Globe-Democrat,* a newspaper that also revealed the story of Harry Overbeck's successful suit of his club and the prescient remark of Harry's attorney that the baseball contract was of questionable legality because it was not drawn up by parties who had equal power. The attorney was correct.

Some letters in the Cincinnati Baseball Collection, written by players trying to negotiate better salaries with their owners, revealed pathetic situations, like the one from a player whose poorly expressed arguments, couched in misspelled words, descended almost to the level of begging — a tactic that of course had no effect on owners, although some of them occasionally acted generously when players' special needs surfaced.

Blacklisting was adopted, we proved, in 1881 at a League meeting reported in the *New York Clipper*. This tool and other restrictions kept players and their salaries under control, thus helping to make the League successful enough to inspire emulation by other club owners.

We gathered early evidence of the move to form the American Association, the league's first successful rival, through newspapers like *St. Louis Republican, Sporting Life, Cincinnati Enquirer, Cleveland Leader* and *Plain Dealer,* and the early guidebooks, as well as the 1881 constitution of the American Association itself, which I discovered in the Cleveland Public Library. The Association and its subsequent war against the National League brought to the fore such picturesque figures as the saloon owner Chris Von der Ahe ("I am der Boss of der Club") and Denny McKnight (who promised "war to the knife").

The resulting trade war between the National League and the American Association spawned organized baseball's first resort to the courts when Cincinnati appealed for an injunction restraining a stolen player from playing with his new club. I read the legal case in Cleveland's law library and discovered that the bill containing the arguments of the plaintiff were stolen from the clerk's office by the Cincinnati Club's attorney and never returned! The court refused to grant the injunction.

In a similar case, when another American Association club lured a player away from the Detroit Club, the player reneged on his agreement, but the court dismissed the case (another that I read in Cleveland's law library), ruling that the contract was invalid and the case prematurely brought.

The baseball trade war was waged not only over players but also over territory. Like birds and animals, the magnates defended territories that they had decided were their own and nobody else's. The newspapers of the cities where clubs disputed territorial rights carried the angry accusations from both sides and quoted freely from each other. Nowadays, newspaper reporters seemingly hate to admit that other media exist and that rival reporters might even scoop them, but in those days writers more often used quotations obtained by others and even quoted and reprinted other newspapers' entire stories or paragraphs from them. League and Association magnates, I was discovering, plotted against each other in their respective meetings, the minutes of which I found bound with the guidebooks. A.G. Mills, head of the National League, also described the League's war measures openly in his letters to the Association.

When enough money had been lost in the war, the two baseball factions, instead of continuing the fight indefinitely—unlike the two sides in the Middle East and in Ireland—came to their senses and stopped the war. In 1883 they divided the spoils, monopolizing all baseball territories and players for themselves.

No sooner did they declare themselves jointly supreme than they were challenged by another league, the Union Association, often contemptuously referred to in the papers as "the Onions." Clubowners on both sides of the fight again stole players freely from each other. And again we discovered colorful characters like Henry V. Lucas ("I am the Union Association. Whatever I do is all right."), the owner of the St. Louis Unions, who used the appropriate metaphor in expressing to reporters his pleasure in player-snatching by saying he enjoyed "going into the enemy's camp, capturing their guns, and using them on your own side." Like Denny McKnight, he viewed disputes about territories and players in military terms, as if France and Germany both wanted the Alsace and decided to fight over it until the strongest side won.

When as a student I read the term "trade war" in American history texts, it caused my eyes to glaze over, since I thought of it as something dull, conducted only by price-cutting and efforts to open new markets. Not in baseball, I found. Here, by getting into the correspondence of some of the participants and the insulting remarks quoted in the newspapers, I discovered that it meant vilification, stealing, and outright lying. Lucas of the Unions admitted to a *Sporting Life* reporter in 1884, "everything is fair in base ball as in war, and I want my share of the fun while it is going on."

All of this was eye-opening to a protected young midwestern woman who had been taught that cheating, lying, and stealing were wrong and who had once believed that these violations of ethical business tactics seldom occurred and were punishable as crimes. The only crime punished in these baseball wars, I decided, was losing.

Trade wars like these challenged the control imposed by the reserve clause. We gathered arguments for and against the reserve: Does it really stabilize the business? Is it really vital for preserving the integrity of the players? Do its flaws hurt players in the ways that many contend? These questions would not really be settled until much later. In presenting the problem we were able to use arguments elicited long after the events we were describing: in the Celler Hearings of 1952, a government investigation of baseball, as well as in the 1958 Kefauver Hearings. We purchased copies of these; in each case Seymour studied the Hearings and I studied the final Report. I then organized the resulting notes. It's revealing about the power base of the game of baseball in this country — the way it's wedged into our economy and the way its ethos is melded into our culture — that proposals for modifying the effect of the reserve clause in organized baseball, proposals made in the 1950s, took so many years and so much criticism to bring into effect.

The Union trade war, like all the others, ended in compromise, the winners (members of the National League) absorbing the most valuable of the losers' property and discarding the rest. Their joint division of the spoils was laid out in a document called The National Agreement. Most editions of this document are in the Cleveland Public Library.

The fragility of this alliance spelled out in the National Agreement was shown in continued disagreements over who owned which players and which territory. Minutes of meetings bound with the yearly issues of the League's and the Association's constitutions or with the annual guidebooks detailed their arguments with each other. Correspondence in the Cincinnati Baseball Collection showed us the way compromises were worked out. The result of the compromises was new restrictions on players.

I began to realize why in matters of dispute between players and owners, Seymour always leaned toward sympathy with the players. That bias continued even into what was then the present (the 1950s), when players were making what most people considered "good money." Clearly, the players, as non-participants in the way organized baseball was conducted and thus excluded from any decisions about its governance, necessarily had to bow to whatever the owners decided upon. Without a strong union, they had no power. The baseball business was the same animal, I saw then, as any other business: if the ownership lacked benevolent feeling toward its employees or restrained them more than the players could accept, the employees would eventually form unions if they possibly could. Otherwise, the owners would certainly take advantage of their weakness in every imaginable way.

In thinking about these wars we were aided by the publication of an insightful pamphlet entitled "Monopsony in Manpower: Organized Baseball Meets the Antitrust Laws," a reprint of an article written by Peter Craig for the *Yale Law Journal* in 1953. Craig explained that monopoly meant complete control of the means of producing or selling a product, but what the baseball owners had devised for themselves was "monopsony," or control of the product or service (the games) through their authority over those who created the product (the players). Because of this monopsony, players had to accept whatever contracts were offered them, or none at all; they had to play wherever the owners told them to, or not at all. This tight control would naturally and inevitably cause an explosion of player resentment.

At that point in our work we found it necessary to lay out the internal problems that our sources showed the leagues experiencing, as revealed in their minutes and in newspapers as well as in correspondence. One was the disagreement about price-fixing. Some clubs wanted to charge less than the agreed-upon admission prices. Others wanted a larger guarantee; some craved a percentage of the gate from the host club. And salaries were being cut, with players classified according to what the owners thought they were worth per year. Other measures to control players were revealed and discussed in correspondence between owners as well as in the papers and occasionally in magazines.

To balance our reporting of the owners' frequent abuse of player control measures, we showed that some players obviously lacked self-restraint: some stayed out all night carousing, arriving for a game with a hangover. I was surprised to see how forthrightly newspapers often reported these cases, as when the *Cincinnati Enquirer* reported that pitcher Leon Viau entered a game drunk, "a head on him the size of a brewery tub," and lost it.

Another legal problem arose when the Metropolitan Baseball Club, located on Staten Island, was ousted from the American Association and obtained an injunction against the move. I found the affidavits in this case in the Cleveland Public Library's Mears Collection. The judge ruled that the Mets must be reinstated, but a couple of years later the issue was mooted when the Mets sold out to Brooklyn. With some Association clubs gradually falling away from it over the next few years, the organization proved too weak to stand against its next challenge.

The notes I organized as "Club Business" made the basis for a chapter in the dissertation called "Club Operations in the Eighties," which demonstrated how owners, managers, captains, and other administrators handled their local work and the problems they faced in operations. My newspaper and magazine research as well as our research into correspondence gave us plenty of examples. A picture of the way fans would see the parks of the day was built from newspaper descriptions. Some fans got their reports at local saloons, as we learned not only from these sources but also from the memoirs of people like the writer H.L. Mencken of Baltimore. Most valuable for learning how a club disbursed its funds was the Cincinnati Club's own records showing its expenses and what they were for.

In connection with club travel we proved that, contrary to some sports writers' assertions, the railroads and the hotels, far from scorning baseball players as clients, actively solicited the business of the clubs. Through diligent research into the baseball guidebooks and newspapers I collected ads of railroads and hotels showing their attempts to attract the clubs and even boasting of the clubs' business. In the dissertation we placed photostats of these ads to back our revelation. We also pointed out the importance of newspapers in promoting baseball.

Even ethnic newspapers reported on games for their readers. My knowledge of the German language (I had heard it spoken since childhood and studied it in high school and college) helped me translate the baseball terms probably invented by German-speaking reporters for those who read the St. Louis paper *Anzeiger des Westens* (Western Indicator or Announcer).

Having already revealed the abuses of the owners in keeping tight control of their players, we had set the stage for describing the player revolt of 1890 that led to a players' league. Nothing like this had ever happened in organized baseball; nor has it happened since, although if they wanted to, I'm sure the players of today could afford to provide their own backing for a players' league and would not need to find "angels." The question of whether they would want to do it is something else. Some have administrative skills and might enjoy using them in forming their own organization, but I've never seen a quotation from a player of today to the effect that "we should start our own league."

The players' organization, the Brotherhood, formed in 1885, led directly to player strikes and the prominence of John Montgomery Ward, the first great labor leader of baseball history. Seymour and I both read his 1887 *Lippincott's* article, "Is the Base Ball Player a Chattel?" with considerable interest, finding Ward's arguments logical and clear. When I discovered the *Players' National League Official Guide* in the Cleveland Public Library, I was impressed with player intrepidity in starting their own league after negotiations with the owners failed.

We found evidence that men with money were eager to back the players' clubs to challenge the League owners in their own bailiwicks. Events of the resulting war were reported heavily in the sporting press, some of which favored one side over the other. *The Sporting News*, we were surprised to note, supported the players against the owners.

During its trade war with the Players' League, the National League, opening its 1890 season seriously weakened by the loss of players, resorted to the courts for redress. The essence of court decisions was that, although the law could not compel a player to perform for the party he originally contracted with, it could enjoin him from performing for another. The contract thus stood in the same dubious position as it had in earlier challenges. And eventually both sides found the ensuing financial losses ruinous, the Players' League collapsing first.

A. G. Spalding, the Chicago magnate and sporting goods manu-

3 — *Getting to First Base*   49

facturer, admitted in his book that neither side furnished the press with correct admission numbers or financial figures during the war, and fans soon became disgusted — as they always did when such wrangles prevented them from enjoying their favorite spectator sport. Disruption of what in the past has seemed stable is always irritating. It wasn't long before backers of the Players' League were bluffed into suing for peace, and again the losers' property was distributed among the winners. Owners also (rather high-handedly, I thought) excluded players from the peace arrangements, which were made only among the backers of both sides. Newspapers reported fully on meetings and on the settlement, in which the Players' League disappeared and the National and American Leagues consolidated their position. Same old same old.

Since we were stopping the chronology at this point in baseball's history, our final chapter described how the game was being played on the baseball field during this era: who the best players and teams were, what changes in the rules for play and in equipment had been made, and which playing tactics were being used by players. To illustrate the equipment of the 1870s and 1880s, I drew some of it by hand, from guidebooks and advertisements. I showed three styles of uniforms, a mouthpiece, two different catchers' masks, a sliding pad, front and back views of a "finger glove," a catcher's mitt, and a square bat (yes, square) of 1882.

Club rules for player behavior, we discovered, included no smoking before the game and no flirting with women while in uniform. Information collected from the guidebooks as well as newspapers proved invaluable for this discussion. I enjoyed discovering and reading an 1888 book called *Hygiene for Base Ball Players*, in which the medical doctor who wrote it, A.E.P. Leuf, recommended significantly that a club manager "compel" players to take a bath at least once a week under his own eyes; Leuf called the practice of showering "dangerous and useless." Perhaps with the shower equipment available in the eighties, it was.

Here we were able to bring in the ethnicity of players as well as the story of the first known black in the majors, Moses Fleetwood Walker, who caught for the Association's Toledo Club in 1884, along with events that demonstrated discrimination against him. We pointed out that other blacks followed Fleet Walker into organized baseball until, following the general trend of the times, baseball closed the doors on their participation, and that after a long dry spell for blacks, Jackie Robinson became the first black in the big leagues of the modern era. In our discussion of umpires we revealed the untruth of the assumption that all umpires have been honest, basing our discussion mainly on minutes of the National League's Board of Directors' meetings.

We ended with a section on the literature of baseball of the era, not only magazines, newspapers, and guidebooks but also books for adults and for children published up to 1890. The New York Public Library, I discovered, contained a great collection of early dime novels, some of them about baseball. What fun it would be to read them all, I thought.

Then the list of materials we used had to be displayed in a written bibliography. I prepared this from bibliographical notes I had kept and sorted into types, including collections, manuscripts, newspapers (thirty-two of them), a dozen club and league constitutions, sixteen articles (but I read a great many more than those listed), eighteen guidebooks, of which many were published annually, other documents, law cases, letters, sheet music, and pamphlets.

Those were only the primary sources. For secondary sources we cited a hundred and eight books (although I examined many more than that) and twenty encyclopedias.

Our appendix appeared in six parts, two of them most important. First we included a copy of the original contract and the secret supplementary agreement of the 1887 Cin-

Paul W. Gates, the chairman of Harold Seymour's doctoral committee at Cornell University, who was instrumental in the history department's acceptance of the topic of baseball for the first dissertation on the subject. The photograph was taken on Gates's retirement in May of 1971. (Photograph courtesy of the Division of Rare and Manuscript Collections, Carl A. Kroch Library, Cornell University.)

ncinnati Club with player Bid McPhee. We also inserted a copy of the contemporary Uniform Players' Contract, which proved impossible to squeeze out of the major leagues of the 1950s but was finally obtained for us (perhaps a bit deviously) by a reporter friend of Seymour's, Joe Trimble, who had once played ball on a boys' team that Seymour coached. Studying this contract proved invaluable in comparing the regulations of the early period with those of what was, for us, the present day.

While I was typing all this, Seymour wrote his preface, acknowledging the help of "numerous individuals and organizations." The preface omits to mention me. No doubt it would have been unwise of him to reveal that I was practically the co-author of this document.

The resulting 632-page dissertation proved entirely acceptable to Cornell University. Nothing like this unique piece of work had ever been done for baseball before. Of course it impressed Paul Gates, Seymour's Ph.D. committee chairman, who was pleased to approve it. We were getting to first base.

But even this achievement did not assure Seymour the doctorate he had been seeking for so long.

4

Delivering the Pitch

To obtain the degree, Seymour still needed to jump another hurdle, one that I couldn't help with: he had to pass an hours-long oral exam in American history administered at Cornell by three members of its history department, his doctoral committee.

We were brought up short by a letter from Professor Paul Gates of Cornell in May 1956 warning that Gates was soon going on leave for a year and so would be unable to join in administering the oral exam after mid-June. "Do you intend to take the exam this term?" Gates inquired.

Although Seymour had satisfied Cornell's residence requirements, he had long overstayed the time allotted by the University for completing all degree requirements. He knew it was necessary for him to reinstate himself with the Graduate School by claiming unusual circumstance: interruption of his work by World War Two, the necessity for taking a job outside academia, and the time taken up by research trips. He did so, and the Graduate School approved his reinstatement immediately, so he decided he must take the exam within a few weeks, before Gates departed for a year's leave of absence.

The exam, to be administered by Gates and two other members of Cornell's history department whom Seymour hadn't even met (replacing two original members who were no longer there), would cover the dissertation and its research only in part; most of it would be designed to uncover Seymour's knowledge of American history in general. He began cramming. We bought and quickly digested new books in the field as he tried to catch up on revisionist historical theories.

Seymour had been away from the study of American history for four years and wondered if he could pass a grueling oral exam handled by three well-known historians. He drove from Cleveland to Ithaca with some trepidation. The day of his exam, he knew afterward that his responses to questions they posed had been acceptable; he felt that he had stumbled on only one answer. After the men had questioned him for hours, they left him alone to talk the matter over among themselves. They delayed so long in getting back to him that he became nervous, worrying that perhaps they were arguing over giving him the degree. Finally they returned, and the first words from Gates were, "Congratulations, Doctor!" When Seymour wondered aloud why their decision took so long to make, Gates replied, "Oh, we approved your degree immediately and then turned to a discussion of something else entirely."

My family attended the proud occasion at Cornell at which the degree of Doctor of Philosophy, the highest academic honor a university can confer, was awarded to Seymour and others in a solemn ceremony. Cornell's promotion department sent out releases, based on information I prepared, that brought national publicity for the first doctorate ever awarded in the field of baseball history. *The Milwaukee Journal* and the *Kansas City Times* were among those reporting, with some surprise, the story of a man who had gone "from batboy to Ph.D. in baseball history."

The *Cleveland News*, the newspaper for which I had worked as copy boy nine years earlier, recognized the news value of Seymour's accomplishment and sent a reporter, Joe Madigan, to interview him at our Lakewood home. Its story quotes Seymour as crediting my help. "Along with his wife Dorothy," said Madigan's story, Seymour had "traveled a lot to collect data." It continued, "His wife has done all the typing, and Seymour credits her as being his severest critic. He insists that it [the dissertation] never would've been completed without her contribution." So although my role as researcher, organizer, editor, and writer remained unrecognized in print, at least my contribution as "data collector," critic, and typist was.

Now we faced the next project: finding a book publisher that would take a chance on publishing something entirely new, a scholarly history of American baseball.

While looking for a publisher, we also had to be concerned with our jobs. University teaching still beckoned Seymour. He itched to return to academia and began applying to various institutions that he thought might be interested in his work. In those days the wife always followed the husband, so when Seymour accepted a position in Buffalo, New York, in 1956, I left the Parma Heights school system and looked for a job in Buffalo.

The University of Buffalo appointed Seymour Vice President and Director of the University's Office of Information Services. In this position he succeeded Sloan Wilson, author of the fifties bestseller *The Man in the Gray Flannel Suit*. His job was administrative rather than teaching, of course, but Seymour hoped to make friends with members of the history department and possibly be invited to do some teaching. That never happened, although he was asked to take part in a radio program on baseball called "The University Round Table." And his "Newcomers Lecture" for the University was entitled "What Is Professional Baseball?" Someone also nominated him as a contestant for the television program called "The $64,000 Question," and although he filled out the producer's questionnaire, it soon became apparent that his baseball knowledge was not of the type suitable for a trivia show. It was just as well that the producer failed to invite him to participate, since later this program was shown to be largely fakery.

Seymour's work at the University of Buffalo, instead of branching into university teaching, turned out to be mainly writing: ghosting the president's speeches and writing other promotional materials for the university. So again my writing skills came into play, especially in preparing articles for the University's periodical called *Pipeline to Business and Industry*, a newsletter comparable to the Better Business Bureau's *Facts*. Seymour also connected with Buffalo baseball to the extent that in 1956 he bought five shares of the Bisons Baseball Club; the stock certificate still remains in the Seymour Collection at Cornell University.

My new teaching position, as director and teacher at a preschool that operated in a church building near our apartment, gave me the opportunity of overseeing a group of University elementary education students who interned as teachers under my supervision. I redesigned the children's preschool curriculum: to make it more challenging and instructive, I brought it closer to kindergarten work by adding prereading activities. I also advanced my speaking career by addressing groups of parents who wanted tips on handling their youngsters.

Our main concern, however, remained getting a publisher for "The Rise of Major League Baseball to 1891." Queries we sent out elicited the interest of Prentice-Hall, but the company thought the topic too limited chronologically, its representative declaring that, for publication, Seymour would have to bring the story up to the present time. We knew that extending the scholarly history of baseball all the way to the present would take many years of research, so we rejected that idea and continued contacting other publishers.

Seymour thought our best bet was the annual December convention of the American Historical Association, where many publishers sent representatives. In 1956 the AHA scheduled its meetings in Cincinnati, Ohio, so we drove there, registering at the Netherlands Plaza and taking the opportunity to meet Lee Allen. Seymour and Lee had begun corresponding early that year, and Lee, then writing for the *Cincinnati Enquirer*, expressed enthusiasm about meeting the man who had just been awarded a doctorate for a thesis on baseball history. We both enjoyed our burgeoning friendship with Lee, a talented writer with a puckish sense of humor.

Lee Allen, the baseball writer who became head of the library of the Hall of Fame in Cooperstown, New York. Lee always welcomed Harold Seymour and me to the library, which then occupied one room above the museum section of the Hall of Fame. All three of us performed research in the Herrmann Collection accessioned by the library. (Photograph courtesy of the National Baseball Hall of Fame Library, Cooperstown, New York.)

The AHA meetings always culminated in a banquet, so on the evening of this occasion we sat at a large round table with strangers and made an effort to become acquainted with them. Seated next to Seymour was a fellow considerably younger than the others, so we wondered how, at his age, he had already obtained a position as a college instructor. On being asked where he taught, the young man revealed that he was not a college instructor but a representative for Oxford University Press. Seymour lost no time in telling him about "The Rise of Major League Baseball to 1891." The young rep's eyes brightened with curiosity. He said he would discuss the matter with his supervisor, Charles Petee, who was also in attendance at the meetings, and he thought Petee might want to pursue the matter.

Petee proved amenable to meeting with Seymour about his idea, so I sat in the hotel lobby in high hopes while the two men met in Petee's room. The Oxford representative, intrigued by the idea of a book on early baseball history, said that on his return to New York he would tell the relevant Oxford editor about it. Within a short time, back in Buffalo, Seymour received a letter from Sheldon Meyer of Oxford University Press expressing enthusiasm for the idea of a book on early baseball history and asking for an outline with some sample chapters. He said the company had published books on British cricket; he didn't see why it should not also publish on American baseball.

Sheldon Meyer, editor of the Seymour books published by Oxford University Press beginning in 1960. Sheldon did not realize, until after Seymour's passing, how much I contributed to the Seymour books. (Photograph courtesy Sheldon Meyer.)

Sheldon Meyer, a Princeton graduate, was then near the beginning of what became a distinguished forty-year career in publishing, during which he would acquire, and supervise the development of, some fifty or sixty important books of history, along with other types of nonfiction books whose subjects interested him. Much later, Meyer would state his requirements for the type of manuscript he looked for:

4 — Delivering the Pitch

> The author has to be someone who knows his subject, who's done the work, who's gone to the sources.... Someone who brings ideas and interpretation to the subject. And the author has to be able to write intelligently, persuasively, and effectively. For history, writing a narrative is essential.

The author of this baseball manuscript qualified on all counts.

We plunged into the preparation of both the outline and the sample chapters. Meyer asked for a slight extension of the time period to be covered: instead of stopping at 1891, could the book cover a few more years, to the establishment in 1903 of the American League as a major league? It could, with more research.

Meanwhile, Seymour had endured his fill of administrative work. He began applying to colleges in New York state for a teaching position, receiving an appointment in New York City to teach at Finch College, an exclusive girls' college mainly for young women from well-off families. I found a position teaching first grade at an elementary school in Pelham, so after less than a year in Buffalo (where it seemed to us that the snow never left the ground) we took an apartment in New Rochelle, the next town up the New Haven Railroad line from Pelham and only about a half-hour's train time into Manhattan.

On September 18 Seymour received a telegram (we had no phone, since Seymour didn't want one) with the news we had been waiting for: Oxford's board had approved the baseball book for publication, and Meyer offered Oxford's contract to publish it. What a thrill! Writing for a prestigious publisher and teaching in New York, his original home, put Seymour in his element.

We had also been producing baseball articles. Our trips from Ohio to New York City, where we researched at the New-York Historical Society and the New York Public Library, resulted in the publication of "How Baseball Began" for the Society's *Quarterly* of October 1956. Our work in St. Louis at *The Sporting News* and the St. Louis Historical Society formed the basis for "St. Louis and the Union Baseball War" in the *Missouri Historical Review* of 1957.

That same year "Ball, Bat, and Bar," about the law and economics of baseball, appeared in the *Cleveland-Marshall Law Review*. For that article, and for the dissertation, I had obtained special permission to use the law library in downtown Cleveland. I learned how to look up legal citations and how to grasp legal terminology. Another article, "Unions

Fail in Organized Baseball," was published in a journal called *Industrial Bulletin*.

By then Seymour's writing style had loosened considerably, and Meyer wrote him to say he was glad to see that for "Ball, Bat, and Bar" Seymour had left behind the pedantic style of the doctoral dissertation. Even more casual was the style used for "Surf Baths and Dumbbells" in *Baseball Digest* of April 1957, a fan article about the colorful methods of conditioning used by early managers during spring training. These methods included games of handball and racquets as well as hiking and dousing each other with bucketsful of salt water at Cape May on the Jersey coast.

Immediately after signing with Oxford, Seymour began his years-long effort to persuade the publisher to list his doctoral degree after his name on the cover and title page of the book, as academic publishers did for other scholars. Oxford demurred, in the belief that displaying an academic degree on a baseball book would hurt sales to fans. Seymour took every other opportunity to show that he possessed the degree, so that correspondents, especially those he asked for information, would understand that his queries concerned scholarship rather than mere curiosity, and that his work was to be taken as a serious academic study rather than the musings of a sports fan. On every letter I typed, he signed his name "Dr. H. Seymour."

This respect that Seymour demanded for the title resulted in an article in which he recommended that academic holders of this prestigious degree use it rather than hide it, as so many did. "Call Me Doctor!" which appeared in *Educational Record* in July 1958, explained the proud history of the academic doctorate and urged that those to whom it had been granted use it on every occasion, as do holders of the medical degree, which is technically on a lower level. The article got quite a play in current journals like *Newsweek, Time,* and *Harper's,* and favorable mentions in the scholarly press like the *AAUP Bulletin*. The American Council of Education was among the groups that reprinted the piece. Only *Time* poked gentle fun at the idea put forward in "Call Me Doctor!" But Seymour's recommendations failed to move Oxford. Not until the second volume, *Baseball: The Golden Age,* was published did Oxford give in on this point.

Another effort that failed was Seymour's attempt to persuade Oxford to include footnotes or chapter notes. At one point he thought he had succeeded, and we spent a large chunk of time at a summer cottage near Monroe, New York, preparing and typing backnotes for several chapters before Sheldon Meyer called a halt to the work, saying Oxford had decided not to publish them. We had to make do with a descriptive bibliography.

During 1958 our ground-floor apartment in New Rochelle, with children screaming just outside the window, became unbearable for people trying to write a book, and Seymour suggested we move into Manhattan, where he worked and where the New York Public Library would more easily be available for our research. That fall we found an apartment in a small and charming building near the Riverside end of West Seventy-third Street; we were told that it had originally been built for the mistress of the business tycoon Charles Schwab.

Now it was my turn to do the commuting, taking the subway each morning to Grand Central Station and riding the New Haven line to my teaching position in Pelham, where I found myself increasingly interested in the conflicting theories about the best way to teach reading to first-graders. I experimented with various methods and always came back to heavy emphasis on phonics, which gave the children the skill in figuring out new words that they needed in order to become independent readers. My experience with early reading instruction gave me excellent background for eventually producing the first books I would write on my own.

Evenings and weekends were spent on baseball research and baseball writing. By then I was typing many of our research notes on my Royal portable, especially those taken on research trips — for example, our spring vacation trip of 1958 to *The Sporting News* office. Although Seymour still did some research, I soon realized that he did not relish research the way I did, so I performed most of it. Not until thirty years later did he admit to a reporter from the *Boston Globe* that he disliked research.

I asked Seymour to read the books and articles about statistics and economics, some of which used prose that I found nearly impenetrable, as well as player biographies, which generally concentrated on the players' technical skills and records — something he already knew a lot about and I did not. We both studied the few dissertations that were beginning to be produced in the field of sport history or related fields, like that of John R. Betts. In general, I took charge of studying the books, and I included my comments and evaluations by recording them directly on the notes I produced.

Seymour's consistent problem in taking notes, I found, was not bothering to split up the information topically. Instead of recording information about each topic on different sheets, he tended to simply summarize the entire article or book on a series of consecutive sheets. But without topical notes, organizing them was impossible. The result of his method of note-taking was double work: I had to study his notes and write new topical notes based on them, notes that covered only one topic so that each could be filed appropriately and linked with the other notes covering the same topic.

I enjoyed tracking down new information. To me research was like a treasure hunt. I doted on following clues offered in the material I uncovered, because they often led me to some unexpected and intriguing information. Sometimes I noticed a phrase that hinted at a connection to still another matter or another source that I could check on, or that presented an entirely new view of the subject, one that challenged common assumptions about it.

At the New York Public Library, a great reference library that quickly became my favorite of all research venues, I was working on the *New York Times* and systematically searching the periodical guides for insightful baseball pieces in magazines like *Literary Digest* and *Outing* and *Collier's*. I checked books and scholarly journals for articles on military history, business history, and popular culture that might possibly include mentions of early baseball play. For the dissertation, Seymour had already studied the Knickerbocker rules and club books as well as the Harry Wright correspondence and account books, and he had gone through all twelve volumes of the Spalding scrapbooks. I studied league constitutions (showing how the leagues tackled internal as well as external problems), the baseball guides (containing unexpected tidbits of contemporary baseball happenings), early boys' books (supporting the British origin of baseball), and even city directories (in order to find certain locations and residents). I pored over old newspapers, quoted from letters and minutes of meetings, and compared and contrasted material in different sources. I even found books in Spanish about the beginnings and the development of early baseball in the Caribbean. The variety of material available on baseball seemed endless. I became skilled at evaluating sources.

4 — Delivering the Pitch

Newspaper research in particular fascinated me. I savored the opportunity of finding out what was happening in America day by day. I performed all the microfilm research except for our research together when we traveled to another city, where we used separate microfilm readers if they were available. In my mind I can still hear the grinding of an old Recordak machine as I turned the handle to locate *New York Times* stories that might prove informative, or searched issues of *The Sporting News* for significant articles.

Only once did I experience an unpleasant moment at the NYPL: when someone stole my note folder. Not my purse; I never put my purse down in the public area of the women's washroom, keeping it hanging from my arm by its strap even while running water in the sink. But once while washing my hands I did put my folder — a brown tagboard envelope tied with cotton ribbon — on a narrow shelf above the sink, and when I turned away to dry my hands, the folder disappeared. I turned back to face only an empty shelf as a young woman quickly exited the room. Luckily, at that moment the folder contained only a five-by-eight pad of paper and a few ideas for possible checking.

This incident revealed to me how desperate some people are, but it failed to disrupt my research at the NYPL, where I particularly enjoyed studying old newspapers. Non-baseball stories and period-piece advertisements in these old periodicals sometimes distracted me from my work, especially those covering important historical developments outside baseball or even presenting new ideas in apparel and furniture, but I always managed to bring myself back to baseball. Much later I recalled the *New York Times* in particular as an excellent source of general events of the day, and I went back to it in order to obtain the framework for my first historical novel and to pick up examples of current developments in popular culture that would fit into that story.

When I discovered that a publisher had reprinted the sheet music of some very early baseball compositions, I tried out the tunes on my piano. Finding that the songs, besides furnishing antiquarian interest, offered considerable musical charm, we attempted to interest record companies in releasing a recording of the music, as played and sung by professionals, but nobody responded favorably to the idea, probably because we neglected to locate appropriate musicians and interest them in performing the songs.

A few other scholars were beginning to write articles about baseball topics. Jay Topkis and Peter Craig, students of law, wrote excellent articles for the *Yale Law Journal* about baseball and the antitrust laws. Articles in the *Kansas Historical Quarterly*, the *Missouri Historical Society Bulletin*, and the *Maryland Historical Magazine* gave information about early baseball in those states. An anonymous author wrote about early Iowa ball in the *Annals of Iowa*. Joseph Overfield of Buffalo, New York, a self-taught scholar, was beginning to publish his work about early baseball on the Niagara Frontier. The scholars John R. Betts and John A. Krout were writing about early American sports and included some information they had found on the development of baseball. The Betts dissertation we used earlier on microfilm had been published in book form.

The material I was collecting fit together like pieces of a challenging puzzle. Organizing the notes for the book, including the new material obtained for the era of the 1890s, brought them into relationship with each other. I enjoyed discovering those relationships. I remembered that as a child, when I played with my friends they always wanted to play teacher while I always wanted to play office, because I liked sorting and organizing pieces of paper bearing information that offered some interconnection to be found. As a grownup working on a book, I found the organization of ideas to be the ultimate in this kind of office work. I organized the notes, all written on five-by-eight sheets of paper, topically into cardboard boxes purchased at office supply stores. Eventually, I collected dozens of these boxes. I never dreamt that all these pieces of paper would some day be considered part of a distinguished university's Rare Book and Manuscript Collection.

The theme of *Baseball: The Early Years*, which I believe is carried out successfully, is that baseball grew from a boyish pastime to an amateur sport for grownups and then finally into a highly-organized business monopoly, therefore losing much of its sporting aspect. Over a period of one century, because of the gradual increase in its attractions for so many people, baseball transformed itself from a minor aspect of American life into a well-recognized part of the economy as well as the culture.

Using the dissertation material as the basis for the first section, I found that most of it fell logically into topics like the beginnings of baseball, the Knickerbockers and their era, the spread of the amateur game, and the organization of the amateurs in an attempt to arrange games more easily. Then came the gradual seeping in of professionalism by the paying of skilled players to play the game. Seymour thought of this as the twilight era of amateurism, so that became its name.

We also wanted to devote space to the infiltration of gambling and "revolving" (the players' practice of going from team to team within a season) as well as "hippodroming" (fixing or throwing games). The Black Sox Scandal of 1919 was hardly the first such threat to the integrity of the game. Player dishonesty and owner duplicity were more common in these early times than most fans of the game realized.

For the second section of the book I arranged the notes into boxes that I labeled league business, club business, and labor relations. As I worked on these notes I found that they often fell naturally into subtopics, which included the challenge of the American Association, resulting in a trade war; the development of the reserve clause and its effects; and the owners' creation of other methods of controlling players who stayed out late before games, got drunk, or impregnated women unintentionally.

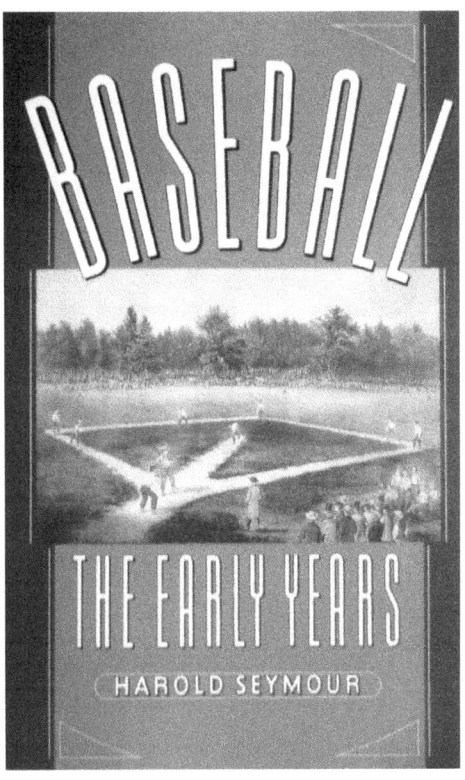

Baseball: The Early Years (Oxford University Press, 1960), based on, and extended from, Harold Seymour's dissertation for Cornell University (1956). I helped develop the dissertation and the book, both of which were the first ever prepared by a historian on the history of baseball. (From *Baseball: The Early Years* by Harold Seymour, copyright 1960 by Harold Seymour. Used by permission of Oxford University Press, Inc.)

The third section formed itself into parts telling of the entrance of the National League into the picture and its eventual alliance with the American Association. Then came the challenge by the Union Association (the "Onions"), who stole the alliance's players but eventually failed as a league; and the development of the blacklist as well other methods of dealing with players, especially during the revolt of the 1880s, when players formed the Brotherhood and the Players' League.

Despite the occasional occurrence of players' strikes and the development of unions, nothing like the Players' League has even happened again in more modern times; despite occasional flareups and even strikes, players now seem more satisfied with their lot, probably because of a strong union, high salaries, and better treatment.

In this section we needed to show, as in the earlier eras, how the game was being played on the field, which clubs dominated the leagues, and who starred in these contests.

Then came the new material for the extension beyond the period covered by the dissertation into the 1890s: how the league monopoly handled players (largely by cutting salaries and instituting suspensions), how they worked out a method of sharing game receipts (using a percentage system), how law cases by dissatisfied club owners were settled, how owners got along (with plenty of bickering over questions like whether to play ball on Sunday), how they made extra money (partly by transferring games to more lucrative venues), and how owners governed themselves (through interlocking ownerships — an arrangement of dubious legality).

The final topic was the entrance of the American League, the trade war between the leagues with its consequent player-stealing, arguments over control of the minor leagues, and the establishment of the settlement to include a three-man National Commission to govern organized baseball. Material on the lives of the players, their fans, and the umpires, along with information about related topics like baseball's impact on other aspects of American life, formed the final two chapters.

Organizing the notes led to my outlining each group of the notes topically so that they would be easier to use in writing. I selected and arranged the material to be used in these outlines, subheading each section for clarity and ease of development. Seymour wrote directly from my outlines, and I edited and revised his writing, which was developing steadily into a smoother, more accessible prose style. For the book I helped him eliminate much of his academic terminology, which in those days seemed appropriate for a dissertation, and instead write more directly, partly by cutting down on the use of the passive voice.

In July we were able to send four chapters of the manuscript to Sheldon Meyer. That fall we returned to Spink's office in St. Louis for research, working late Saturdays and Sundays on *The Sporting News*. By then we were familiar figures to the sports writers, and I must have seemed a much less exotic creature than I had on my first visit to this wholly-masculine enclave.

For women to enter sports writing, at least on the level of the major leagues, was proving as unusual as hitting a game-winning homer in the last of the ninth inning with the bases loaded. My early heroine, Doris O'Donnell, made news in 1957 when she tried to report a ball game from the press box at Fenway Park and found her way barred by the Boston baseball writers. The *New York Times* headlined its story on her with a comment that seemed to support the men's desire to retain their territorial rights: the headline writer called the press box "Where Woman's Place Is Not."

Doris O'Donnell, reporter for the *Cleveland News* when I worked there as a copy boy in 1947. This photograph was taken about the time Doris tried unsuccessfully to report baseball games from the press box at Fenway Park, where the male journalists refused to admit her. (Cleveland Press Collection, Cleveland State University Library, Courtesy of Bill Barrow, Special Collections, and Dr. Glenda Thornton, Library Director.)

Back in 1949, when I first walked into the newsroom of J.G. Taylor Spink's baseball newspaper, that was certainly "where woman's place was not." But as with other advancements, the change soon became less disturbing. Entrenched inhabitants of sports newsrooms eventually got used to seeing people who didn't look exactly like them.

Jean Ardell, the California writer, in a 1994 letter to me, commented on the historical lack of women in the sports media: "How often such voices have been muted, the press box and broadcasting booth being sacred ground [reserved to men] until quite recently." Although I didn't realize it then, in the forties the journalist Mary Garber of the *Winston-Salem Journal* was forced to sit in the stands with players' wives instead of in the press box with the other reporters. And of course the effort to allow women reporters into a baseball park's clubhouse and locker room with other reporters lasted into the 1970s. Women like Doris and Mary felt that their "place" was wherever they needed and wanted it to be.

In July of 1959, we completed the book's manuscript and submitted it for publication. We were delivering the pitch.

Meyer responded by accepting the manuscript in a congratulatory note to Seymour, declaring that he had found "genuine enthusiasm for your project in the [editorial board] meeting.... You have produced a most readable manuscript.... It strikes us as an important contribution to the study of 19th century American society."

Meyer also sent the final manuscript out for review to John Kieran, who for years had written the *New York Times* column "Sports of the Times." Kieran replied by writing Meyer that the work "shows evidence of enormous research," calling it "invaluable" as well as "the best detailed history of the rise of baseball that I have yet encountered." Meyer also sent the manuscript to Professor Harvey Wish of Western Reserve University, who reacted by saying he was "greatly impressed" and that the work "rings true as solid research."

Oxford had already begun promoting the book, and in April the veteran newsman Howard K. Smith invited Seymour to be interviewed on videotape at New York's Tavern on the Green, as part of a long television program Smith was producing called "What Does Baseball Have That Other Sports Haven't?" I wasn't invited to the taping, but when the film was shown on ABC-TV at the home of friends a few nights later, we watched it with them. Smith built the show around an interview with Seymour, but the director or producer also inserted into it, at various points, clips from filmed interviews with Jackie Robinson, Casey Stengel, and Chuck Thompson. Seymour performed well, replying to a broad set of baseball queries ranging from baseball's organization to the pitching styles used by players.

One topic Smith asked about was baseball's effect on social life; to exemplify its effect on language, Seymour pointed to the common use of baseball images like "born with three strikes on him," trying to "get to first base with her," and "they don't belong in this league," which were commonly used even by people who weren't particularly baseball fans. He answered many questions about baseball as a sport and as a business.

Smith also asked technical questions about the way the game was played. At one point, when Smith asked him how various pitches were produced, Seymour began demonstrating as well as explaining, and the director then inserted an animated clip showing the ball whirling through space and revolving, just as Seymour was showing how grasping and delivering the ball affected its trajectory. For those early days of television, it was a dramatic moment in the show, so when *Sporting News* reviewed it on April 18, 1962, the reporter made much of this sequence:

> An interesting feature of the program was an explanation by Dr. Seymour of the various deliveries of pitchers, illustrated with a camera set behind home plate. As Dr. Seymour described the action of spitters, curve balls, sliders and other pitches, a dotted line followed the flight of the various deliveries to the plate.

That September, while expecting proofs, we submitted the Preface and the Bibliographical Note describing the extensive research done for the book. For illustrations we sent in historical photos of early baseball players, teams, and club owners, most of them collected from sources found in the New York Public Library, but we also used the Culver picture agency in New York as a source. In addition, we provided a copy of Adrian "Cap" Anson's 1884 player contract. Oxford directed an artist to re-draw my chart showing the increase in number of clubs represented at player conventions of 1857 through 1868, and his drawing became one of the illustrations.

The Preface explained that because this book was the result of scholarship, it punctured old assumptions that sports writers had copied from one another over the years, thus clearing up questions about the game's origin, for example, and about the workings of the reserve clause. The book placed the national game firmly in American history (said the Preface), showing baseball moving from its beginnings as a simple boy's game in a predominantly rural society into a highly skilled game of professionals who performed for the entertainment of paying urban spectators. In doing so, baseball was reflecting similar changes in other aspects of American life, like the movement of early business toward cutthroat competition, monopoly, and trade war, and the changes in attitudes toward blacks as the Civil War receded and as the trend toward separation and exclusion escalated in the nineties.

In the last paragraph of his Preface, Seymour acknowledged the cooperation of various libraries and historical societies as well as permissions granted to use quotations. He also paid tribute to my help, saying that his wife "contributed her time, knowledge, and patience in all stages of the work. It is not too much to say that without her, the book would never have been finished." I appreciated this general recognition, not really expecting it to include a detailed description of my equal or even predominant responsibility for the research and my heavy contribution to the writing itself.

Galley proofs (and those were the days when proofs were still in the form of galleys) began arriving in groups during September, and I was appalled to find that the copy editor hired by Oxford to edit the book had made many errors in her work. She knew much less about grammar and writing than I did, so she had inserted errors that I needed to correct. Seymour read the galleys, too, but I made the corrections, including those he asked for. In my first letter to the copy editor I asked for 29 changes. In the second group of galleys I asked for 56 more. It went on like this for an entire month of proofing. A few requested changes had to do with technical baseball matters or with improvements in the writing that we wanted, but most involved the copy editor's work. All the corrections we asked for were made; I believe that Leona Capeless, who supervised the copy editing department at Oxford, saw to that.

Seymour asked me to write the required index, so as soon as page proofs arrived, I used them to write the index, the first one I had ever written.

In those days publishers took nine months — the length of a pregnancy — to produce a book, so *Baseball: The Early Years* appeared in the spring of 1960. For the first time, basic historical research techniques had been applied to the subject of the national game in a book published by a scholar. Instead of remaining the purview of sports writers and other journalists, baseball had also become the object of historical treatment. It had been raised to the level of other aspects of American history, like national land policy, or labor history, or political history.

We knew that *Baseball: The Early Years* was an unusual accomplishment, but still we wondered: how would reviewers receive it?

5

Right Off the Bat

Reviewers sat up and paid attention to the unique qualities of *Baseball: The Early Years*. By 1960, Lee Allen, journalist and author of baseball books, was in charge of the library of the Hall of Fame at Cooperstown. Lee volunteered to review *Baseball: The Early Years* for the *New York Times* as "a landmark in the writing of baseball history." In his letter to the *Times*, a copy of which he sent us, Lee said he'd read the book twice, calling it "extremely valuable" and "uniformly excellent," pointing out that it was "thoroughly documented, yet rich in anecdotal material."

Lee's resulting review in the *Times* called *Baseball: The Early Years* "a solid work, meticulous in its restraint" and declared that it described baseball personalities "with a fine flavor." To Lee it was apparent that Seymour had "conducted his research exhaustively." He thought the author was fair to "even the most parsimonious of the game's entrepreneurs, and the reader cannot escape the impression that he is secretly amused by them." Lee added, with his characteristic irony, that "It is barely possible that *Baseball: The Early Years* will influence libraries and historical societies to treat baseball with less condescension."

In the same issue of the *Times*, the *Sunday Book Review* printed a biographical summary of Seymour's life, emphasizing his baseball experiences (as batboy, college player, and bird dog) rather than his work. The description noted one anomaly: that the book was published by Oxford University Press, "which theoretically should be sticking to cricket. This isn't a willful case of if you can't lick 'em, join 'em, but can be set down to an interest in Americana." Accompanying the brief summary of Seymour's life was a cute sketch, purportedly of Seymour, as a baby in a carriage wearing a baseball cap and waving a Giants pennant (Harold Seymour was born in Manhattan, then moved to Brooklyn), his proud parents standing by in 1890s costumes (close: Seymour was born in 1910).

Newspapers around the nation recognized the value of *Baseball: The Early Years*, especially its difference from the books produced previously by sports writers. The *New York Telegram and Sun* pointed out that "unlike many of the so-called histories of baseball, which merely repeat the same tired legends," *Baseball: The Early Years* is "a serious and dramatic study of the game." The *Newark News* declared that the book was "in a different league than previous baseball histories." John Barkham of the *Saturday Review* Syndicate, using an apt figure of speech, wrote, "Right off the bat, let me say that this history of baseball stands in a class by itself." He called it "the best I've ever read on the subject ... informative and myth-shattering ... crammed with revelations ... a uniquely valuable contribution to the game."

Many reviewers picked out and commented on the assumptions of earlier baseball writers that *Baseball: The Early Years* had turned upside down. John Barkham pointed out that the book "demolishes many a cherished myth," mentioning that it proved Jackie Robinson was not the first black man to break into major league baseball and that the honor belonged to Moses Fleetwood Walker. The *Detroit News Call-Bulletin* pointed out that "Professor Seymour has put the final crusher on the legend" that General Abner Doubleday invented baseball in 1839 by presenting proof that the game was played in London, England, as early as 1744. In fact, declared the *Sunday Oregonian,* the book "exploded a dugout full of myths."

But a Michigan paper disagreed, stating that the author "isn't debunking, he's just getting at the facts." Putting it even better was the *Chattanooga News-Free Press*, which said the book "clarifies many misconceptions" and "unravels a maze of legends." Some reviewers seemed surprised to see their heroes shown as human. The *Chicago Sentinel* thought the book contained "some shockingly revealing pages." Others, like the *Baltimore Sun*, praised the book's "impartial attitude" and "analytical approach."

Librarian Robert W. Henderson, who had written an important article on early baseball, wrote generously about *Baseball: The Early Years* for the *Journal of the New-York Historical Society*, describing the book straightforwardly as "the first scholarly history of baseball," one that is "an extension of the Ph.D. degree ... which adds to its authority while in nowise diminishing its readability." Henderson stated prophetically that the book "will remain ... the basic reference for baseball history."

Other reviews paid tribute to the book's solid and extensive factual base. *Baseball: The Early Years* "represents a tremendous amount of research," marveled the *Cincinnati Enquirer*. A reviewer for the *Washington, D.C., Army Times*, astonished at the revelation that so much baseball was played in the military services during early American history, said *Baseball: The Early Years* was "fascinating" and "the most thorough and entertaining of all the books written about baseball's early years." The *Baltimore Sun* called the book "a literary home run," while the *Chicago Tribune* said the book "gives life to the dusty records of the last century" and "manages to cover a tremendous amount of ground without becoming weary or wearisome."

The writing style of the book received its share of praise, too. The *Chicago Sentinel*, for instance, realized that the book was "not the usual kind of sports writing — and not the ordinary sort of book, either! [but] a history, a serious one, well-written, emphasizing baseball as a business, not a game."

Amazingly, one baseball owner also reviewed *Baseball: The Early Years*. William E. Benswanger, former president of the Pirates, wrote in the *Pittsburgh Press* that the book is "of greatest interest to real old-timers." He recognized the author's "intensive research" and said Seymour had produced a work that "deep students of the game" would find "engrossing." The book, he thought, was "a worthwhile exposition of historical background ... necessary ... in order to understand present-day development." He thought it "a highly useful book for the student and for the collectors of baseball lore." Benswanger seemed to believe that the book would be of use mainly to antiquarians, not realizing that owners of the sixties, and those still to come, might find it a cautionary tale.

Ford Frick, then Commissioner of Baseball, wrote Oxford after receiving a complimentary copy of *Baseball: The Early Years*, saying that he'd looked through it "with a great deal of interest," remarking that the book "seems to be a solid and factual presentation of baseball," as of course it was. If Frick had lived to read the third volume, *Baseball: The*

People's Game (he died in 1978), he would probably have liked that book even more, because about *Baseball: The Early Years* he commented insightfully that most researchers "forget that they are writing about an institutional game and confine themselves too much to organized and professional baseball. The real value of our baseball," he said shrewdly, "is the impact it has had on our people both as spectators and participants." Harold Seymour and I would, in the third volume about the amateurs, devote ourselves to making exactly that point.

Historians, too, appreciated the book. Professor Donald Grove Barnes, with whom I had studied at Western Reserve University, wrote for the *American Historical Review* that *Baseball: The Early Years* is "a serious study of the game" and "a good book," one that "both historians and ordinary baseball fans will enjoy." Barnes never knew, of course, how much a former student of his had contributed to this "serious study," for he did not realize that Seymour's wife had studied with him. Professor Carl Wittke, another Western Reserve instructor, wrote in the *Ohio Historical Review* that *Baseball: The Early Years* was "an important volume." He admired its "prodigious research" and said, "Seymour knows and loves his baseball, and he knows his American history, and so he has given us what is without question the best book on the subject."

Several reviewers recognized that the author's devotion to the game had made its contribution to the book. The *Louisville Times* recognized that Seymour was "an incurable fan." The *Jewish Exponent* believed that "only a person with a life-long love for the game plus a scholar's insistence upon fact and documentation could produce such a volume." The *San Francisco Chronicle* said the book was "faithfully and lovingly told," one based on "the first Ph.D. thesis on baseball by a right-handed former batboy." None of these newspaper reviewers ever suspected that not only a former batboy but also a former newspaper "copy boy" had contributed to the development of both the dissertation and the book.

Many readers assume that because a book receives favorable reviews it makes a good deal of money. Untrue. The three Seymour baseball books, although eventually considered classics, never did well financially or even made up for the money we spent producing them, money we earned through our day jobs. The books were labors of love — as are so many creative productions.

The best experience of publication came one day when we were walking south on Fifth Avenue toward Thirty-Fourth Street and, glancing to the left, noticed that a bookstore — I believe it was Scribner's — had decorated its entire store window with dozens of copies of *Baseball: The Early Years*. We were so astounded that we just stood there and stared. We never thought of going inside and offering to sign copies, or calling Oxford's attention to the phenomenon, or even snapping a picture. Instead, the image of that moment remained in our minds.

We celebrated publication of *Baseball: The Early Years* by taking our first trip abroad together. Seymour had traveled through Mediterranean countries during a cruise his parents paid for after he graduated from college in 1934, but I had never been farther away than Canada. At the invitation of a former Finch College student of Seymour's, Marcy Atkins, daughter of the well-known Cleveland fight promoter, Larry Atkins, we joined her and the lawyer she had married on a tour they planned, visiting most of the same places they visited. We stayed in Europe for seven weeks, getting acquainted with Florence, Venice, Naples, Sorrento, and Rome, Italy, and with Copenhagen, Denmark; in Germany we drove from Munich to Garmisch, stopping at Oberammergau, Dachau, and Heidelberg, and we drove the Rhine and Neckar valleys to Frankfort. We visited Amsterdam, Holland; Madrid and Toledo, Spain; Zurich and Lucerne, Switzerland; and Paris and Nice, France. In England we drove through the Cotswolds and enjoyed London, Cambridge, and Oxford, England. We met many Europeans and soaked up the atmosphere of Europe, which I savored.

At Oxford, Seymour and I gave ourselves the pleasure of stopping in at the headquarters of Oxford University Press, reveling in our connection with Oxford as an ancient center of learning. The Press representative who welcomed us promised to give *Baseball: The Early Years* "a good display" when copies arrived from the publisher's New York branch. Seymour, who had once dreamed of attending Oxford — his mentor, Sherman Plato Young of Drew University, who died in 1954, had spent a semester there — found it immensely satisfying to know that he had been able to attract Oxford's attention to his work.

In the famous Bodleian Library at Oxford I bought a souvenir postcard illustrating the game of cricket as shown in a Dutch manuscript dated circa 1340: it showed a monk wielding a bat and facing a nun about to throw the ball to him; in the outfield, waiting with raised arms, stood two more monks and two more nuns. Another evidence of early ball games in history.

A piece of sport information came to me unexpectedly when I was looking for something to read one evening at an out-of-the-way German *pension*. While browsing in an old German-language encyclopedia, I came across an entry for *Schlagball* (literally, hit-ball), which through its description I soon realized was the same game, or practically the same, as baseball. Since the innkeeper could offer me no typewriter, I copied the entire entry by hand, with bibliographical information, for addition to our growing collection about ball games abroad. Encountering this description made us more aware of the probable interrelationships of ball games worldwide.

Some of the sights I saw and people I met on this trip would inspire me much later in my own writing. I never forgot, for example, the sensation of becoming lost in the maze at Windsor Castle, or the thrill of seeing Stonehenge as it loomed on Salisbury Plain while we approached via the highway. At that time it was still possible to walk up to this mysterious and ancient monument, and it was one of the structures that I sketched excitedly. I took pleasure in reading about speculations on, and research into, those who occupied Europe during prehistory. Much later, I would find the opportunity of pursuing this interest through research.

Not neglecting the relevance of other sporting events to history, on July 16 we attended a cricket match at Lord's Cricket Grounds and watched Middlesex play South Africa, and later we were spectators at a *corrida* in the Plaza de Toros in Madrid. Cricket seemed to me like a polite, stylized pageant, complete with tea break; bullfighting like a cruel and bloody dance, with torture and killing reminiscent of the ancient Romans under the Caesars. By comparison, a baseball game appeared to me as a rule-directed contest of high skill and great intensity, a sort of practice for the competitive life of business in America, its fans as knowledgeable and serious as its practitioners.

Even before publication of *Baseball: The Early Years*, Oxford proffered a contract for the second volume, then named *Baseball: The Modern Era*, a book planned to bring the Seymour history of baseball into what was then the present (to 1960). We plunged immediately into the research with another trip to Cooperstown.

The main purpose of the Hall of Fame in those days was to display its collection of museum items. That part of the establishment failed to interest Seymour. "Who would ever want," he wondered, "to go to a baseball museum and see Babe Ruth's old jock strap?" Well, obviously, lots of people, although I never did spot a jock strap there. As for the library, it was still thought of only as a minor adjunct to the museum section and did not even have facilities for photocopying.

Lee Allen was now in charge of the library. He had been given the title "Historian of the Hall of Fame," and he delighted in it. The genial sports writer always welcomed us to his lair above the museum, and by that time he was addressing Seymour by his baseball name, "Cy." Lee once remarked with pleasure that we were "the only three in the world" who knew, from a story in the 1889 *Enquirer* that both Lee and I had noticed during our separate research stints on that paper, that seventeen-year-old Zella Coleman once caused catcher Edwin Bligh to be arrested on a charge of being the father of her unborn child, about which the newspaper reported that she had "yielded to his unholy desires last May." (Despite the old-fashioned wording, the story has a certain modern ring to it.) Lee and I had both found this quote irresistible and weren't surprised to discover that we had both recorded it in our notes.

The library looked the same as it had when we first visited — much like a high school classroom. The wall behind the director's desk was fitted with shelving containing books and boxes of manuscript; the rest of room contained only a few tables and chairs. Although the library had limited space and facilities, it had just accessioned the valuable Herrmann papers. August "Garry" Herrmann had been the head of the National Commission as well as the president of the Cincinnati Club, so the material he collected contained many documents relating to the history of the Commission as well as the history of his club. As usual, both Seymour and I worked on the research, each taking notes on different boxes of the collection so that we could cover all 72 of the boxes of material.

Lee was using the collection himself, for his next baseball book. In fact, at one point all three of us were using the collection at the same time. Working in the same room with Lee made obvious to us the difference in the way we as scholars approached the writing of a book from the method used by Lee and other sports journalists. Lee wrote much of his book first, before doing the research, then looked for information that would support his statements, filling in with details and quotations. ("I'm writing about the Merkle play," he would mutter. "I wonder if there's anything here about that... .")

We, on the other hand, worked mostly from the opposite direction.

As scholars, we performed the research first, sorting the resulting notes into topics. Then, as the material was being combined with the notes from other sources on the same topic, an outline of it began to take shape. But we did not write the book before organizing and analyzing the material we had gathered. In other words, instead of deciding in advance what we would put in the book, we wrote about what we had learned through research. Friends who heard we were doing research on baseball history would ask us, "What are you looking for?" The answer, of course, is the same one given by Detective Columbo: we would know when we saw it. What we found is what steered the formation of the book's outline.

Besides spending summers researching, we also made research trips during holidays. We went back to Cooperstown at the end of January 1961, to complete our work on the Herrmann Collection, Seymour arriving a few days before I did because he had several days off between semesters, whereas I took a bus from New York's Port Authority on Friday afternoon, arriving at Cooperstown during a snowstorm that delayed my arrival till midnight. We worked as late as we could both Saturday and Sunday.

One of the topics we knew in advance that we must address in the next book was the notorious Black Sox Scandal of 1919, in which some of the players of the Chicago White Sox accepted bribes to lose the World Series. To perform research in Chicago — mainly, in the *Defender* and the *Tribune* — at that city's Public Library and Historical Society, I wrote the librarians of both institutions saying I would be there during the Christmas holidays of 1962. Travel for research was not always comfortable. We found our hotel near the Chicago Historical Society a bit primitive and could hardly wait until our stay was over because of roaches spotted in the bathroom. At one New York hotel where we stayed, the door to our room was so ill-fitting that it could not be locked. But that wasn't as appalling as another New York hotel where Seymour's bed had fleas; he had to appear on television the next morning, so I gave him my bed and slept on the floor.

During the Chicago visit, I performed the research while Seymour attended the American Historical Association meetings taking place there. It must have been at this AHA meeting that Seymour had the encounter he remembered much later for an interviewer. He met a couple of historians who spoke to him there, asking him where he taught and what he wrote. They seemed surprised, he said, and even acted condescending, when he mentioned that he had written a book on the early history of baseball. Asking who published it, he could tell they expected it to be some small, unknown publisher taking a chance on an odd subject, or even a vanity press. When he announced that his publisher was none other than Oxford University Press, "it was like slapping them in the face," he recalled. "They couldn't believe it."

This triumph over condescension gave Seymour great satisfaction. It also demonstrates that scholars in the field of American history in the 1960s retained the traditional view of their field. Even after the publication of *Baseball: The Early Years*, baseball history, and sports history in general, appears to have earned little standing among historians and in university departments of history. Anything that seemed to fit into "social history" was less valued academically than political history or economic history. The rubric known as "popular culture," where baseball history might be bracketed, was still a distant cousin to the standard branches of history, most which were often given geographic rather than topical names (American history, European history, English history—Seymour taught these). Sport history may or may not be among the topics mentioned within such courses.

For Oxford to embrace the early history of baseball as a publishable subject probably made no difference in attitudes toward acceptance of the subject of sport history as a part of the study of American history. This attitude would continue far into the future. In 1983 sports writer Leonard Koppett, after attending his first conference of sport scholars, wrote a column of appreciation for their work in which he mentioned that they were "fighting the same uphill battle" that practitioners of women's studies faced because "they are too easily shrugged off as dealing with a triviality." And in 2003 Dr. George Gmelch, a professor at Union College in New York, speaking at one of the annual Cooperstown Symposiums on Baseball and American Culture, remarked, "It's tough to establish legitimacy when you teach about baseball unless you're a tenured professor at a prestigious institution."

So in the 1960s, the first book of sport history, *Baseball: The Early Years*, was hardly known in academic circles, and we never heard that instructors even used it as supplementary reading for courses in American history. Professor Mel Adelman believes that in the United States, history departments did not begin offering sport history courses before the 1970s.

Instead, the study of sport history generally entered the curriculum through university departments of physical education. The history of sport is sometimes included within courses centering on the history of physical education, although it is now offered separately as well. Seymour himself envisioned sport history as an aspect of American history rather than as part of the study of physical education. After all, baseball and other sports arose and grew up in America separately from physical education and without the benefit of information from that field, so they might more accurately be considered a historical phenomenon than an aspect of physical education. Although in Europe sport clubs may be close historically to instruction in physical education (as with the Turnverein), in the United States the connection of sports with physical education appears to be a secondary development rather than a primary one.

Seymour himself never had the opportunity of teaching a course in the history of sport, although when he taught at Finch College he once took students of his American History course on a field trip to Yankee Stadium, after first presenting a lecture on the history of American baseball and preparing the students about what they should look for. Today at Cleveland State University, formerly Fenn College, where Seymour first thought of teaching sport history in the late forties, the catalog still omits any listing for a course in sport history.

While we were working on the second volume, Seymour handled some research interviews on his own. One evening in June of 1962 he spent an evening in New York with Eliot Asinof talking about the Black Sox. He reported to Lee Allen that Asinof "lives just down the street" and that he "knows more about the Black Sox than I do." In December of that year Seymour saw and interviewed a player named Danny Gardella at Al Roon's, a New York club that had become a hangout for men with an athletic background, getting some insights into Gardella's 1940s suit against organized baseball, which we hoped to cover later. Gardella had left his club for a larger salary in the Mexican League, and on his return to the States he found that he had, like others, been banned from organized baseball for five years. He challenged the legality of the ban, but lawyers eventually settled his case out of court, so organized baseball's status outside the purview of the antitrust laws remained safe for a while longer.

Most interviews we performed were handled jointly. Together we visited and interviewed ex-player Ben DeMott at his home in Peapack,

New Jersey, on the Labor Day weekend of 1962, as guests in the home of the DeMotts. And when Albert "Happy" Chandler, former baseball commissioner, agreed to a phone interview from his home in Versailles, Kentucky, we prepared the questions together, and I typed them. Seymour used them on the phone, and I transcribed Chandler's replies. Later that month we viewed some short baseball films at the archives of WNEW-TV studios in New York, where I took notes. Seymour especially enjoyed watching an RKO film on modern bat-boys, whose experiences contrasted greatly with his own. Boys of his era did not write nice letters of application for the job; they simply tried every possible tactic to make themselves personally known and useful to the clubs.

George "Specs" Toporcer, baseball player, manager, and longtime friend, whom Harold Seymour met through Branch Rickey. Seymour was a "bird dog" for Toporcer. Some of Seymour's protégés made good in organized baseball through Toporcer's teams. (Photograph courtesy of the National Baseball Hall of Fame Library, Cooperstown, New York.)

One baseball contact of Seymour's went back to his college years. George "Specs" Toporcer, who had been the first infielder to wear glasses, was the manager of a Cardinals farm team, the Red Wings, in Rochester, New York, back in the late thirties when Seymour brought a couple of his best young players to spring training camp for tryouts. Seymour had retained his contact with Toporcer and even bird-dogged for him (a bird dog is a scout for a scout). George, who had since lost his sight, corresponded with us by mail, typing his replies to questions we posed to him. He and his wife Mabel lived on Long Island, and we occasionally saw them socially. The two men loved to talk baseball. Once at the Torporcers' home Mabel and I emerged from the kitchen to view a shocking sight: both men sprawled on the living room floor! We were relieved to learn that they were simply comparing notes on the correct way to execute a hook slide.

Another time George Toporcer, Seymour, and I attended a game at which stars of the past were honored. Because of George's status as an ex–major leaguer, we had very good seats. When I saw athletic-looking men entering the stands to sit near us, just behind the dugout, I noticed a familiar face. "There's Hornsby," I commented.

George, surprised that I recognized any player from that era, asked "How do you know it's Hornsby?"

I had to admit: "It's those dimples. I've seen his picture enough to recognize him by those dimples."

Getting information for the new book was not always easy. When we wrote the office of the baseball commissioner for a copy of organized baseball's booklet describing its player pension plan, Charlie Segar responded negatively, and Ford Frick stated that the information was "restricted." Realizing we needed to continue our work on *The Sporting News*, we tried to buy microfilmed copies, but C.C. Johnson Spink replied that the company owned only one copy of the film and suggested we purchase a set for $536.00 — a figure that was out of the question for us. Seymour had applied for, and received, a research grant from the American Council of Learned Societies, but that amounted to only $500.00. We subsidized our own research and writing. Oxford had given Seymour a small advance on royalties, but that didn't go far. An award called the Alumni Achievement Award from Drew University, Seymour's undergraduate college, was bestowed in 1962 but came with no accompanying funds.

Then Seymour was released from Finch College, the president giving as his reason that he feared Seymour, with his left-of-center tendencies, would take the students down a road he disapproved of. Seymour was shortly hired instead at Mills College of Education, also in New York, where again he taught young women. But that job proved impermanent as well, and finally we decided to leave the city in favor of the area where we had several times rented a summer cottage: in Orange County, just to the north. I found a teaching position in Warwick, New York, and we located a small home in nearby Chester. Seymour then interviewed at Orange County Community College in Middletown and was taken on as instructor in the Evening Division. Here he had some of his best history students, and I enjoyed reading their papers, which I marked up before Seymour read them. The students were pleased to find themselves learning as much English as they did history, and they began to realize the importance of clarity in presenting their ideas.

5 — Right Off the Bat

While I was teaching at Warwick I became a book author in my own right. A new method of teaching reading phonetically by means of a temporary alphabet caught my interest. This method, designed by Sir James Pitman (of Pitman shorthand fame), used an alphabet in which a separate symbol represented each of the 44 sounds of English. It was called the Initial Teaching Alphabet, and the children used it to become familiar with the way symbols represented language sounds; near the end of the school year they made a transition into standard typography, usually at a third-grade reading level rather than a second-grade, thus advancing their acquisition of reading by a full year.

I attended a workshop to learn how to use the new system and induced the principal to let me introduce it into my classroom. He in turn persuaded the superintendent to select a few classrooms of each Warwick school to try the method as an experiment and learn whether the I.T.A. children would out-perform those of other Warwick first-graders in reading. (They did.) My work with the Initial Teaching Alphabet launched a considerable correspondence with Sir James and led me eventually to other education projects.

While using I.T.A., as usual I prepared supplementary instructional materials for the rather sparse published set available, and I saw quickly that the students also needed more practice material, which I created in the form of short stories built on known sound-symbols, so that the children could read the words and sentences themselves and thus experience the thrill of becoming independent readers.

Realizing that other teachers who taught reading with I.T.A. needed this sort of material, too, during the Christmas vacation I took a bus to the office in Pennsylvania of the head writer, a college instructor in education, to show him the materials. He approved them and sent them on to the publisher, a branch of Pitman Publishing, who bought all ten of the stories I had written and published them as short books, paying me a flat fee of a hundred dollars each for publication rights, plus another hundred for a short teacher's workbook containing suggestions for using the books.

I then went to the editor of one of the two newspapers published in Warwick and volunteered to write and draw a weekly comic strip in I.T.A. so that the many Warwick children learning to read with the new system would receive additional practice in an entertaining format. The editor paid me five dollars for each strip, and the six-year-old pupils of the three I.T.A. classrooms discovered that they, like their older siblings, could also read the "funnies." Later I re-sold these comic strips to a children's magazine, which republished them.

That year I spoke on I.T.A. at a meeting of the local chapter of the American Association of University Women, and at an I.T.A. conference at Lehigh University, where I met Sir James Pitman and other educators important in the I.T.A. movement. That same year the Pitman Publishing Company sold the rights to my ten children's books to Grosset and Dunlap, which republished them for the general market, selling copies by the hundreds of thousands — for which I was entitled to receive no royalties, since I had relinquished the copyright. I saw the books selling in department stores and supermarkets, but after a while I forgot about them.

My work on these children's books had one immediate effect and one that proved long-term. First, a newspaper reporter for the local *Newburgh Evening News* actually included me in his story about Seymour and his work. For the first time we appeared jointly in a photo, captioned "Chester Writing Team," but ironically, the writer never mentioned that I assisted Seymour with his books; instead, the caption of the photo described Seymour as checking the progress I was making on mine! Other Seymour interviews had always failed to mention

Working at my portable typewriter with Harold Seymour in the yard of our home in Chester, New York, in 1965. The reporter-photographer thought Seymour helped me with my writing, when actually the situation was the other way around. (Photograph by Mike Krawetz from the *Newburgh Evening News*, July 24, 1965. Courtesy of the Division of Rare and Manuscript Collections, Carl A. Kroch Library, Cornell University.)

me except occasionally, in passing, to recognize my existence; no book reviews, among the dozens that appeared about the three baseball books, ever mentioned my contribution to the work.

The one long-term effect of the publication of these ten children's books would not become evident until thirty-five years later, when I suddenly learned, from the people who had grown up with them and doted on them, that some of these books had become classics.

Our main concentration remained on baseball research for the second volume.

6

A Whole New Ball Game

Publishers brought out many landmark baseball books in the sixties, seventies, and eighties, and we examined them all, taking notes as we added them to our shelves. They included Leonard Koppett's *A Thinking Man's Guide to Baseball*, Fred Lieb's memories as a baseball reporter, Herbert Hardwick's book on Effa Manley and her contribution to black baseball, Robert Obojski on the minors, Donn Rogosin's work on black players called *Invisible Men* (which was at first only in the form of a dissertation), Gerald Scully's *The Business of Major League Baseball*, Robert Smith's and Karl Wagenheim's biographies of Babe Ruth, Roger Angell's *The Summer Game*, Jim Bouton's *Ball Four*, Bill Veeck's autobiography, Robert Peterson's *Only the Ball Was White*, William Brashler's *Josh Gibson*, Leverett Smith's *The American Dream and the National Game*, and Donald Honig's *Baseball When the Grass Was Real*. University presses other than Oxford University Press had entered the field of baseball history and baseball biography, producing serious and solid works demonstrating considerable ingenuity and scholarship.

Seymour's baseball reputation had begun to build. Living in the New York area meant invitations to be interviewed on radio and television programs centered there, like Jackie Robinson's and Roy Campanella's. The Robinson show aired May 21, 1960. Jackie had obviously been prompted, for his first question to Seymour was, "You say I wasn't the first black big leaguer. Then who was?" Seymour explained that the honor belonged to Fleet Walker and that Robinson's achievement was to become the first in the modern era. Seymour was a guest on Jack Sterling's radio program and on Long John Nebel's all-night talk show, answering phoned-in questions about baseball until long past midnight, when calls finally began to slow down. Roy Campanella seemed to enjoy chatting about baseball with Seymour on his program, called *Campy's Corner*.

Living in or near Manhattan also made it easy to advance our research considerably, especially research in a topic that intrigued me increasingly: foreign baseball. In the New York Public Library I had been discovering a great deal of material on the early contacts of American amateur baseball players and teams with Japan as well as the growth of baseball in the Orient.

For years I'd been interested in the Japanese culture and had become intrigued with the way baseball filtered into it during the Meiji era of the 1860s and '70s through American diplomats and others working in Japan. I enjoyed Robert Whiting's *The Chrysanthemum and the Bat* (1977) as well as the Ruth Benedict book that preceded it, and I liked reading Japanese literature. Always fascinated with linguistics, I had even learned to speak a few words of the language and to read a little in its romanized form (*Romanji*). I searched books for mentions of early contacts with baseball and began writing to Japanese sources like the Japanese Baseball Commissioner. I communicated, in Seymour's name, with Wasedo and Keio universities about the American and Hawaiian tours of their baseball teams in the 1900s, and I sorted out and organized my evidence of early baseball play by American military clubs in the Orient. My collection of information on early Japanese baseball began to grow.

At one point Professor Junji Kanda, an aide to the Japanese Commissioner of Baseball and a correspondent of ours, visited New York. We obtained an interview with him, held at the offices of the Fifth Avenue importers Masaoka-Ishikawa, but when we met him we soon realized that his letters to us in English must have been written by someone else, for he knew hardly any English. Brief replies to a few of our questions came through his friends and translators, the importers, but we learned little from the interview, although Professor Kanda seemed to appreciate the few pleasantries in Japanese that I was able to contribute to the occasion. I was sure, however, that in the second volume we would need to include a great deal on early Japanese baseball, and I kept plumping, despite Seymour's lack of interest, for scheduling a research trip to Japan.

Learning the way baseball started and developed abroad intrigued me. Although baseball grew out of games that probably originated in Europe, after the closing of the frontier Americans began exporting their version of the game. I was collecting and organizing all the material I had found on early baseball in other countries, adding to it by writing for information. Using Seymour's name and describing the volume we were preparing, I wrote to baseball organizations in Europe, the Caribbean, and South America, obtaining material on past and present baseball activities from helpful contacts in England, Belgium, France, Nicaragua, and Italy. The information they sent us about the introduction to baseball in their countries, along with other research I performed on the topic, is still in the files of the Seymour Collection, for we eventually found it impossible, for space reasons, to fit in anything about foreign baseball, either for Volume Two or Volume Three, except for mentioning contacts made by American teams who visited other countries.

In fact, it soon became clear that the amount of material we were collecting, and I was organizing, for the modern age of baseball (1903 to the present) could not possibly be covered in one volume in the detail we were planning to write it. We explained the situation in a long letter to Sheldon Meyer at Oxford, and the company then rewrote the contract, calling the newly-conceived book *Baseball: The Golden Age*, which we thought might bring the story of the major leagues through the 1930s, with the understanding that a third volume, for which we continued to collect material, would be written about the majors from the thirties to the (then) present. This was a whole new ball game.

A development in Seymour's teaching changed our situation once more. During the school year 1964-1965, Dr. Harold Shively, the director of the night sessions at Orange County Community College in Middletown, told Seymour he had been asked to start a new community college just north of Boston. Shively asked Seymour to go with him to the new college as head of its history department. We left in May of 1966 and bought a home in West Newbury, Massachusetts, from which Seymour would commute to Beverly, where the new college had been built. After our arrival in the Boston area, Seymour appeared on a television program, *Boston Forum*, talking baseball with Palmer Payne. He was also interviewed on radio by Mike Wallace, a nationally-known and respected newsman, who complimented him afterward on a good performance.

While at North Shore, a new institution still without academic traditions, Seymour wrote a piece for the college's commencement program explaining the meaning of the colors and styles of the academic costume — particularly the hoods worn by the college's professors — that those attending graduation ceremonies would observe during the ceremonies. This informative article, called "Modern Scholars in Ancient Garb," continues to be reprinted annually.

By that time, Seymour thought, colleges might be ready to seriously consider adding a course in sport history to the curriculum. So after getting settled at North Shore Community College he proposed a sport history course. I typed the proposal, entitled "Teaching History through the Medium of American Sports History," dated July of 1966, which contained a justification, an outline with procedures for handling the course, and even ways to evaluate the students' work. He submitted the proposal without much confidence and, predictably, it was rejected.

Harold Seymour at North Shore Community College, Beverly, Massachusetts, where he became head of the history department in 1966. (From a photograph that appeared in 1966 with a story from an unidentified Massachusetts newspaper. The image comes from a clipping in the Seymour Collection of the Rare and Manuscript Collections, Carl A. Kroch Library, Cornell University.)

Our move gave me the opportunity of rethinking my choice of occupation. By 1966 I had burned out as a teacher. After sixteen years in the classroom, I no longer enjoyed the work. Determined to change careers, I decided to study for an education doctorate at Boston University. I had already started work on a degree with a course at the University of Buffalo; in Boston I registered for another, a late-afternoon course with a professor at B.U. who specialized in reading instruction. I was also commuting to perform baseball research at Boston's wonderful library and publishing articles on reading instruction in education magazines as well as stories in children's magazines.

So at West Newbury, instead of taking a new position immediately,

I paused to work full-time at home for a while, organizing our baseball notes and outlining them for use in the second volume. I did not keep the outlines I had prepared for Volume One. The huge amount of paper we were collecting influenced my decision to toss these outlines. After all, when a book is completed, one discards early drafts; that's the usual drill. Not realizing that they could serve a purpose later, I failed to save them.

For Volume Two I had refined my technique of preparing these outlines. I began outlining substantial topics in great detail, using only those notes I thought useful. One outline still extant, called "Sunday Ball 1900–19," shows how I did it. I selected information general enough to open the topic and used it for introducing the material. Then I began writing, using the material as if I were writing the book itself, but adding, in parentheses, a brief notation of the source immediately after the quotation or my paraphrase of it. The source might be "Barrow to Herrmann 3-22-15 in Herrmann Correspondence" or "*Times* 12-9-27" or "Lieb in *Sporting Life* 7-18-14" or "*Sporting News* editorial 8-5-15." Some sentences contained several such parenthetical citations, inserted right after the phrases they were documenting. I was sure that inserting these sources in the outline helped in evaluating the statement I had written.

I organized the topic I was outlining by using subheads, with the material under each subtopic usually written chronologically. My outline for the topic "Sunday Ball 1900–19" is twenty-six typed pages long. I gave Seymour the outline to study, and he annotated it, then used it to write pages 359–366 of Chapter 18, "Hallmarks of a New Era," in *Baseball: The Golden Age*. The wording of the information that appears on these pages is not substantially different from the wording of the material on my outline.

As I prepared these outlines I fitted them together logically, finally writing what I called "outlines of outlines," which summarized a group of interrelated topics so that they could be more easily used to write a chapter on the main theme they supported.

After working at home for nearly a year I began to think about my next position. My interest in the preparation of teaching materials led me to the idea that perhaps I should seek a job in the field of educational publishing. Having already prepared and published materials in that field, I knew I could contribute to it.

6 — A Whole New Ball Game

The new emphasis in reading instruction was linguistics, and since the subject interested me deeply, I studied it independently, then applied for a position to the Reading Department of the reputable old education press, Ginn and Company, with offices in downtown Boston. Ginn, founded in 1867, published the famous Dick and Jane series, which had taught many American children to read.

During my interview at Ginn, I found that I had applied at an opportune time, for the company was about to start preparing an entirely new reading series with a linguistic emphasis. I was hired immediately as an editor and, as I demonstrated my special competence in linguistics, soon became senior editor in charge of the linguistic program for the series, which would create new instructional materials for children in kindergarten through sixth grade. In consultation with the senior author of the series, Dr. Ted Clymer, and especially with the linguistics advisor, Dr. Roger Shuy, I devised a graduated program in which the new series could introduce word analysis techniques that fit in with the latest discoveries of linguists about the relationship to reading instruction of the acquisition of language sounds and the letters that represent those sounds.

To handle my new position at Ginn I had to deal with an hour's commute each way five days a week between West Newbury and Boston, so I turned this to my advantage by bringing work to do on the train; luckily, I have always been able to work on trains and planes. As a senior editor I also utilized my writing skills, first in preparing reports and instructional memos and, second, in communicating Ginn's new reading program to the education community. The position of senior editor required some travel and considerable speechmaking, not only to the editorial staff and to groups of salesmen but also to teachers, especially at conventions of the International Reading Association, which were held in various American cities.

As I handled the responsibilities of my new position, I began to realize that the work offered me much more scope for my abilities than teaching did and was helping to broaden and develop me in ways classroom teaching could not. I found the job both challenging and satisfying.

One of the salient topics in reading instruction at the time was the problem of teaching reading to black children who came to school speaking a nonstandard dialect. Teachers reported that these children found it difficult to learn reading from text that represented pronunciations and sentence constructions unfamiliar to them. In studying the problem and the methods used in addressing it, I began to realize that the children's dialect, which interfered with their acquisition of reading, must relate to languages their ancestors had spoken. I decided to learn about the languages brought to America by the blacks who became slaves, for I was sure that the heritage of these languages was the source of the children's dialect. It followed that if the interference from the dialect was clarified, teachers could more easily address the children's speaking differences and thus help them learn to both speak and read in the standard dialect. I performed the research on this topic at the Boston Public Library, where I was doing baseball research anyway. In researching various African languages and their relationship to the inner-city dialect, I used the skills I had developed through my work on baseball history.

The result was my most-reprinted article, one that would continue to appear in various books and other publications over and over for twenty-five years thereafter: "Black Children, Black Speech," initially published in *Commonweal*, whose editor told me later that the magazine had never received so many requests for permission to reprint, or received them over such a long period of time.

The article revealed why inner-city children spoke as they did, demonstrating that they were not "making errors in speaking English" but speaking the English language exactly as black children had been learning to speak it for generations: in their own dialect, developed under the influence of the African languages spoken by their ancestors. I showed that their speech was comparable to the dialects of English used by other immigrants.

Another article I wrote at this time proved almost as popular and was even more closely related to my work at Ginn. It explained the difference between the phonics approach to reading and the newer, more linguistic approach, known as decoding. It showed reading teachers why and how the new linguistics approach was more logical and easier for children to grasp. This article, too, received many reprintings in various books.

My work in educational publishing stimulated my thinking so much that I published frequently in education journals. Before I even joined Ginn I had written for the *Journal of the Reading Specialist* and *Grade Teacher,* but while I worked full-time as an editor I was publishing in magazines with wider readership, like *The Reading Teacher, Education*

6—A Whole New Ball Game

Digest, Journal of Reading, Elementary School Journal, Elementary English, Instructor, and *Young Children.*

My main writing job, of course, remained my work on the forthcoming baseball book. I continued to use the Boston Public Library on vacation days, occasional weekends, and even sometimes at lunch breaks. Oxford was amazingly patient about delays in meeting deadlines — which were not, we discovered, really firm, as they were in the printing of a newspaper or magazine, or in the publication of a reading series. For the new Ginn reading series, every volume with its supplementary material had to be ready at the same time, so a large number of editors and writers worked on it at once, and their work had to be closely coordinated, since each book and piece of material in the program was related to those written for children and their teachers working at the previous level and the next level. With the baseball book, only two of us worked on it, and although Sheldon Meyer commented briefly on chapters we submitted, the decisions on what to include and how to treat the material were essentially ours. Even working as steadily as we could, carrying full-time jobs made the work slow going. So eleven years passed between publication of the first volume in the series and the appearance of the second.

It was satisfying for us both when Meyer wrote on January 28, 1966, "You have pulled together an enormous range of social and business history within a few chapters. I am amazed at the way you are constantly improving, and synthesizing material. You have done a superb job of bringing under control the vast range of material."

7

The Knuckleball

Organizing *Baseball: The Golden Age* made for a task that was different from the task presented by organizing *Baseball: The Early Years*, since we had no dissertation to work from. Yet the material falls almost naturally into an organization that is partly topical but also chronological, since the book necessarily carried the story of the major leagues forward chronologically from the end of *Baseball: The Early Years*.

The opening chapter establishes baseball's importance in American life as both sport and business in the beginning of the twentieth century. Citing newspapers, magazine articles and books, we showed that, for American boys and men and sometimes for women, their being fans of baseball was taken for granted in the America of their day. These fans looked to the structure of professional baseball to set the rules concerning the way the game would be played and presented to the public.

Restrictive practices, especially the reserve clause in the player contract, remained at the heart of the system under which the professionals operated. We demonstrated that the clubs' assertion of territorial rights (essentially, "I won't let you sell professional baseball games in this area; I'm declaring that it's mine") supports and reinforces player control.

The chapter describes and explains the administration of this structure by the National Commission, set up by the two major leagues in 1903 to carry out the National Agreement by arbitrating all disputes. One of the surprising facts revealed by my research into the background of members of the National Commission came from Lincoln Steffens, the investigative journalist and famous "muckraker." His revelations of corruption in major American cities included reporting a conversation he overheard between August "Garry" Herrmann, the Cincinnati Club owner and also Commission chairman until 1920, and George B. Cox, the Cincinnati political boss who was also one of the owners of the Cincinnati club. In this exchange Herrmann admitted to Cox that he was merely the tool of the political boss. One cannot help wondering what this admission meant for the way the Cincinnati Club furnished entertainment to citizens and the way the Commission made its decisions.

A gregarious sort, Garry Herrmann gave many parties. But the dominating member of the Commission was Ban Johnson, who had created the new American League and gave it strong leadership. Johnson and Herr-mann, I discovered, were also drinking buddies, and their personalities contrasted greatly with that of another Commission member, Harry Pulliam, a sensitive soul who within six years committed suicide.

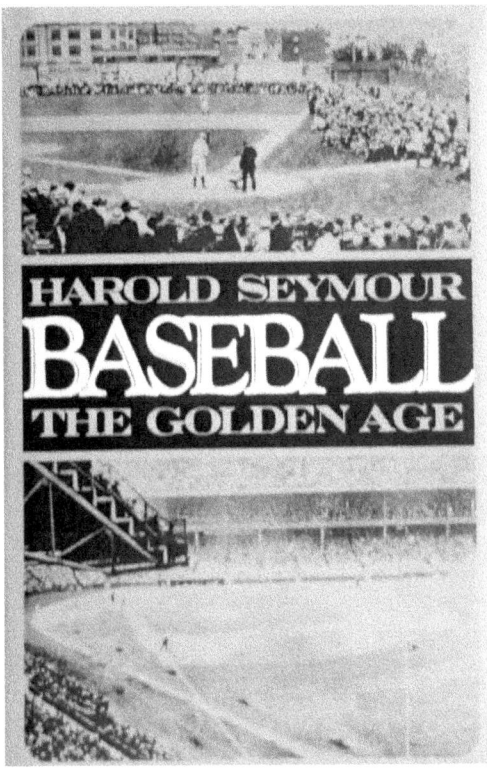

Baseball: The Golden Age (Oxford University Press, 1971), the second volume in the Seymour series, developed by Seymour with my substantial help. (From *Baseball: The Golden Age* by Harold Seymour, copyright 1971 and 1989 by Oxford University Press, Inc. Used by permission of Oxford University Press, Inc.)

The Commission had to face several player problems and a number of disagreements among owners, who often tried to take advantage of each other. Because of Cooperstown's acquisition of the Herrmann Papers, we were able to present the details of many disputes and their often-private settlements. We were the first researchers to work through the Herrmann Papers systematically, and the work paid off in clarifying the inner workings of the Commission.

The second chapter covered the way the individual club owners did business. Remarkably, unlike modern owners, these men generally admitted that they were in the baseball business for the money. They obviously wanted to be viewed as businessmen. It was intriguing to notice that they even tried to look and act like the successful entrepreneurs of the period, complete with cigars and the typical large bellies draped with gold watch chains.

National League owners often gave only lip service to their own rules and even undercut their own league president in his decisions. The fact that some clubs in both leagues owned stock in other clubs made for suspicions concerning the fair outcome of games in which interlocking ownerships prevailed. Might an owner who had stock in a rival team influence it to lose against his own club? Or vice versa? Nobody could tell. Revelations of all these machinations on the part of club owners in a chapter entitled "Politics and Partisans" were to provide many surprises for readers.

It's intriguing to consider that in 2001, when Jim Bouton accepted election to the Baseball Reliquary's "Shrine of the Eternals," in a witty speech he predicted — only partly with tongue in cheek — that in the future, following the general American trend toward mergers and acquisitions, one company would own all of the baseball teams. The owners would thus legally be able to

Harold Seymour in June of 1960, during one of our research trips, pointing to the sign, erected by the New York State Highway Commission, at Doubleday Field, Cooperstown, New York, that reads: "DOUBLEDAY FIELD/WHERE BASEBALL/WAS INVENTED AND/FIRST PLAYED IN 1839." The Seymour books helped disprove this claim. Doubleday Field is also the final resting place of Harold Seymour's ashes. (Author's collection.)

cooperate in controlling players' actions as they desired. This prediction may not be as extreme and ludicrous as it sounds. After all, the owners were beginning to approach that point in the 1900s with their interlocking club ownerships.

In a short chapter that followed the presentation of the club owners' business, we explained the complicated relationship among the owners of baseball clubs, a system in which they must both cooperate and compete to present entertainment; otherwise, the regularly-scheduled games that kept fan interest going would be impossible. The system they used to maintain their relationship included a variety of restrictive practices: not only the reserve clause and territorial rights but also the newer draft and waiver rules (for obtaining and keeping players), arrangements for splitting ticket sales (the owners cheated each other in reporting attendance), and arrangements with other businesses like transportation and other sports and entertainments that were coming to the fore. I discovered material in the New York Public Library's Theatre Collection about baseball movies and shorts, even about instructional films. The players, I learned, earned nothing for permitting themselves to be filmed in the World Series, despite an announcement by the league that they would be paid for their appearance.

Following this chapter we presented one giving details of the way the individual owners ran their own club businesses—how they built their parks, for example. In this era the magnates seem not to have thought of trying to blackmail their local city governments into giving them money to help build their baseball parks. Construction of those parks, we discovered, often caused them problems with labor unions or, conversely, with organizations that opposed labor unions, depending on whom they hired to do the work. Either way, they got complaints. To schedule games they preferred mid-afternoon for a starting time, in order to get husbands home for a 6:00 P.M. meal because, as Chicago Cubs president Charles Murphy said, "We must cater to the wives and cooks ... and try to get our patrons home in time to keep peace in the family." His statement assumed, of course, that "wives and cooks" cared naught for watching baseball themselves.

We had collected information about park equipment as well as playing equipment, and we learned that the parades of player carriages (this was still the era of carriages) from hotel to ball park and back were discontinued because they exposed visiting players to jeers and missiles from local fans, who could evidently be as hostile as they can be today. At the park, lineups and changes in them were announced by a man using a megaphone; Seymour had himself seen this done in his youth at Ebbets Field.

Game promotion attempted by the owners included buying brief ads in the newspaper, starting knothole gangs, and holding special days like Ladies' Day, when presumably "wives and cooks" would be catered to. But I discovered that club owners permitted both Suffragettes and Anti-Suffragists (those opposed to allowing women to vote) to make money on selling special tickets! Owners could be even-handed about promoting fans' agendas. Women, although welcomed as paying fans at baseball parks, didn't get the vote nationally until 1920.

Fans at baseball parks could already purchase all kinds of food, drink, and tobacco in the park: my favorite example was the sandwich with "translucent" ham that a reporter complained about. (It cost him five cents.) Harry Stevens, already the leading concession entrepreneur, was building his empire and being described as driving a "swell" auto and living in a "palace." Owners were making money from Coca-Cola and from an agreement with Western Union in which it furnished baseball news to subscribers to a news service. Owners were also rich enough to hold their meetings at New York's most famous hotel of the era, the Waldorf-Astoria.

Players came in for description in "The Making of a Hero." We showed that, even at this early period, some fans were following the stars to spring training sites. Barnstorming in small towns fed fans' baseball interest, as did boys' books of the period that I searched out and read — books that idealized players as demonstrating all the old-time virtues that Americans claimed to believe in, like honesty and self-reliance. The hundreds of magazine articles I read as a result of my study of the *Reader's Guide to Periodical Literature* often portrayed players as models of "clean living and quick thinking." In this chapter, however, we described many of their less savory exploits.

Not all Americans could rise to the professional level in organized baseball, no matter how self-reliant they were. American Indians could, however, aspire to that level, and so could some Jewish men — or men presumed to be Jewish. But black Americans certainly could not, and when Cubans were imported, men with dark skin were excluded. In the Herrmann Collection I found evidence of the Cincinnati Club's efforts to ascertain, for fan consumption, proof that the Cuban players being hired were "genuine Caucasians." The Club ownership assumed that fans desired to see on their team only those players with white skin.

Sportswriters of the period, we found in analyzing their comments, often suppressed or at least euphemized the less admirable exploits of players. In connection with player misbehavior, we discovered that the newspaper terms "malaria" and "rheumatism" for player illnesses were actually synonyms for syphilis and gonorrhea. Proof was found in the Cincinnati Club's correspondence concerning certain players and in talking to former players, who told us about the cases of "social disease" they knew of. Sexually-transmitted diseases and those who contracted them remained unnamed in the public press. But then, how often do we see them mentioned on today's sports pages?

Although reporters kept some escapades quiet, writers of articles and books might reveal their oddities. Ring Lardner's depiction of baseball players gently parodied the unsophisticated minor leaguer whose letters home displayed his gullibility and his limited education. Many years later, while I was preparing my web site, *www.HaroldSeymour.com*, I reread letters written to Seymour in the 1930s by the young men he had helped get into organized baseball; they wrote him of their experiences and successes in the minor-league cities in which they were playing, and I was struck with the similarity of these letters, in tone and expression, to those created for *You Know Me Al* and *A Busher's Letters*. I realized then that Lardner had caught the lingo, the sentence structure, and the sentiments of these artless young fellows perfectly.

In the chapter "A Ball Is a Ball Is a Ball," we used notes we had collected describing the way certain prominent players and managers did their work. I outlined two boxes of notes that I had labeled "The Game on the Field," from which we prepared "Stars and Galaxies" as well as "A Ball Is a Ball," with the help of a six-page outline I prepared, explaining the topics in these boxes, annotating each point, and writing transitions into chapters. In characterizing the famous managers John McGraw and Connie Mack, Seymour had the advantage of having seen both of them in action on the field — in fact, on Brooklyn's Parade Grounds he had himself been known to fans as "McGraw" because of his similar style of club management. Now I helped him perfect characterizations of these men that later came in for much praise from reviewers.

To explain which clubs and players dominated play in the era 1901–1920, we decided to write about each season and its stars. To demonstrate the disparity of competition in this era, as certain clubs took more than their share of the pennants and some never won at all, at Seymour's request I prepared information for a chart to show the pennant winners over the years in each major league. We also collected photos of star players and clubs, paying premium prices for those from New York agencies like Culver and Brown Brothers for the use of their file photos but obtaining photos less expensively through the Boston and New York Public Libraries and the Hall of Fame Library at Cooperstown.

We then showed, in a chapter called "The Seeds of Union," that the methods the owners used to control players made it easy for abuses to creep in. Our notes from the two collections of manuscript relating to the Cincinnati Club helped document these abuses, but newspapers recounted them, too. Law cases, Congressional hearings, and papers in George Toporcer's possession, which he kindly lent to us, furnished details.

These abuses left organized baseball open to the formation of Davy Fultz's Fraternity, a players' union. They also led to having players stolen away by the next challenger, the Federal League, which in 1914 offered a more liberal player-relations policy than did organized baseball. Players who were proffered more money and agreed to leave their clubs for a Federal League Club were said to be "jumping" their contracts. They signed with clubs that they hoped would be able to pay them better. Legal cases I studied helped interpret events and, significantly, showed once more that organized baseball's contract lacked mutuality and so could not be enforced. In newspapers and magazines I found and savored clever little poems like:

> Sing a song of dollars:
> A pocket full of kale;
> See the players jumping,
> Hear the magnates rail.
>
> Soon the season opens
> Salary coming due
> If it's not forthcoming,
> Jumpers will be blue.

The inevitable end of the two-year trade war with the Federal League arrived in the usual way: the winners absorbed the losers, so the

7—The Knuckleball

players, no longer with a choice in the matter, had to sign with their teams even if their salaries were cut.

Our analysis of attendance figures of this period showed that, although organized baseball's clubs drew fewer fans in 1914, the onset of World War One didn't cause the drop in attendance, as some writers believed; after all, the United States didn't enter the World War until 1918. In fact, fans were still going to baseball games in goodly numbers. Those writers who saw only the lowered attendance figures had simply forgotten to add into the equation the attendance at Federal League games, which probably attracted many fans who had stopped going to American and National League games, since the Feds for a while fielded many good teams.

One important event of the Federal League war took place in the courts, when the Federal League charged organized baseball with being a monopoly, citing the anti-trust laws. Of course, it is a monopoly, but so many important people fear to disrupt baseball that the monopoly will probably never be destroyed.

We discovered and read the briefs and transcripts in the case of the Baltimore Federal League Club versus organized baseball, which revealed the terms of the settlement along with details of the BaltFeds' finances and the Federal League contract. But the Feds may not have realized that the judge in the case, Kenesaw Mountain Landis, was a devoted baseball fan. He informed the Feds' attorney of his "shock" at the labeling of players as "labor" and the suit's attempt to "tear down" a "national institution." Landis then stalled the case for a year — until the trade war was over and any ruling mooted. It seems likely that baseball owners never forgot this service to their business by the sympathetic Judge Landis, and when they decided several years later that they needed a "dictator," he became the lead candidate.

From this topic we moved into the way another war, The Great War (as World War I was then known), affected organized baseball. The league heads argued for keeping baseball going during the War and exempting players from the draft, although *Stars and Stripes* disapproved of the plan. To avoid the draft, players swarmed into steel mills and shipyards, where they played with industrial teams, nearly causing another trade war. It's not true, we found, that the government forced the owners to shut down during wartime. Closing or staying open was left up to organized baseball, so the owners merely shortened the season, releasing their players early without paying them for the rest of the season and agreeing secretly not to steal players from each other. Reductions in players' World Series shares caused a brief strike, for which players were later penalized.

Reading the case of the BaltFeds against organized baseball revealed the surprising fact that in 1918 some clubowners approached Chief Justice Howard Taft to be Commissioner and that he said he would have accepted if the American League had not prevented his appointment.

The owners, it's clear from all their wrangling, fought almost constantly over players and finances. Those who lost players George Sisler, Scott Perry, and Carl Mays because of the decision of the Commission could not accept the ruling. We found the revealing correspondence in the matter of Sisler bound with the BaltFeds legal case. Torrid meetings on the part of the owners led only to a tenuous peace in 1920, at which point the country suddenly learned that the World Series of 1919 had been crooked.

Nothing has fascinated baseball writers and fans more than the Black Sox Scandal of 1919. When I was an English student, I knew little about 1919 besides its use as a title in a John Dos Passos trilogy and a reference to the "fixing" of the World Series that year in F. Scott Fitzgerald's *The Great Gatsby*. But as soon as I began working on baseball history, I learned about that series of numerals as a powerful symbol of appalling deception and enduring disappointment. In fact, an entire book, Daniel Nathan's *Saying It's So*, was published in 2003 about the obsession of journalists, historians, novelists, filmmakers, and fans with this subject. Probably the two best studies published of the scandal itself, before *Baseball: The Golden Age* appeared in print, were *Eight Men Out* by Eliot Asinof (1963) and *The Great Baseball Mystery* by Victor Luhrs (1966). We studied both, of course, as well as everything else we could find on the events and the people involved, including magazine articles, newspaper reports like those in *The Sporting News*, the *New York Times,* and the *Chicago Tribune*, along with hints from the guidebooks, the book written by Bill Veeck, clippings in the Scully Collection of the Chicago Historical Society, and biographies of the notorious gambler Arnold Rothstein and the attorney called "The Great Mouthpiece," William Fallon. After reading all this, however, we still had to make our own presentation of the events. Analyzing this material hardly solved the mystery of exactly what happened, and I doubt if every detail will ever be known, but our research gave us a lot more than anyone else had uncovered to that point.

In pondering how to present the scandal, Seymour relied upon my chronological outline of the way the matter was revealed to the public in the press: he decided to write the story as it unfolded to fans in the newspapers. Even without knowing for sure who was crooked and who wasn't, it's a riveting story. More than thirty years later, in 2003, Dr. Steven Riess, presenting a re-evaluation of the Seymour books, called this presentation in *Baseball: The Golden Age* "Seymour's outstanding discussion of the Black Sox Scandal."

A player who, to fans, represented the tragic aspects of the case is Joe Jackson, one of those fired from the league for accepting gamblers' money but who may not have sabotaged his team. Researchers and fans have often asked me what Seymour meant when he wrote, "I once asked Shoeless Joe Jackson about the scandal, and he named one of the 'honest' players and suggested I see him." Until now I have been reluctant to clarify Seymour's remark, but I finally decided that in this book I would reveal the answer to the fans' question.

Seymour's first wife and her family came from Greenville, South Carolina, Jackson's home town, and Seymour was there often in the forties, before I knew him. After Jackson's dismissal from organized baseball, he operated a store in Greenville. One summer day Seymour brought a baseball to the store and asked Jackson to autograph it. The player accepted the ball and replied that if Seymour would return the next day, he could pick up the ball with Jackson's signature on it. Seymour realized that, as had long been suspected, Jackson was illiterate and would have his wife sign the ball for him.

The next day, when Seymour returned for the autographed ball, he got up the nerve to ask Jackson about the scandal. Jackson bristled and replied, with sarcastic emphasis on the name, "You ask *Mr. Eddie Collins* about that." From this response Seymour gathered that Collins, one of the "clean Sox," had known in advance about the "fix" but did nothing about it. Collins might even have considered joining the cabal but decided against doing so. Probably, nobody will ever know whether Collins, the captain of the team, occupied a suspicious role in the "fix," but others suspected he did. I was amazed to discover, for example, that after the accused players were indicted, on an occasion when the Clean Sox who were their teammates had dinner together, Collins was quoted as saying, "We've known something was wrong for a long time, but we felt we had to keep silent because we were fighting for the pennant." That remark, I think, lends credence to Jackson's accusation hinting at a cover-up by those who, like Collins, were pretty sure of an attempt at crookedness but didn't want to disturb the status quo, since it might jeopardize their own livelihood.

When I give lectures nowadays about my historical novels, I remind my audiences that what historians have supposedly discovered about the past is hardly the ultimate truth. I point out that it's merely one layer, a veneer that may contain distortions and even falsehoods. "The journey into our past is one we can take only superficially," I always tell them. "We'll never know everything that once happened." Nothing makes this bald fact clearer than trying to delve deeply into an event like the Black Sox Scandal, whose details remain elusive no matter how much time and energy is spent on extracting them, analyzing them, and trying to resolve conflicting pieces of evidence. Attempting to get at the ultimate truth of the affair is like attempting to avoid being surprised by the approach of a knuckleball.

Since *Baseball: The Golden Age* was published in 1971, more material on the scandal has been unearthed by diligent researchers, particularly by members of the Society for American Baseball Research (SABR). But probably the salient fact about the matter is the enormity of it all. The scandal deeply dismayed baseball fans, who wanted to believe that the national game was above reproach. The owners, who had for a long time desired to change their method of governance, used the scandal as the pivot for the change to a different type of ruling authority.

But, as we showed in the fourth section of *Baseball: The Golden Age*, a section we called "The Tarnished Image," baseball gambling and even crookedness was not fresh in 1919. It had been going on, and news of suspicious events had often been muted or covered up, since early in the century. The 1919 scandal differed only in that it was simply too large, and involved too many important names, to be downplayed. Adverse public reaction had to be dealt with.

The scandal did not cause the appointment of Judge Kenesaw Mountain Landis as Commissioner, as long thought by earlier writers; it was merely, as I believe we proved, the last straw in a series of arguments among the owners that led to their dissatisfaction with the three-man Commission. Besides, long before the revelations of the Black Sox

Scandal, the owners were already considering a plan to appoint outsiders to a new position that would govern the leagues in organized baseball. So when they sought and obtained the services of Landis, they were ready to acquiesce in his demand for absolute power to take action on problems rather than to merely recommend action.

After the Black Sox revelations but long before the trial, Landis declared publicly that the accused men, no matter what the courts decided on their guilt, would never get back into baseball. He placed all eight accused players on the ineligible list.

Seven players were indicted, the case against the eighth being dismissed for lack of evidence. Ten gamblers were indicted, but they either vanished, changed identities, played sick, or denied any participation. The players and two gamblers were acquitted in the courts, but afterwards Landis declared once more that the accused players, even though acquitted, would never get back into organized baseball.

From the evidence we had accumulated, we were sure that the accused men had met with gamblers and received money, but whether they actually carried out the plot to throw the games is unclear and will perhaps always remain obscure. We showed, in the three chapters of *Baseball: The Golden Age* relating to the scandal, that Chicago White Sox owner Charles Comiskey certainly bears some of the blame for the players' actions. Probably, so does the gambler Arnold Rothstein.

When in 2003 Gene Carney, a SABR researcher, visited Cornell University to examine our notes relating to the Black Sox Scandal, he wrote me afterward that he found the experience enlightening. In going through those files for more than five hours, he learned something about the way Seymour and I put it all together, remarking:

> I loved reading the comments, questions, and !!! scattered about. It reminded me that historians do not simply assemble facts, they also evaluate them; they report what happened, but also what might have, could have, or should have been done.

Carney realized from reading our notes that the task of collecting and analyzing this material took a great deal of thought. Others are still pondering these events and looking for more clues to what happened.

For *Baseball: The Golden Age*, we demonstrated that in the new era of the twenties, baseball was affected by forces like the growing importance of the automobile, the radio, and rising income among all workers.

Baseball players continued to press individually for better pay and often objected to being traded. Our being able to quote directly from their correspondence with owners — much of it found in the Herrmann Correspondence — made their requests seem more immediate and real.

One of the more interesting players was the talented Hal Chase, probably the most crooked player of them all. We found fascinating material about him the year we lived in Buffalo. His Federal League contract and other documents were filed in the Erie County Clerk's office. Other legal material helped in the writing of this volume: the transcript of testimony in the trial of Lee Magee, another cheater, was in the Herrmann Papers. In Cleveland's law library I read details of the story of Bert Hageman, who objected to a salary cut when he was traded, in a law case pursued for him by Davy Fultz's Baseball Players' Fraternity. The case dragged on for five years, and Hageman finally won.

I enjoyed reading all the biographical material about Landis that I discovered. He was surely a free-wheeling egotist who flouted the law in favor of making arbitrary decisions that were often overturned later. He failed to resign his position as a Federal judge until fifteen months after being appointed head of organized baseball and not until an official Congressional complaint against this unbecoming greediness became public knowledge. In the twenties Landis banned several other players for life when evidence against them seemed sufficient to him.

Correspondence among owners about these cases greatly strengthened our use of the material found about them in the newspapers; there's nothing like reading the original words written by the participants for revealing their real feelings about these cases.

Players' and owners' betting never stopped, of course. In those days the Yankees were checking racing results between innings, and Rogers Hornsby gambled away thousands of dollars on horses. Some later players, like Pete Rose, enjoyed betting, but so did owners of the earlier era, some of whom refused to stop doing it. The Cobb-Speaker scandal of the twenties may be the best place to look for parallels with Rose's case. Ty Cobb and Tris Speaker were "permitted to resign" in the face of betting charges and then reinstated when Landis ruled that the two were "not found guilty of fixing a ball game" — rather a backhanded way of saying, "We have no proof that they are crooked players." Their judgment was surely flawed, however; pretty solid evidence exists that they bet on baseball. Nonetheless, these players were still elected to the Baseball Hall of Fame. Should personal character count in election of stars to the Hall of Fame? If it should count, what level of perfection should we expect of our baseball heroes, and who should decide upon that level? No satisfactory answer to those questions has come to the fore.

Material we found on Ban Johnson's ejection from his position at the head of the American League made for a rather touching yet classic story: the downfall of a once-powerful leader who had stayed in his job too long. We collected considerable material on Johnson, thinking of writing an article about him, but when Gene Murdock dropped in to visit us in Cleveland, we learned that he was at work on what turned out to be an excellent biography of Johnson, so we abandoned the article idea.

Although *Baseball: The Golden Age* was devoted to the major leagues, we knew it would be necessary to give some attention to the majors' relations with the minor leagues and with the burgeoning "farm system," a system in which a major-league club formed a relationship with a minor-league club that developed players for it exclusively. Branch Rickey was forming a whole chain of such agreements with minor clubs, in classifications from AA all the way down to D, sending players up and down the ladder at will. Landis saw this system as comparable to the "chain gangs" of the penal system, but since it did not break baseball's rules, all he could do was to watch for infractions and release players who had been ill-used. In describing the actions of Landis, Seymour, who was continually improving his writing skill, came up with the phrase "selective severity," a term I thought particularly apt.

Since the game on the field in the twenties was dominated by the exploits and personality of Babe Ruth, we used him as the fulcrum of the book's final section, in which we discussed changes in the balance between pitcher and batter caused by manipulation of the ball's resilience as well as by such rules as the one against the spitball. Seymour's favorite player was not Ruth but Cobb, since he thought that the style of play common before the advent of Ruth was much more conducive to fast infield moves and exciting plays around the bases. He enjoyed the display of athleticism, skill, and even ballet-like motions that the Cobb style of play seemed to demand. To fans of the era before Ruth, including Seymour, that was real baseball. Competition for home runs necessarily cuts back on these displays of infield activity and seems to make for long periods of dullness punctuated by very short periods of high excitement over towering homers, which are now underscored by fireworks and screaming. Whether these short periods of high excitement compensate for the dullness and the loss of displays of infielders' skill is a question that Seymour answered in the negative.

Since Ruth's ability to hit the long ball enabled him to take unusual advantage of the new curbs on pitching, he soon became the star of the game. His off-the-field hijinks had to be mentioned, too, although many of his personal failings were so unsavory that we simply omitted them — the details reported, for example, by a former roommate. After all, Ruth's main contribution to baseball lay in his striking accomplishments on the field, which forever changed the way the game was played. I'm sure that, if we had reached the point in baseball's history of treating the contribution of Joe DiMaggio, we would have handled his life the same way, downplaying his disturbingly unlikable personality, which a recent biographer, Richard Ben Cramer, has uncovered for fans.

We ended the book by describing the disparity of competition in the era of the twenties, as demonstrated by the way New York clubs dominated both leagues and some teams never won pennants at all. From the graph I drew showing this disparity, Oxford directed an artist to prepare one for the book. In this final chapter, to describe the dominant personalities of the period, Seymour used his advantage of having seen many of the era's players on the field himself and having been batboy for Wilbert Robinson's Dodgers. He also added his conviction that the boys' teams playing on Brooklyn's Parade Grounds cemented the relationship between kid ball and the Brooklyn team, beloved by local fans despite incompetent play and few wins. He believed that these feelings of close relationship between the boys and other fans with their local major-league players was reflected in other cities, during the era when baseball retained an emotional grip on America that may never again be attained.

Baseball was becoming a recognizable business, too, much like others of the era, with the same kind of trappings. To illustrate the nature of baseball ownership in that era we included, as an appendix, a list of some of the equipment owned by a club. It included ten dozen fire buckets, caps and badges for employees, four player benches, a hand lawn mower and a horse-drawn mower, and — to accommodate certain contemporary habits of men — nine cuspidors.

8

Two Strong Innings

Readers may assume that Seymour's personal experiences and his resulting love for baseball led him to idealize baseball history of the era covered in *Baseball: The Golden Age* by exaggerating its importance in American life. But I believe that the details about baseball history in the early twentieth century as presented in this book give full credence to the description of baseball's prominence in America life during the period it covers.

The theme of the book is that during the first three decades of the century, baseball consolidated itself from a basic economic structure established in 1903 into a national institution experiencing a "golden age" through its strong emotional grip on our culture.

In our Bibliographical Note, which we wrote in lieu of footnotes or chapter notes, we described the plethora of material examined and the libraries and other institutions where the material was found. We also evaluated some of the new and much better baseball books then appearing, like Larry Ritter's collection of transcribed tapes, *The Glory of Their Times*, in which he interviewed retired players, thus saving a valuable resource for historians as well as making a good book.

The presentation of our Bibliographical Note avoids introducing sentences with the phrases like "I read" or "I used," which are usually employed by authors, because Seymour himself did not look at much of the original material; by then I was handling most of the research. Since my taste tends toward social history, I found myself particularly interested in general leisure sources like Larrabee and Meyersohn's book, *Mass Leisure*; memoirs like William Bohn's *I Remember America*; and books on journalism like Stanley Walker's *City Editor* and Stanley Woodward's *Sports Page.*

Both of us read histories of the period like those of the historians William Leuchtenburg, Arthur Link, and Frederick Lewis Allen, as well as memoirs and biographies of persons who lived through those times. Nelson Algren on Chicago, George Wharton Pepper on Philadelphia, and Lloyd Morris on New York were all worth examining. Among the thousand or more articles I read, I particularly enjoyed E.J. Kahn's well-known 1959 piece on Coca-Cola for the *New Yorker.* I relished my perusal of old issues of once-popular periodicals like *Collier's, McClure's, American Mercury, American Magazine, Life, Independent, Munsey's, Outlook, Everybody's Magazine,* and *Saturday Evening Post,* all of which offered something that could contribute to the work of portraying baseball in the era.

In his Preface to *Baseball: The Golden Age,* Seymour acknowledged more individuals than he had in *Baseball: The Early Years,* mentioning, among others, George Toporcer and Lee Allen. His last sentence was, "Finally, I express gratitude to my wife, Dorothy Zander Seymour, who not only contributed her knowledge and professional skills to all phases of the work but exercised such patience with the author as to make Job seem like a chronic complainer by comparison."

I think the last clause refers to something I was refusing to recognize but knew was there: Seymour's increasing irritability, which would eventually contribute to long periods of depression. This irritability seemed to arise largely from his work situation. At some point I realized that he was no longer enjoying his teaching; he complained constantly about the college. I finally persuaded him to leave teaching and spend full time at home writing while I continued working full-time as an editor in Boston. That meant he was alone at home in West Newbury for about ten hours a day—not the best situation for such a reclusive person who did not make friends easily. But I hoped that removing the distractions of teaching would lead to increased focus on his work. That did not materialize.

But finally, everything came together, and *Baseball: The Golden Age* was published in 1971. We were so eager to see how it looked that we opened our box of books right at the Post Office, admiring the fine gold-and-black jacket on the hardcover edition (paperback editions of both volumes weren't printed until 1988). Oxford's clipping service kept us informed of the reviews, which were uniformly excellent. Again, reviewers recognized the special value of this baseball history as compared with those written by writers untrained in scholarship. Oxford invited us to New York for a dinner meeting at Sardi's with the advertising manager, Gerald Sussman, and paid for the weekend, during which Seymour was interviewed on radio shows.

The quality of *Baseball: The Golden Age* seemed to surprise reviewers, who summoned up the ghost of classic authors of the past for comparison with *Baseball: The Golden Age*. The *Times Literary Supplement* of London, England, called it "fascinating" and "a remarkable book" by "a highly intelligent writer," comparing Seymour to the great historian Hazlitt and calling him "a learned prose Pindar." Writer Robert Cantwell of *Sports Illustrated* started to prepare an article in which he called Seymour "The Gibbon of Baseball" but died before he could complete the piece. Another British paper, the *London Guardian*, recognized the book's solid analysis of the economics of baseball — as did the *Chicago Sun-Times*, which called the book "as indispensable to economists as it is to the enthusiast of so-called sports."

The amount of research displayed in the book came in for special praise. *Business Week* called it "splendidly researched," and the *Chicago Sun-Times* spoke of its "exhaustiveness" and "diligent research." The *Independent* of Long Beach, California, praised the book's combination of a "lively touch" with "deep research." *Publishers Weekly* declared the book "definitive" and said it was "noteworthy for its thoroughness." Ron Fimrite, quoted in the *Seattle Post-Intelligencer*'s supplement called *Book World*, opined that "no one has ever explored the national game so zealously." Of course, no one person could have done all the research necessary for the writing of the book. That the work was the result of collaboration, with most of the research done by Seymour's wife, remained unrevealed.

The writing, too, of *Baseball: The Golden Age* brought praise. The *News-Tribune* of Tacoma, Washington, asserted that the author "has managed to keep the readers entertained as well as informed." In Cleveland, Howard Preston of the *Plain Dealer*, whom I knew in the forties when he was a reporter on the *Cleveland News*, called Seymour both "a painstaking researcher" and "a thoroughly readable writer." Howard never knew that most of the research was performed by a woman who, as a girl in the newsroom, responded when he called "Boy!"

As with *Baseball: The Early Years*, this second volume's revelations of chicanery provided another surprise for reviewers, who had doubtless expected something closer to the fan histories of the past, which did little more than celebrate the exploits of sports heroes. The fact that Seymour revealed his love for the game while presenting its blemishes intrigued readers.

Despite the objectivity demanded by scholarship, Seymour's nostalgia for his early days as a player and fan certainly crept into the writing. Sports writer Shirley Povich put it this way in the *Washington Post*: the author's "love for the game is inescapable. So is his determined objectivity in exploring the rascally aspects of it."

Thomas Lask, reviewing the book in the *New York Times*, warned readers that in *Baseball: The Golden Age*, "commonly-held beliefs are destroyed or challenged," and that although the book is "not a debunker's manual," it "makes ignorance [of baseball's past] indefensible" and opens "a weighty ledger for the scrutiny of all." The *Boston Globe* reviewer realized that although the author "idolized baseball," he "treats the participants as a historian should: dispassionately." The *New York History Journal* stated that *Baseball: The Golden Age* "combined a fan's love for the game ... with a researcher's interest." Jonathan Yardley said the fact that Seymour is "obviously and ardently a fan ... does not blind him to the greed, mendacity and callousness of owners," which the book points out with "devastating documentation." Ron Fimrite of *Sports Illustrated* noticed that the author's "obvious affection for the game has not deterred him from recounting ... greed ... buffoonery ... and chicanery." And Professor Robert Beisner in the *American Historical Review* called Seymour "that rare person, a batboy-turned-iconoclast, not only a scholar but a baseball nut."

The lack of source notes in *Baseball: The Golden Age* failed to elicit complaint, even from academic reviewers. That the book was so obviously based on scholarly research seemed to alleviate, in the minds of readers, the necessity for footnotes or chapter notes. I'm sure their perception was aided by our effort to display sources within the text, because, as before with *Baseball: The Early Years*, we slipped sources right into the body of the story when it seemed natural to do so, especially crediting secondary sources when their author's ideas were used. We wrote, for example, "A few months later Johnson acknowledged in *Baseball Magazine* that..." (p. 207), and "Not until 1956 did Chick Gandil present in

Sports Illustrated his version..." (p. 331), and "*Sporting News* came as close as any to forthrightness when it announced that..." (p. 106). This manner of crediting sources helped readers understand that, like *Baseball: The Early Years*, this book was research-based.

One of the special features of *Baseball: The Golden Age* was the biographical sketches of important people of the period. We particularly enjoyed characterizing a person like Landis in a paragraph or two. Joe Overfield, who studied and wrote about Buffalo baseball history, pointed out that the book did "an exceptional job of portraying the leading characters" of the period, featuring "striking portraits" of Landis, Ruth, Ban Johnson, and others. The *Boston Globe* reviewer thought the author had "a knack of bringing personalities alive." Thomas Lask made the same observation, saying the book "restores flesh and blood to men who have too long been cartoons from a sportswriter's imagination." Professor Franklin Ford of Harvard particularly admired the "careful assessment of Landis."

Above all, readers seemed to find *Baseball: The Golden Age* absorbing reading. Although solid and "exhaustive" history, said the Virginia Kirkus Service, it was also "of interest to the average fan." *Business Week* found it "filled with delectable details," and the *Boston Globe* described it as "irresistible." To the *Chattanooga Times* reviewer the book was "thoroughly engrossing."

Reviewers often remarked that the book brought home to them the importance of baseball in America. *Publishers Weekly* called the book "fascinating" and said it was noteworthy not only for its thoroughness but also "for the way its author relates the sport to American life." Thomas Lask thought the book would "grip every American who has invested part of his youth and dreams in the sport." And Professor Ford believed the book displayed "admirable balance between history of baseball as a game and history of baseball as a business," thus "giving baseball its due as a genuine force and outlet for the emotions of millions of people."

Perhaps the most satisfying review came from sports writer Leonard Koppett, himself the author of several thoughtful books. Koppett showed complete understanding of the accomplishments of *Baseball: The Golden Age*. In reviewing the book for *The Sporting News*, he covered all the bases, declaring,

> Anyone interested in baseball history should be grateful to Harold Seymour.... What is so valuable about Seymour's work is its method. He is a trained historian working from original sources as well as from previ-

ously published material. It's not putting anyone else down to say that Seymour is the first author to put that kind of training and research techniques fully to work on baseball history. The result is something special.... Seymour was the first ... to attack the subject comprehensively. Nowhere else is there available so informative, so clear, so reliable and so well-ordered an account of what really went on. You can't possibly understand the reasons for today's baseball structure, or the forces at work in baseball's past, without going through the material Seymour has sifted. [In sum, he said, the book performed] an invaluable service.

Sports Illustrated's Book Club boxed the second volume with the first, for sale as a set to its club members, its promoter summarizing them as "widely acclaimed by sportswriters and critics as the most comprehensive survey of the game ever to appear"; the writer then went on to say, "Seymour's carefully documented and well-researched books will be with us for many years to come as the sport's only definitive history and most lively reference work."

Looking to the future, the *Providence Sun-Journal* declared that the author "has now pitched two strong innings and is a good bet to take the baseball-history series." That prediction proved correct. But the third volume, planned to bring the story of organized baseball through to the last inning, would not come near that goal. It would instead move off the subject of organized baseball entirely and go back to the beginning of the game's history to explore something that no book had ever attempted: telling the story of the way amateurs — everyday Americans — played the game themselves.

For some time we remained unaware that, in 1971, an organization was forming in Cooperstown that would become important to both of us: the Society for American Baseball Research (SABR), a group of serious fans, writers, researchers, and statisticians who created an association to study baseball and disseminate information about it. SABR quickly grew to include academic scholars, and eventually we would find it useful to know about the work of these men (at the time, all of them were men).

Our research trips to the library at the Hall of Fame in Cooperstown continued, as the library itself improved its scope and as its holdings became more valuable. Clifford Kachline, a former sports writer we found easy to work with, directed the library at that time. Another source of material was proving expensive: we found it necessary to purchase back issues of *The Sporting News*. Frequent trips to the newspaper office in St.

8 — *Two Strong Innings* 113

Some shelves of books at the library of the Baseball Hall of Fame, Cooperstown, New York, as it looked in 1972. By then, Harold Seymour and I had already been using it for research for twenty-three years, and we continued doing so for fifteen more years. (Photograph courtesy of the National Baseball Hall of Fame Library, Cooperstown, New York.)

Louis, necessitating costly stays in hotels, had become non-economic, so having our own copies seemed like the only solution.

At first we tried to circumvent Spink's policy of not selling microfilm to individuals: Seymour persuaded the college librarian at North Shore to write *The Sporting News* office to ask if the film could be sold to the institution instead. But Spink replied, in the fall of 1972, that he no longer supplied microfilm even to libraries, giving as his reason that libraries had every roll in their possession stolen! So instead, from a collector in Ohio we bought a large set of hard copies, covering the years 1949–1961, and paying only $50.00 plus shipping — a bargain. Of course, we had long been subscribing to the newspaper as well, and we saved our subscription copies, too. When Spink later changed his ruling on selling microfilm, we bought many reels of the newspaper on film, along with our own desktop electric microfilm reader, which I used myself (Seymour declined to use the device, finding that it tired his eyes).

In our research and writing we had to this point paid little attention to the other major historian who was writing on the history of baseball, David Voigt. When *Baseball: The Golden Age* was about to appear, the editor of the *Journal of American History* asked Voigt to review it for the *Journal* while at the same time asking Seymour to review Voigt's book. Neither author was aware of this arrangement. The *Journal* then published the two reviews in tandem. Seymour thought the device was simply trickery, and his editor at Oxford, Sheldon Meyer, was so incensed that he lodged a formal complaint with the editor.

To prepare for that review I studied Voigt's book carefully, checking footnotes with their sources and finding a great many errors, contradictions, and lapses. In the resulting report I wrote for Seymour, I made more than two dozen points. Seymour also looked through Voigt's book and made some notes. He then studied my report, checking off the points he wanted to use. After writing the first draft of the review, Seymour handed it to me for editing, as was our usual procedure, so the review is again the result of our collaboration.

At this time we were working on what we thought would be the third and final book in the series on the history of baseball, believing we could fit into it everything from the 1930s to what was then the present. So we studied everything we could think of that might help in covering and interpreting events like the business problems of the depression, the triumph of the farm system, the acceptance of night ball and radio, and the domination by the Yankees.

Seymour had been a fan during the era of the thirties and the forties, so he knew he would be able to do a good job in describing the game as it was played on the field during the period when DiMaggio came to represent excellence in play. We would certainly be devoting space to wartime baseball, showing how it differed from similar events of World War I. We worked on the final breaching of the racial barrier with the acceptance of Jackie Robinson, the challenge of the Mexican League, and the changes in the Commissionership. Seymour's phone interview of Happy Chandler and our long interview in New York with Marvin Miller, head of the players' union, and his colleague Dick Moss would be helpful, we thought. I typed a manuscript ten

8—Two Strong Innings

pages long containing my notes from the Miller interview, and Seymour annotated it.

The advent of blacks in the modern major leagues represented a story we were eager to write. That theatrical promoter Bill Veeck had brought Larry Doby to Cleveland while we were still living there. In fact, Doby made his debut with the Indians on my nineteenth birthday; I was being courted by Harold Seymour, and we attended the Indians game together. I remember the tension in the park as Doby, obviously nervous, tried desperately to make it as the first black on the team. Just watching him press so hard while at bat made me nervous, too, and I was glad to learn later that he made it with the team and that his career lasted for years.

I studied Robert Murphy's union, the American Baseball Guild of 1946, and began a file of teams that were transferring to other cities in the seventies, along with another file on the entirely new major-league franchises resulting from expansion of the leagues to include them. When the Dodgers left Brooklyn and the Giants left New York, Seymour became one of the many who, appalled at the sundering of long tradition, found the change difficult to accept. We took many notes on the new metropolitan team proposed by Bill Shea to fill the gap left by the beloved Dodgers.

While we were trying to collect and organize the material on the majors (along with their relationship with the minors), we continued to collect information about the amateurs and semipros. In fact, we had never stopped collecting this material. More closely connected to social history, in my opinion, than the story of major-league baseball, the information we continued to encounter about amateur and semipro ball proved compelling. More was constantly being discovered about this vast ocean of unrecognized amateur play that underlay and fed interest in the major leagues. The colorful stories unearthed by locals interested in their own city, town, and country baseball history proved irresistible. We could not ignore them. So all the while we were planning to write about major-league baseball from 1930 to 1960, we were still finding fascinating material about children and adults who played the game on their own, with little sponsorship or none at all. And we kept adding to this collection of information, which covered every era, including the eras we had already covered in *Baseball: The Early Years* and *Baseball: The Golden Age*.

A European trip in 1968 took us to Ireland, Sweden, Germany, and Holland. As we returned on the *Rotterdam,* Seymour dictated notes on an idea for a short book to be called *Twelve Who Made the Game,* which would feature a dozen figures that he believed shaped the American game of baseball most directly. We never got around to the writing of this book, but we did have one permanent outcome from this trip. We found that we had fallen in love with Ireland, and Seymour proposed that we move there.

Ireland, especially the quiet and rural West, beckoned as a place conducive to writing and welcoming to writers, even giving them tax benefits. Living there, we figured, would be relatively cheap. Seymour had calculated that we would be able to manage financially with his Social Security checks, some income from investments, whatever I could earn by freelancing, and the small royalty checks we received from the baseball books — they never sold as well as we and Oxford thought they might. Good reviews do not always translate into good sales.

The publishing company I'd been working for had moved out of Boston to Lexington, thus necessitating a more awkward commute. I had never bothered to learn how to drive a car, so Seymour drove me part way, and I was picked up at a meeting point in a car driven by another editor. The commute had begun to wear on me. I believed that this might be a good point for me to leave full-time editing, and I thought that, no matter where we were living, I could pick up writing and editing assignments to supplement our income.

But before that we made another trip, this time to and through Austria and Germany to Berlin (it was startling to actually experience the Berlin Wall and the tensions around it), and home on the *France,* a ship that would many years later prove fateful in my life. So would the Austrian tour. The notes I took at the time of this trip, and the mental images, sketches, and snapshots I returned with, became central to the background of a historical novel I produced more than twenty years later.

Our only trip in 1971 was a winter flight to St. Maarten for a week of rest. But in the fall of 1972 we acted on our interest in Ireland, seeking and finally finding what we believed we wanted in a cottage near the market town of Ballina, in County Mayo, in Ireland's West. Coming home on the *Queen Elizabeth II,* we made our plans. In 1973 we sold our house and car and shipped our entire library and some furniture to Ireland, where we knew practically nobody.

8—Two Strong Innings

Seymour had been able to obtain Irish citizenship by proving descent from Irish grandparents on his mother's side, and establishing that proof gave us the right to permanent Irish residence. The cottage we had bought near Ballina was being modernized, but the work was done according to "Irish time"—much more slowly than we were used to. It wasn't finished when promised, so we moved into the incomplete shell and camped there while the bookshelves and closets I had designed for the carpenter were being built and while the house was being painted and wired for electric heat. Finally, after our goods arrived by ship at a Dublin dock, and we purchased some hand-made Irish furniture and had Irish woolen draperies made, we settled in.

My office in this charming little house was the biggest I'd ever had. The bookshelves I designed and watched the workmen construct worked beautifully. Each room in the cottage had its own fireplace—luckily, because the electric panels used for heating the house doled out only the smallest trickles of heat, and the dampness of the climate meant that I was continually washing the kitchen walls with bleach to discourage mold.

Learning that teachers at a school in nearby County Sligo named *Scoil Ursula* (the Ursuline School) were using the Initial Teaching Alphabet to teach their pupils how to read, I initiated correspondence with them and received an invitation to visit. Seymour and I took a bus to Sligo City, and he remained at our hotel while I visited the classrooms of Sister Perpetua, who taught four year olds, and a Miss Coen, who instructed five year olds, observing how the teachers handled the introduction of reading. I gave the teachers a set of my I.T.A. books for use as supplementary readers.

How did we manage our research in American baseball at that distance? Not very easily, with such limited communication facilities. We received the Sunday *New York Times* and *The Sporting News* by mail. The nearest phone was a couple of miles away, at the post office, since in Ireland the phone service is part of the postal service. The wait for installation of a personal phone was two years. At our request, Cliff Kachline at the Hall of Fame sent photocopies of needed guidebook pages that gave seasonal overviews. Baseball correspondence came to us from other baseball contacts: Bowie Kuhn, the new baseball Commissioner, and Marty Appel of the Yankees.

At my urging, Seymour joined SABR. Stanley Grosshandler, then an officer of the organization, issued the invitation to join the association and initiated correspondence with Seymour. We began learning much more about the work that other baseball scholars were engaged in. When we received listings of their presentations at meetings, I marked those I thought might be helpful, and when Seymour agreed, I then wrote to ask for copies. Without fail, these scholars kindly sent us copies of the papers they had presented, and we found that their work was supplementing our own nicely. We had suddenly become part of a circle of scholars in the field of sport history.

When the local newspaper editor learned about Seymour's unusual background through information in a release I sent him, he published a story calling Seymour "The Baseball Don" and "the foremost living authority upon the American game of baseball," explaining that we had left the United States and its "frenetic pace" for "the peace and tranquility of Mayo and friendliness of the people." That Irish peace and tranquility sometimes grew into a sense of isolation, and the almost-constant dreary weather became a bit wearing. The slow pace of Irish life, although conducive to thinking and writing, meant that house repairs didn't get done in what we considered a reasonable period of time. But living there was a great adventure, and my interest in Irish history, culture, and language was fed. At the small local library, although it was heavy on Irish fiction and of course lacking in any references to baseball, I found a great deal of information on Irish life, including Irish sport, which revealed its brutal side as well as its deep connection with nationalism.

Ensconced in my self-designed office in our cottage in County Mayo, Ireland, 1973, where I organized and outlined material for *Baseball: The People's Game* and freelanced as editor and writer. (Author's collection.)

8—Two Strong Innings

As I'd hoped, I did receive freelance writing and editing assignments, both in Ireland and by mail from the States. I consulted on an Irish reading series, revised a set of reading workbooks for an American publisher, and began corresponding with Clarence Barnhart of dictionary fame, eventually consulting for him on his children's readers. I performed an analysis correlating his reading system, *Let's Read*, with the basal system published by the largest commercial publisher of children's readers, Scott Foresman. Clarence reprinted my *Commonweal* article on black English. And I was asked by an American publisher to review a manuscript being considered for publication as a textbook.

Seymour, too, received assignments. With my editorial help, he wrote a piece on Babe Ruth for the *American Biographical Encyclopedia*, one on Clark Griffith and another on Grover Cleveland Alexander for the *Dictionary of American Biography*, and baseball articles for the *Jefferson Encyclopedia* and *Chambers's Encyclopedia*. He also wrote entries for the *Oxford Companion to Sports and Games*. These paid assignments took attention away from our work on the third volume, but they also helped a bit with finances.

While living abroad we read in our slow-to-arrive copies of the *New York Times* about the resignation of an American president and about a gas shortage that made small cars appear like a great advantage to Americans lucky enough to own them. It all seemed like a distant story until suddenly the American government intruded on our own lives with a notice to Seymour that, according to the Society Security Administration's interpretation of the rules, he should not be receiving government checks while living abroad. His checks, which we depended on, were stopped.

Angry, Seymour complained in writing, but his arguments were discounted. Determining to make a quick trip back to the States to object in person, we timed our travel so that I could attend the International Reading Association meetings in Boston in order to make more writing and editing contacts. We went to the offices of Senator Ted Kennedy to register Seymour's complaint and ask for advice. Kennedy's representative told Seymour to marshal all his evidence and write at great length, explaining not only why the money should be restored but also emphasizing that a Social Security representative had assured him in advance that he was entitled to get his checks no matter where he was living. On our return we spent a lot of time preparing this long letter.

Finally, through the intervention of a law judge, the decision was reversed, and Seymour's checks were restored. But he would not be placated. The whole matter soured him on living in Ireland and increased the number of his bouts of depression.

As for me, loneliness sometimes got the better of me. But it was more than loneliness; it was regret that I had cut off a promising career in publishing, where I might have gone much further. And it was regret that I had almost completely submerged my creative and professional skills in Seymour's work rather than in developing my own.

9

Curve Ball

More stateside recognition came to Seymour while we lived in Ireland: C.C. Johnson Spink wrote that he looked forward to the publication of the next book, and his newspaper declared that Seymour was "probably baseball's definitive academic historian." For the first time the *Dictionary of American Scholars* listed Seymour among its entries.

But general recognition among historians and among baseball people for Seymour's unique contribution to knowledge would for a long time continue to elude him. One reason for his continued relative obscurity may have been the amount of time that elapsed between publication of the books. *Baseball: The Early Years* came out in 1960, and *Baseball: The Golden Age* not until eleven years later. Another nineteen years would elapse before the third volume made its appearance, so a new generation of baseball fans, ones who might never have heard of the first two books, would learn of the third.

In returning to the States we agreed that instead of moving to the North we would try living in the warm American South. From a book on retirement spots we selected Fairhope, Alabama, and by 1975 Seymour was being interviewed for a story in the local paper there, for I had always carried out his promotion, along with my own. When each book was about to be published, I prepared information for the news release by Cornell's promotion department and listed the names and addresses of persons and publications to notify. Wherever we moved, I made sure that the local newspaper knew of his arrival and his importance as a scholar. I avoided mentioning myself in any of these news releases.

We bought a tape recorder/player, and Seymour tried dictating his writing, after which I transcribed it. Reaching an acceptable first draft through dictation seemed to take a long time and several retypings, however, so I believe this method of writing hindered rather than hastened the work. The machine proved more useful for recording baseball radio programs, which I transcribed later. One transcription took twenty-seven pages of typing, and the typed version still had to be worked on afterwards because, in order to file its information topically, I had to take separate notes from it on each topic covered by the program.

Besides using the tape recorder I also continued to use the microfilm reader. We were buying microfilm other than copies of *The Sporting News*, especially the dissertations that were starting to be produced by young scholars interested in sport history and emboldened to write in the field by the knowledge of Seymour's doctorate from Cornell. And I collected many magazine and journal articles and took notes from them. It was in Fairhope that we bought our first television set, so we saw some remarkable baseball in games for the pennant races and in the World Series that year. Even I, a self-styled non-fan, found myself enjoying them.

Our residence in Fairhope did not last long, however. We found the area lacking in stimulation and decided to move to the Upper South. First we bought a small home in Mars Hill, North Carolina, a college town, where we never really fit in. While we lived there I took the opportunity of using the college archives and found evidence of early baseball play there.

It was during our residence in Mars Hill that we became convinced that we needed to change our research focus. Our collection of material on amateur and semipro ball had become so large and so intriguing that we found our interest veering in that direction. We collaborated on a long letter to Sheldon Meyer at Oxford, explaining that Seymour wanted to break off the story of the majors to write about the amateurs and semipros in a book like no other on the market. It would tell the complete story of baseball outside the majors and minors, the story of the way everyday Americans in all walks of life played baseball for fun and sometimes for a little profit. Sheldon acquiesced and issued a new contract for what would become *Baseball: The People's Game*. This volume would provide a surprise pitch for fans expecting a third segment of the history of major-league baseball. We would be throwing them a curve ball.

Selling out at Mars Hill, we moved to a comfortable apartment in Asheville near the Grove Park Inn. As usual, I found the local library useful. One of my discoveries was fascinating material on baseball play during the building of the Panama Canal—a dramatic story in itself. The librarian even stored our bulky newspaper collection for us. In our apartment we each had a cozy office and felt that we were moving ahead, except for the times when Seymour's bouts of depression kept him from being responsive to anything. I was also receiving more freelance assignments in writing and editing, some from my former employer, the publisher Ginn and Company, in Lexington. I wrote, for example, entries and definitions for a children's dictionary.

Then I received an offer to return to that publishing house as a senior editor. Ginn and Company planned another new reading series and needed experienced editors to take over the production of groups of related books and workbooks. I would be supervising younger, less experienced editors and the writers being hired to create the books. Ginn and Company offered

Baseball: The People's Game (Oxford University Press, 1990). As with the previous two volumes in the series, I was deeply involved in the preparation of this book and wrote a large section of it myself. (From *Baseball: The People's Game* by Harold Seymour, copyright 1991 by Harold Seymour. Used by permission of Oxford University Press, Inc.)

to pay our moving expenses to the Boston area. I persuaded Seymour that it was time to return to the American North, pointing out that we would be near a great research library again and that, with a salary coming in once more, we would be doing better financially; he would still be able to write at home in comfort.

We found an apartment in Newton that was part of a private home but accessed via a separate entrance; the landlord lived in the other part of the house. Here Seymour's study was on the main floor and my office was in a finished basement, a room large enough for my six-foot work table and many of the books and articles I used for reference. To reach Ginn and Company in Lexington, I took a subway to the end of the line, where I and others were picked up by a company van for the trip to the publisher's office building.

Baseball work that I performed dating from this period includes a thirteen-page chapter-by-chapter review of the textbook *Saga of American Sport* by John Lucas and Ronald Smith, which Seymour had been asked to review for the *Journal of American History*. My analysis compared the work of the authors to that of John R. Betts, who does much more listing of sporting events and omits to knit them into American history. I also evaluated Lucas and Smith's sources and the way they used them, and I critiqued both their coverage of the subject and their writing. Seymour used my work in writing the review, which I then edited. The importance of the Lucas and Smith work lies in the proof that a need for it had surfaced, so in at least some American universities, sport history had by the 1970s become an acceptable subject for study.

Another piece of work I handled was a review of a biography of Josh Gibson written by William Brashler. The Historical Society of Western Pennsylvania asked Seymour to write this review. My notes are five pages long, covering contradictions, repetitions, comparison with Brashler's fiction, weaknesses in historical validity, and the lack of source variety. I also mentioned Brashler's jargon and forced writing. Seymour checked off each of my points as he used them for his review, after which I edited his work.

When Seymour was asked to write reviews of Charles Alexander's biography of Ty Cobb and Eugene Murdock's biography of Ban Johnson, I read and studied those books, writing an eight-page evaluation of each, covering the authors' excellent work as well as their errors and omissions. (Thirty years later Alexander would win an award called the Seymour Medal for another book of baseball history.) Seymour studied my reports on these books, underscoring the parts he liked best and even commenting "good" next to some of my remarks — the way he would on college themes. The resulting collaborative reviews, which I edited as usual, were published together. Gene Murdock then wrote Seymour of his gratitude for the kind words about his book.

Seymour was also asked to review a scholarly manuscript for

Louisiana State University. Again I prepared a chapter-by-chapter commentary, and Seymour used it to write an evaluation, which I edited.

An interview I obtained at this time for Seymour with the local Newton paper calls him "baseball's designated historian." But the historian had become so sedentary that he hardly left the house. He spent most of the time sitting in his armchair in his study, smoking his pipe, and reading, usually in the field of American history. He did little work on *Baseball: The People's Game*. My suggestion that he seek help for his depression was met with scorn and refusal. I worked evenings on baseball, but I worked mostly alone. He did receive some recognition when his 1956 article for *The New-York Historical Society Quarterly*, "How Baseball Began," was reprinted in Scribner's *The Armchair Book of Baseball*, edited by John Thorn, who used the lead-in headline, "The game's premier historian on the game's central question!"

By then our baseball files were huge. We ordered, and kept in our files or on our shelves, dissertations that I took notes on, along with many baseball guidebooks and handbooks, all of which required study. The local library in Newton borrowed books and dissertations through interlibrary loan for me to study. I managed somehow to keep up with it all. One day, in perusing the local newspaper, I read an advice column about successful working techniques: the advisor directed people to perform only one task at a time. I laughed aloud at this remark. Is there any woman who is also a writer (I asked myself) who actually does only one thing at a time? Women must have been the original "multitaskers." While studying or composing or editing, I always had something else in progress, either a load of wash going or food cooking or baking in the oven or both. How could any woman get everything done without simultaneously performing multiple tasks? Even today, women — including women writers — are still responsible for most of the household tasks. They would never accomplish anything in their field if they waited for a "free" moment in which to do it.

I had long ago discovered for myself that checking the footnotes of applicable articles in the American Historical Association's journal (which we received through membership) and other journals (those we sent for whenever they sounded like possible sources) offered clues to still other articles that might include information about early baseball games of various types. I then attempted to locate those articles in libraries or by mail. This technique served me well in preparing *Baseball: The People's Game*.

By writing for information and publications, I had received what amounted to a full library of materials for working on at home. I spent Saturdays in the Boston Public Library, and there I found and studied periodicals like the *Army and Navy Journal* and other military journals, the *Amateur Journal, Indian Boys' and Girls' Club News*, and other boys' club periodicals. I read *Recreation Magazine*, which had started as *Playground*, from 1909 through 1941, and many other periodicals from the era of the 1860s (when available) through the 1930s. My boxes of filed notes proliferated, and my bibliographical notes on articles I read and used took up two file boxes.

In those days the Boston Public Library employed a system of book delivery much like Cleveland's. Patrons, after identifying a wanted book in the files of the library's catalog room, filled out a form with the book's date, author, and call number, then looked for an open seat at a numbered spot on a table in the reading room. That number, too, had to be recorded on the form. Then the patron went to a central desk and handed the form to a librarian, all the while hoping that, in the interim, nobody would take that numbered spot. Then patrons had to remain at their numbered places and wait for a library page to bring the book.

I soon learned to begin ordering a new group of books, about six at a time, before I was finished studying the pile of books that had already been delivered to me, so that I would never have any "down time" but would be kept busy reading and taking notes even while waiting for the delivery of the next batch of books. I found it wise, too, never to leave my notes, pen, and folder at my numbered spot while bringing book requests to the librarian, since some people in libraries would pick up anything that looked useful. Instead, I left a small sign that read, "This seat is taken."

To speed my library research I also got an acquaintance to search for and find the library call numbers and location of more than a hundred books that I listed and typed for her on an eight-page form I had devised. We paid her fifty dollars to find and jot down those numbers. A couple of other people did similar favors.

We originally conceived of this third baseball book as including children's amateur baseball plus grownups' amateur and semipro ball. The topics then expanded as the number of our ideas about who played the game increased. We discovered from the notes I had been taking that, although we were cutting off the story before the 1939 advent of the Little League, many other groups sponsored baseball for children before that date. What I was finding out about the American Legion's sponsorship of boys' baseball became increasingly disturbing, as the information in unimpeachable sources (mostly, the Legion's own records) proved that this organization used boys' baseball not so much to help boys but to teach its own version of "Americanism" and do so "under cloak of a sport code." The Legion admitted that the reason it sponsored baseball was to instruct boys and their families in what it considered "good citizenship" and to attract members to its own organization. The Legion even convinced the leadership of organized baseball to contribute money annually for several years in order to forward its efforts. Tracking down the details of this story proved enlightening.

Because associations like the Legion promoted baseball for boys in the era long before the era of the Little League, we knew we must give attention to them in this section of the book. What transpired, it eventually became clear, was gradual local and regional growth in the groups that were taking over boys' baseball, so that when the Little League came on the scene, the stage was already set for complete national domination of the boys' game.

The Little League (although we didn't have the space to demonstrate this in the book) eventually contributed to the decline of spontaneous team formation by the boys themselves. It also caused parents to expect the children's teams to perform like adults' teams. A hint of times to come lay in the complaint of a plain-spoken Worcester eleven year old, whom we quoted in the book: "With so many men and women around telling you what to do, they get on me nerves." Adult intervention, which we showed to be incipient in the era of the nineteen twenties and thirties, would make for problems in the forties between and among parents, their children, and the boys' baseball organizations like Little League. In 2001 one boy's father even caused him to enter the League games fraudulently; he was two years older than the League's rules allowed. Cheating like this stems from trying to conduct boys' baseball for them by superimposing adult rules upon children's play. What started as a benevolent effort to provide play space for boys ended as a device for controlling them.

The limited description of college baseball included in *Baseball: The Early Years* gave way in this new book to the full description of what amounted to semipro play as colleges and universities, first banning or ignoring student play, gradually paid attention to it and eventually decided to use baseball to promote and publicize their institutions. I wrote to many colleges and universities for information on their earliest baseball history and even received good photos for use in the book. Amherst, for example, sent a photo of an 1873 team, its stern-looking members resplendent in dark uniforms. The Dartmouth fellows playing in 1866 looked thoroughly gentlemanly. Saint Bonaventure sent a picture dating from 1892 with two players who later became famous as professionals, Hugh Jennings and John McGraw.

I included the black colleges in my requests, writing, for instance, to Tuskegee Institute, Moorland-Spingarn Institute of Howard University, and Wilberforce in Ohio. It was then that I discovered the interesting Washington-area competition that grew up among local black universities. Our work on early black baseball had started as early as our New York City years, with a visit to the famous Schomburg Library, then located at West 135th Street in Manhattan, where we found many old clippings about black players and their games. Research at the Boston Public led me to the transcribed recordings made of people who had been slaves or were only a generation away from slavery, and I was startled and gratified to discover that, according to their memories, blacks were playing ball even at this early period in our nation's history.

Industrial ball and down-home baseball developed much more extensively for this book than we thought it might, as I came across stories uncovered by researchers writing about fellows who played in their own local areas. Photos of industrial play that I found included those less formally posed than for military and college ball, including one showing some California players traveling to an amateur game by stagecoach about 1892. Textile baseball was so extensive, both in New England and in southern states, that the textile industry teams formed entire leagues, and their clubs traveled around the area to compete. When I studied steel company ball, I picked up a photo of earnest-looking fellows from Buckeye International, an Ohio company, wearing mostly overalls. Writing to the White Motor Company of Cleveland (my home town), which sponsored a famous club that won the 1914 championship of the city industrial league, I received copies of the company's house organ of the period and a photo of the winning team. I was writing many letters and receiving much cooperation from colleges, companies, and institutions.

Military play proved to be much more extensive than we thought it was. I selected military histories for reading, to get background, and searched for histories of sport in the various services. We were delighted to see a photo of the 1873 baseball team at Annapolis, in their harlequinesque uniforms, that included the father of Fleet Admiral W.F. Halsey, a photo that came from the Naval Academy Archives, and I even obtained a picture of a ship's team of a similar era, the photo taken right on board the U.S.S. *Powhatan*. I can't imagine when or where that team got a chance to play, since the U.S. Navy didn't set up formal competitions among fleets until later. The Military Academy sent us a photo of the West Point team of 1901 that included Cadet Douglas MacArthur.

Then I came across mention of the popularity of baseball in prisons. Nobody had developed that story, either, and it occurred to me to read prison histories to see how prisons changed enough to begin permitting, and then sponsoring, baseball play by inmates. Did they ever play outside the walls, I wondered? And by writing to prisons for information on their sports history, I was surprised to learn, from their records, that they occasionally did. What more proof could there be of baseball's standing in our culture than the trust of prison authorities that love of the game could keep criminals from trying to escape, despite the opportunity that travel outside the walls offered?

Reading the current works in American history had always been part of our general background reading. We had both already studied Robert Wiebe's important book on the progressive era, *The Search for Order* (1966). Wiebe's interpretation of the emerging leaders as people trying to make sense of their world by forming groups that eventually disintegrated in favor of others seemed to play out in the leadership of organized baseball as we portrayed it *Baseball: The Golden Age*. Now we also read Gabriel Kolko on *The Triumph of Conservatism* (1977). The work of Daniel Boorstin and Frederick Lewis Allen was familiar to us. Richard Hofstadter's solid work emphasizing the positive aspects of American history was tempered by studying Howard Zinn on the less attractive events of American life. These books helped in understanding the setting in which amateur baseball developed. Advancing the field of history, I was reminded, always begins by piggybacking on the work of others.

For each of the topics we were covering, it now seemed necessary to read more specific background material to understand the way baseball could have sprouted in particular American institutions and why. To get a better sense of the development of school baseball, I brought home stacks of books on the history of education, memoirs by early educationists like William A. Alcott (in which we discovered that some of them played ball, too), information about the playground movement, and city histories.

By reading about the work of Frederick Law Olmsted I learned of the campaign to include active sports like baseball in the new public parks being constructed for cities, parks originally designed as places for quiet contemplation of rural beauty. Those who wanted places to play within those parks succeeded in changing the plan of Central Park to include baseball diamonds. I studied the early efforts by philanthropic groups to improve the health of immigrants, since settlement workers, too, saw sports as a way of reaching "underprivileged" youth through the "boys' club" movement, church groups, and the YMCA. Seymour's own experience with his boyhood chums in finding opportunities to play in the Brooklyn of his youth fit in perfectly. He joined a church as a young fellow mainly because it offered, along with a baseball club, free uniforms for players. By the 1920s, I noticed, the schools themselves were sponsoring baseball.

To grasp the way baseball worked its way into college, besides histories of education I read individual college histories and memoirs of early alumni (discovering that the writer Oliver Wendell Holmes, among many, played ball at Harvard in the 1820s), and found baseball springing up in eastern colleges in the 1860s and the West in the 1870s, as a distraction from intense studies. The University of Cincinnati sent us evidence of early play found in student yearbooks and newspapers. We learned that, at first, students controlled the earliest teams themselves, through associations that collected funds for equipment. In the 1880s administrators were changing their view of college sport from a disruptive to a unifying force, so from there it became an easy step to actually taking over baseball for the college's own reasons.

To understand the inception and development of town teams, it seemed necessary to refer to studies describing the gradual dissolution of the frontier and the growth of towns. A baseball team could, it soon became clear, focus and develop local loyalties that led to, and heightened, area rivalries. Research in historical societies' journals brought out many examples of informal play in every part of the country before the

Civil War. I discovered colorful team names like Bug-eaters, descriptions of elaborate uniforms with peg-topped pants, articles in scholarly journals about games played by the fathers of the Mormon Church, and residents' memories of early games on fields pockmarked with holes dug by gold prospectors.

Soon came the burgeoning Fourth of July celebrations with annual games remembered by many. The yearly company picnic usually featured a baseball game; as a child I had attended one in which my father played ball, and growing up two blocks from famous Euclid Beach Park in Cleveland made me aware of the many companies that held their annual picnics there; they used a baseball game as the centerpiece of the event. Improvement in transportation stimulated inter-town rivalries, the hiring of ringers, and the advent of paid town teams. I was getting a picture of early American life, with communities developing cohesion partly through baseball.

To fit industrial ball into general American history, it was important to study the growth of American industrialism, how at first its repressive nature—its monotony, its lack of any creative aspects—inspired workers to find moments of leisure and fun away from work. I read about Frederick Taylor and the influential system called "Taylorism," which demonstrated how to manage every moment of a worker's time for the greatest efficiency—an approach that viewed a worker as a mere cog in the manufacturing process.

Making work interesting and even enjoyable hardly fit into the efficiency theory of Taylorism. But eventually this view of the worker became modified, and the desire for efficiency gave way to the desire to forestall employee dissatisfaction. Baseball, at first banned from the workplace, was gradually seen by industrial plant owners as a method of cutting employee turnover, preventing unionism, and possibly increasing production. As early as the 1860s some employers already sponsored teams. Employees formed clubs in white collar as well as blue collar establishments, in railroads, among tradesmen, even in company towns, and owners began thinking of club sponsorship as part of the approved paternalism known as welfare capitalism.

Companies started to seek out good players and employ them. Later, this search for skilled players stepped up, especially during wartime; players could escape the draft by performing war work, and the companies gained prestige from their presence. The information I unearthed about professional players turning to industrial ball to escape military service during the Great War called to mind an incident from my youth when my father, who was working at a Cleveland defense plant, Jack & Heinz, during World War II, told me with pride that one of his fellow workers was Frank Pytlak, a former Cleveland Indians player. Company owners and employees were happy to have him there.

At this point in the book it seemed necessary to devote separate attention to those teams that formed independently and were moving from amateur ball to the partial professionalism known as semipro. Some of these teams formed in towns; others grew up in cities and formed leagues. A few independents became so strong as to challenge the power of minor- and major-league clubs. And the proliferation of such semipros — often teams with special personalities, like the House of David, whose members sported long beards — led to the formation of large associations like the National Baseball Federation and popular national semipro competitions like the *Denver Post* Tournament. The truism that in America, two people who get together form a club, and two clubs form an association, continued to prevail in baseball outside the professionals.

In researching the important national semipro organizations like the *Denver Post* Tournament, I found that these competitions played a large part in broadening opportunities for both white and black semipros during the Depression era. They even made it possible for ex–major leaguers to continue participating in baseball, though often it was as coach or manager. I enjoyed collecting material on events like the 1934 *Post* Tournament, in which Satchel Paige, pitching for the House of David instead of for a black team, beat the excellent Kansas City Monarchs, with whom he had often played. I delighted in uncovering such curiosities as the fact that Leslie Mann's International Baseball Federation of the late thirties already included Britain and Japan, and that in 1938, with international tensions building, the Federation's English team, composed mostly of Canadians, beat the Americans.

Getting background for military involvement in baseball required reading about the formation and organization of the American military services, thinking about the possible connection between sport and war, and finding out when military organizations began playing games both informally and as organized teams and leagues. Again, such play began spontaneously, we found, before the Civil War and even during it.

My notes showed that military posts, particularly in the West, developed teams as a way to alleviate routine, and officers started sponsoring baseball "to safeguard against breaches of discipline." American imperialism, as developed through the theory of Manifest Destiny and as demonstrated in the building of the Panama Canal (where much baseball was played), brought baseball wherever the military visited, including Japan of the 1870s. Soldiers taught Filipino children to play just after the insurrection of 1900. In Hawaii, where a local periodical referred to baseball play as early as 1840, the Hawaiians were playing against soldiers in 1860. Cubans who studied in the States brought the game back to their island in 1857, and servicemen played Cubans at Guantánamo after the Spanish-American-Cuban war.

Some notes I had collected about prison ball led me to investigate how baseball play got into American prisons. When and how did games breach prison walls? I read the books of famous prison reformers like Sanford Bates, Lewis Lawes, and Thomas Osborne. I learned about early thinkers like Zebulon Brockway, who introduced calisthenics and playing fields to incarcerated men. By the 1880s, I discovered, reformatory and prison leaders were attributing beneficial properties to baseball. Again, the admission of baseball to this institution was gradual and launched by forward-looking administrators.

I thought the yearning for baseball equipment among young fellows in reformatories that I read about was touching, but nothing made me think more about the American government's policies toward marginal people than the books I read concerning the way baseball was used in institutions for "Americanizing" young Native Americans. To understand what went on in the early boarding schools for aborigines, I read biographies and autobiographies detailing their humiliations, discovering that these children were often dragged away from their parents, incarcerated with youngsters of other tribes with whom they were unable to communicate, suffered their hair being cut off and their familiar clothing to be replaced, and were forced to discard all their own customs and learn those that meant less than nothing to them. It was astounding to discover that, despite all this, although a few ran away or committed suicide, most of them adjusted to their constricted new life, and many even excelled in sports. Some became stars on all–Native American baseball teams like the Nebraska Indians (I saw a book about this famous independent club in the Library of Congress on a visit to Washington in

1954), and a few of the best Native America players advanced to the big leagues. The resilience of the human spirit is amazing.

For background on black history I started with the work of Lerone Bennett. Our need to search for the beginnings of black baseball led me to study the rise, before the Civil War, of a group of free middle-class blacks in the Northeast, where they not only created their own businesses, they also formed baseball clubs. Some years previously, we had been lucky enough to discover, in the Pennsylvania Historical Society, the papers of the black Pythians detailing their Knickerbocker-like organization of the 1860s. The club's attempt to join the whites in the National Association of Amateur Base Ball Players met with predictable refusal. It proved to be a poignant story. But that rejection failed to stop the rise of black clubs, especially in the East, with consequent formation of their own leagues.

The South, too, spawned black clubs, as scholars were beginning to show. The black colleges that grew up in the Washington, D.C., area formed a surprisingly active baseball league. I also found some examples of "white" college teams that included blacks. In the 1880s, my notes demonstrated, blacks entered minor and major league clubs, and Fleet Walker appeared to be the first to get into the majors, but by the 1890s, when American institutions were reacting against the entrance of blacks into the life of the nation, organized baseball gradually eliminated all its black players, and blacks were forced to form their own professional baseball associations, which the majors condescending labeled as "semipro."

I had long been collecting information about blacks playing in schools, as members of teams sponsored by the National Recreation Association, on public playgrounds, and in groups initiated by the YMCA and by churches. Biographies of prominent blacks, like that of James Weldon Johnson, helped me get an idea of what it was like to form and belong to a popular black club. I read the biography of the well-known black educator, E.B. Henderson, and discovered his work in sports and games in the Washington, D.C., schools. Personal contacts brought unexpected information: a teacher I had met through Ginn and Company who was the widow of Lorenzo Dow Turner, a University of Chicago linguist, gave me a photo of her late husband as a young player on a black team formed by steamship company employees in Fall River, Massachusetts. Just investigating black publications like *The Crisis* and *Southern Workman* brought me several gemlike bits of baseball information.

Checking studies of black soldiers, I discovered a book written by a black player about his regiment and its rivalry with other black military clubs.

My study of the background for each topic we were covering, such as the military and colleges, led me to write background material that Seymour could use to fit baseball into the general development of the topic. But when he did so, he tended to use too much of it, making the chapter or chapters lopsided by emphasizing background over baseball. In each case I trimmed the background somewhat, but when Meyer noticed the same problem and requested more trimming, I cut it back severely so that on each topic the narrative moved more quickly into the part specifically about baseball.

I found myself deeply involved in studying the way baseball affected everyday life in America and thereby obtaining a solid base in American social history. Then suddenly my day job changed.

10

Relief Pitcher

Soon I would have even more time to work on baseball history. At Ginn and Company the reading series I had been hired to work on was approaching completion, and most of us brought into the company to produce that project were terminated. I was one of them. Much older and more experienced in publishing than most of the company's editors, I was at risk anyway because by firing me the managers saved a bigger salary than they would in letting some of the younger editors go.

For a time I received workers' compensation while I cast about for another publishing position, but when the compensation period ended without my being hired by another nearby company, I decided to freelance instead, so I began contacting those who I knew would be interested in my skills. Publishers of education texts and other nonfiction books responded quickly by giving me writing assignments and editorial work in educational publishing and other fields like ESL, English as a Second Language. The well-known publisher Little, Brown and Company became my most frequent employer for editorial work, and for that company I edited texts in English and sociology written by college professors.

More time at home meant more time for baseball research. Most of my library research took place at the Boston Public, where I discovered the annual reports and proceedings of the conventions of the Playground and Recreation Association and even earlier materials showing institutional attention to the play of children. The BPL also yielded material on early government Native American schools, where I found evidence that efforts to "civilize" these hapless young fellows were made mostly through baseball and band. Realizing that some of these schools were still operating, I wrote to as many as I learned about and received catalogs and some historical material about early baseball from places like Haskell's Indian Junior College. At this time we took at least one more research trip to Cooperstown, staying at the Worthington House in May of 1984.

It occurred to me that I wasn't utilizing one of the most famous libraries in the Boston area, Widener Library at Harvard, which was only a subway ride away. But Widener permitted nobody except students and faculty to use its library. How could I get into this valuable source of knowledge? By inquiring of my editorial colleagues, I discovered that one of the people I was working with on the writing of a set of education materials was taking a course at Harvard. She offered to lend me her library pass. So, assuming her identity temporarily, I got into the great Widener under false pretenses.

By checking the Widener catalog under the topics I was working on, I discovered some exciting material: the original reports of prison wardens and directors of children's institutions. These included early reform schools, not only in the Boston area but in other states as well. The dates of the reports ranged from 1851 up to 1940. I wondered whether these reports mentioned recreation; perhaps baseball had penetrated these institutions, too.

Not only did these documents mention baseball, they revealed why the directors wanted to use baseball with their charges, how they believed baseball helped the children, on what occasions the children were permitted to play, and even how much the directors were spending on baseball equipment (a pitifully small amount). I took that subway to the Widener Library in Cambridge day after day, for a good part of the summer, to mine the collection for detailed information apparently available nowhere else, and I savored the pleasure of its discovery.

I also used other Boston libraries, that of the Congregational Christian Historical Society and the Unitarian Universalist Association, both of which offered some material on early sponsorship of baseball by their religious groups. Even the local Newton libraries offered material new to me. And while I was still at Ginn, which carried a membership in a private Boston library called the Atheneum ("the Ath"), I got permission through the company librarian to use this exclusive library as well.

Of course, we continued to collect material about the major leagues of the current period, assuming that we would return to that topic after completing *Baseball: The People's Game*. We accumulated a lot of information, for example, on the Flood Case, in which Curt Flood as an individual bravely challenged the reserve system and put at risk organized baseball's traditional position outside the antitrust law. The eventual advent of free agency, which gave players the right to sell their own services, represented an important change in baseball's structure that we knew would need to be addressed after *Baseball: The People's Game* was completed.

That is, if we ever completed it. The research kept building, and the organization of materials continued, but the writing moved slowly. The only trip we took at this time was back to Ireland for a couple of weeks. There we toured prominent sites and visited our local acquaintances. I particularly enjoyed Dublin's National Museum, with its great variety of historical and cultural objects. I would visit it again much later, for research that was as yet hardly even the size of an atom in my mind.

After about a year of freelancing in Newton, I began to think of the Boston area as too expensive for two people neither of whom was bringing in a full-time salary. We covered day-to-day expenses through income from our investments and Seymour's Social Security checks, plus my free-lancing income, but our resources began to look meager. Continuing to pay rent under these circumstances irked me, anyway; I preferred having our own home, so that expenditures for housing would contribute to our own equity. I thought of a move to a less expensive area but one that would still offer access to important research facilities.

Recalling that some Ginn employees had vacationed enjoyably in Monadnock County in New Hampshire, an area just northwest of Boston, I researched the college town of Keene and thought it sounded attractive. Keene was on the bus route to Boston — an advantage necessary for continued research. After contacting realtors there, I persuaded Seymour to take a bus trip with me to Keene and look at houses, a group of which seemed within our price range. We settled on a house at the end of a residential cul-de-sac, one in which I could arrange an office for each of us. With the help of one of the friends I had made at Ginn and Company, we moved there in 1987.

By then I was generating most of the research ideas, performing nearly all the research, and preparing chapter outlines that were about as close to the final chapter drafts as they could be. An outline I prepared covering our notes on black youth, including black colleges, reached 170 pages, including the source notes for each statement. Reference librarians at the local Keene library constantly serviced my needs for interlibrary loans of books and microfilm, and I used the library of the local college as well.

While living in New Hampshire I came across information indicating that women played baseball very early in one of the famous Seven Sisters colleges. Higher education, I knew from reading histories of the subject, was believed in the America of the eighteenth and nineteenth centuries to be valuable only for men. Women, although assumed to be strong enough for child-bearing and for running large and complex households, were thought too delicate for the strain of formal learning, which might unduly tax their constitutions. (Or perhaps learned women, who might come up with fresh ideas, could challenge men's control of society!)

Those whose families could afford to educate their daughters and realized that young women, too, might benefit from learning (and that society could in turn benefit from including learned women) created institutions solely for females who wanted an education. What about physical education, sport, and recreation at these colleges? I wondered. Were they part of the curriculum of these exclusive institutions? And when was women's softball introduced?

After reading background information on women's history, I began sending out a few preliminary letters to women's colleges. Then I came up with the idea of research into their archives to find out about all this more specifically, particularly since the earliest women's colleges were located primarily in New England. The work I would soon pursue on the story of women's baseball would prove momentous for my future.

By the time we moved to Keene, I knew that something was seriously wrong with Seymour. His depressions had become almost continuous. He was gradually withdrawing from the work and spending time in his study unproductively. Yet on the occasion of our final meeting in New York with Sheldon Meyer, our Oxford editor, he refused to permit me to attend the meeting, as I usually did, stating that he was going alone and insisting that I remain behind in our hotel room. No doubt Seymour realized that our actions as a writing partnership were at odds with the way the books were being presented: as the product of Harold Seymour alone. So he thought he could establish his individual responsibility for the books by handling this meeting with Meyer independently, although in the past I had always taken part in them, and for years our letters to Meyer had referred to us jointly: "We are making steady progress on the organization of volume 3.... Please let us see this frontispiece again after it is redrawn....We would like to see a layout. We cannot okay it yet." The joint working relationship we had displayed with Oxford for so long would hardly be counteracted by one meeting with the editor.

I believe that, as Seymour sat in his office smoking his pipe, he was instead thinking back into his past. It was at this time of his life, both in Newton and at Keene, that he jotted down a number of ideas for what he called his "nostalgia book," recording stories he had already told me: about his coaching of boys' baseball on the Parade Grounds, his moments as batboy for the Brooklyn Dodgers, and his years at Drew University, an institution that he felt had never appreciated his contribution to sports there. I encouraged him to write about these matters. Eventually, after his passing, information about them would appear on a web site I wrote, *www.HaroldSeymour.com*. But now, from his notes about his childhood adventure with Wilbert Robinson's Brooklyn Club at Ebbets Field, I constructed drafts of "Big-League Batboy," which he finally completed and published in 1988 in *Sports Heritage Magazine* (reprinted that same year in *The Brooklyn Bums Newsletter*), and "Books Before Baseball," published in 1982 by a SABR magazine, *The National Pastime*. Feedback from the publication of these pieces, I believe, helped show him that people at least recognized what he had done in the past.

"Big-League Batboy" is the best kind of nostalgia, with its details about what Seymour called "Wilbert Robinson's colorful incompetents" and the way he and his boyhood pals figured out methods, legitimate or otherwise, to get into Ebbets Field to see them. It tells some stories about the Dodgers that are unavailable elsewhere. As an illustration, the article even contains a snapshot for which Seymour posed on Ebbets Field while pretending to snag a grounder; this snapshot, his only memento of his days with the Dodgers, was unfortunately misplaced by the magazine editor and has since been lost. I persuaded Seymour to include, at the end of the piece, some remarks about the significance of the experience to him.

"Books Before Baseball," although its theme is the need for college athletes to realize the superior importance of getting an education, is also nostalgic, since it describes his experience at Drew University as the student who ran the university's first team and who gradually realized that even baseball, his great interest, must bow before the importance of learning.

Recognition came also, in an offhand way, from organized baseball. When A. Bartlett Giamatti, an academic who became baseball's commissioner, spoke on "Baseball and the American Character" at the Boston Public Library in 1985 under sponsorship of the Massachusetts Historical Society, he quoted Seymour and referred to "his excellent history of baseball, to which I am [for this presentation] throughout indebted." Seymour basked in this praise and wrote Giamatti to thank him, whereupon Giamatti responded appropriately.

Seymour had also desired to establish, at Drew, a trust fund in his name, to be used to sponsor lectures in sport history, partly as a way to call Drew's attention to his contribution to its sports development. But because Drew University never seemed much interested in the planned gift and never formally announced it, he finally withdrew it in annoyance and turned instead to Cornell University. He felt grateful to Cornell, first for granting him a fellowship when, during study for his master's degree, he needed that financial support, and even more for having the foresight to recognize that baseball was worthy of scholarly study and that his unique work in the field merited a doctor's degree in history.

Seymour began working on the idea of a gift to Cornell in 1980 and talked to several Cornell representatives over the following few years. With my assent, in 1988 he arranged to bring a Cornell representative to our home to discuss the matter in detail and to produce a document that would put all our savings into an irrevocable trust for Cornell, from which we, during our lifetimes, would receive only the income that would eventually pass, along with the principal, to the University. I was a bit startled that he would use all our money to perpetuate his own name (who will remember *my* name? I wondered) but went along with his idea because it seemed to focus on the main interest of both of us since our marriage: the history of baseball.

With the advice of Cornell's trust representative, and with me sitting in at the meetings (held in my own little office), Seymour set up the Harold Seymour Annuity Trust Fund, which provided for a Harold Seymour Graduate Fellowship Endowment in American History. The Trust

Fund would underwrite a fellowship to graduate students in history and would establish the Harold "Cy" Seymour Sports Lectureship.

The lectureship was planned for sponsoring, after his and my passing, one or two presentations each academic year, to be delivered by qualified faculty or professionals in sports-related fields. These lectures would present aspects of the development and significance of sports. The Trust also set aside funds to catalog and maintain our sport history archival materials — all of our books, microfilm, documents, and notes — which Seymour wanted sent to Cornell after his death. He hoped that this gift of materials would stimulate other scholars interested in the field to contribute similar archives so that eventually a sport history center, like those established at some other universities, might be formed.

I saw no valid reason to challenge his wishes in this matter. I had no children to whom I might leave my money or possessions (assuming any assets would be left for posterity); his own children, fully grown and established in life by then, evidently needed none. As for our baseball materials, I thought of no justification to hang onto them, assuming that I survived Seymour, for I still harbored the idea that baseball was his field, not mine, and that he should plan the ultimate destination of our baseball library.

Cornell recognized this gift appropriately. The university's newsletter, *Cornell Alumni News,* published a substantial article recognizing the planned gift. Cornell's president, Frank H.T. Rhodes, wrote Seymour to express his warm appreciation, adding,

> I understand that your sports history archive will ultimately come to Cornell, and I know that researchers of the future will derive great benefit from its presence here.
>
> This is indeed a splendid commitment, and especially significant to the University because of its association with a Cornellian who is a pioneer in the field of sports history. I know of the painstaking research that has gone into your work on the history of baseball, and I am deeply touched that you have chosen Cornell as the recipient of the lectureship and the archival materials.

The University Librarian, Alain Seznec, wrote Seymour,

> Sports and, most especially baseball, is an important part of the social history of the United States. Your leadership in recognizing this fact and your pioneering efforts to bring sports within the purview of scholarly research has provided important insights into our society. In the future, when your

sports history archive comes to the library, the level of access and bibliographic support that we can provide scholars and students because of your generosity will undoubtedly advance this field further still.

Cornell's appropriate recognition of this gift may have eased Seymour's mind somewhat about the paucity of public acknowledgement of his unique contribution to scholarship. But it failed to improve his mental health. He must have realized that, because he had chosen to stay largely aloof from other scholars who had entered the field, he remained isolated from them: why should they beat a path to his door? His attitude toward them had been made only too plain in his preface to the paperback edition of the second volume, written in October of 1988 at Keene, where he displayed his vexation with those few who made minor criticisms of his work or used parts of it without crediting him, sometimes writing almost the same words. He quoted Jonathan Swift, implying they were "wicked" and should be "ashamed."

I could not persuade him to avoid venting his increasing testiness in this manner. And I realized that his personality changes were probably the result of an insidious illness. His work abilities, along with his body, had weakened greatly. Although at first he tried to write from my outlines, he soon gave up even this aspect of his work, admitting that he could no longer do it. We exchanged roles: I wrote, and he reviewed my work, making editorial comments. I became the relief pitcher.

With a small legacy from my mother, who passed away the year we moved to Keene, I bought a computer, despite Seymour's disapproval, thus speeding my production of the writing and greatly easing the task of preparing new drafts. He also disapproved when I obtained a credit card and a small hand calculator, since he believed that people should do without such devices, but I decided I must have them for convenience. For the first time I insisted on having a telephone in the house, placing it in my own office, where its ringing would probably not be heard in his own study on the other side of the house. My office, being a former porch, included an outside door, so that I could (and often did) entertain visitors without disturbing him — he had become quite antisocial. This separate entrance proved invaluable when I began to develop local business contacts.

As I soon did. My main employer, aside from Little, Brown in Boston, became a Walpole publishing house called Stillpoint, which produced spiritual and self-help books. Stillpoint contributed to my technological advancement by giving me a fax machine that the company was discarding in favor of a more sophisticated model. For Stillpoint I edited the books written by the company's co-owners, Caroline Myss and Meredith Young-Sowers, as well as other manuscripts Meredith selected for publication by the company (since Caroline soon left to develop her own separate and distinguished career). Stillpoint had published the classic *Diet for a New America* by John Robbins and was bringing out the books of other writers like Norman Shealy, Charmaine Wellington, Dan Millman, and Gary Kowalski. I edited these authors' books for Stillpoint. Gary was one whose thank-you note written to me after I completed my work with him remarked that his book "benefited greatly" from my suggestions and that "For me the process of re-writing and re-working the manuscript was the equivalent of a short course in expository writing, and I think I am a better writer today as a result of the experience." With Stillpoint I developed a close relationship that continued long after I had left Keene.

Besides editing for publishers I also connected with the two local newspapers. *The Keene Sentinel* published two of my short stories, the better of which is "Aidan's Luck," a tale inspired by my residence in Ireland, and the editor also hired me as an occasional freelance feature writer. I wrote about the new trend in home offices, about current fashions, and about the many adults learning successfully at the various educational institutions in and around Keene. I enjoyed interviewing a broad segment of the community for these stories and others I would write later.

While living in Keene I also published three more books of my own. In 1987 I published, with Patrick Groff, a textbook for reading teachers called *Word Recognition: The Why and the How*. For this book I obtained the publisher Charles C. Thomas of Springfield, Illinois. Dr. Groff, a professor of education at San Diego State University, and I held similar opinions about the importance of showing children how to figure out new words independently, and he suggested that we prepare the book together. We worked by mail, never having met in person, and we put together a program that demonstrated how to make children aware of the way words are constructed. We included lessons that would help the children recognize word-parts quickly and accurately. For this book I wrote the chapter about teaching word recognition to children with linguistically-diverse backgrounds, as well as writing sections of other chapters. I also edited and revised the entire manuscript. I discovered that

Working on *Baseball: The People's Game* at my first computer in my office at Keene, New Hampshire, 1989, where I completed the book myself. (Author's collection.)

Dr. Groff preferred a rather academic style that I found difficult to replicate in the sections I contributed. The book never sold well, but perhaps it helped some teachers assist their pupils in learning how to read.

More to my taste is the book I suggested to Paul Keene, the country's first organic farmer. For at least twenty years I had been buying organic products by mail from Paul's Pennsylvania company, Walnut Acres, and enjoying the essays about country living that he included in his catalogs. It occurred to me, while we were still living in Newton, that a group of the better essays, if well edited and organized, would make a charming and enlightening little book.

I persuaded Paul to work with me to cooperate on a project in which he sent me a large carton full of his catalogs, from which I selected essays I thought suitable, sent him edited versions for his comment, then worked out an organization for the book. When I had the sections arranged, I wrote introductory and bridging essays for each section. Then I wrote the preface, prepared the front matter, put it all together, and found a publisher: Globe Pequot Press. Paul gave the book a title taken from a tombstone he had once seen: *Fear Not to Sow Because of the Birds*. I worked with the publisher on organization, corrected the proofs, and saw the book through to publication in 1988. Paul and I shared the copyright and royalties.

Although the book made no money, I treasure it partly for its valuable thoughts about nature and our relationship to it. I never met Paul in person, but I feel as though I know him well. He contributed much to the environmental movement without ever having been connected to it formally, for his descriptions of life as an organic farmer appeal to our most authentic desires for a wise relationship with nature. The book is full of simple but deep philosophical thoughts about the future of the world, such as his assurance that "our fate is in large part in our own hands." One reviewer described *Fear Not to Sow* as "delicately arranged and exquisitely thought out ... a nice little volume perfect for browsing while reclining in a sunlit wicker chair." Another reviewer said the book is "inspirational in the best way ... a sampling of quiet wonderments."

Fear Not to Sow Because of the Birds (Globe Peqot, 1988), essays that I prepared for publication with Paul Keene, the country's first organic farmer, who did most of the writing for the book. (Author's collection.)

The third book I produced at this time stemmed from my interest in showing children how to use logic, which is vital as an aid to reading comprehension. The book is divided into four parts: Sequencing and Comparing, Classifying, Understanding Relationships, and Grasping High-Level Concepts. Each part contains several enjoyable activities in game form for primary teachers to use in giving pupils experience in organizing and understanding relationships. My own

10— Relief Pitcher

interest in analyzing and organizing ideas, as put to good use in my work with baseball research, helped me write this book, published by a company I had done considerable editing for: Scott, Foresman and Company. The editor, Chris Jennison, who also researches and writes books in the field of baseball, gave this publication a title taken from some of the activities suggested in the book: *Toad Charts, Paper Faces, and Other Ideas for Visual Comprehension*. The book sold moderately but within a few years went out of print.

I viewed these small writing projects, produced over a period of two years, as side issues to my main work on baseball history. They gave me an outlet for my own individual ideas outside the field of baseball and within my own expertise. They also kept me from feeling that I was using all my creative juices on someone else's work.

Toad Charts, Paper Faces, and Other Ideas for Visual Comprehension (Scott, Foresman, 1987), one of several books for teachers written when my name was still Dorothy Z. Seymour. (From *Toad Charts, Paper Faces, and Other Ideas for Visual Comprehension* by Dorothy Z. Seymour ©1988 by Good Year Books. Used by permission of Pearson Education, Inc.)

Since I still did not drive a car (we no longer owned one, anyway), bus trips would be necessary for me to perform the research I had in mind into the topic of college women's participation in baseball. I began writing letters to the oldest women's institutions to find out which of the Seven Sisters might reveal baseball in their history. My letters led to research at Mount Holyoke, Smith, and Wellesley, along with the receipt of valuable material by mail from other colleges. I arranged bus trips that would keep me away from home for only one or two nights, so that Seymour would not be alone for long. As always whenever I was going to be away, I prepared his meals in advance. Seymour wrote Sheldon Meyer about a recent trip to Cooperstown where "We did get a few nuggets of information" and "We also took some bus trips to New England colleges where some excellent new information was uncovered." Actually, it was I who took those bus trips.

The Mount Holyoke College History Collection alone, I found, included valuable letters of students and alumni, dissertations, notebooks, handbooks, student scrapbooks, typescripts, yearbooks, annuals, pamphlets, and questionnaires. I discovered early references to baseball play in several parts of this rich collection. Material at Radcliffe, Smith, and Wellesley also proved informative. Besides finding evidence of women's baseball play through research trips, I received great cooperation from many colleges through the mail.

The five resulting chapters about women's baseball covered not only its beginnings in colleges, they devoted space to other baseball play on the part of women. To develop these chapters I first read widely in the history of women, women's education, women's health, and women's participation in sports and physical education. The education of women remained recent enough even in my own college days that my undergraduate institution, then called Fenn College, which was a coed institution in Cleveland, used in its promotion a description of Fenn Tower as "the building that your boy will remember as one of his college homes." Although not a boy, I remembered Fenn Tower, too — as the place where I worked in the college newspaper office.

Early advocates for women like Elizabeth Cady Stanton and Catharine Beecher pushed the boundaries of opinion on the physiology of women. From the common assumption that females were weak and delicate grew the ideas of early educators that they needed physical development through gymnastics. It may have been women's enjoyment of bodily movement in gym classes that caused them to form sports clubs, including baseball clubs, as early as the 1870s on their college campuses and outside them. I reveled in coming upon stories about women who experienced the delicious feeling of doing something physical, something slightly irregular and nonconformist. This feeling was reported by early women baseball players, for example, at Vassar and Smith.

Although for years these baseball clubs remained outside the physical education curriculum, eventually, as in the men's colleges, they were incorporated into the instructional program. But in the case of women, whom most educators still considered too weak for hardball, the schools and colleges permitted only the less demanding version that eventually evolved into softball. Besides, prejudice against competition caused female physical education instructors to frown on intercollegiate play and often to ban it.

Because I had been for years collecting evidence of women's play, I was able to incorporate into my outlines stories like those revealing women's early participation in baseball reporting and scoring (Doris O'Donnell of the *Cleveland News* was in 1957 only trying to do openly what earlier women had done secretly or at least quietly).

I also showed that when women first formed exhibition teams and traveled around the country, newspaper reporters assumed that team members all had "loose morals" (though I saw no evidence that men's traveling teams all demonstrated high morals!). Stories from papers of the 1890s about women's exhibition teams wearing scandalously short costumes brought to mind the later outfits of the women's All-American Women's Professional Baseball League, which were adopted for a different purpose: the teams of the 1890s wore short skirts in order to look attractively sexy, whereas the women's clubs of the 1940s and '50s, who were serious players rather than participants in exhibitions, wore them because of the league requirement that they look feminine rather than masculine.

The 1890s spawned some serious women players, too, and it was satisfying to reveal the comments of knowledgeable male fans and players admitting their skill. I liked being able to present the story of excellent players like Alta Weiss, Elizabeth Larrabee, and Elizabeth Murphy. It was surprising to discover that some society women, too, played baseball on their own estates; that might have come about because they had played it at college. Their experience contrasted nicely with material I had found about girls playing ball in reformatories.

I even picked up a story of high school ball among the girls of Manito, Illinois, when, while attending a tea at the home of the Keene State College president, I met the president's mother and, learning that she had played baseball, asked for the opportunity of interviewing her. The story she told of clearing out a field full of prickly pear in order to play ball impressed me with the girls' determination, as did her remark that in playing baseball "we had a glorious time." I knew by then that I had missed a lot in never having developed an interest in sport.

When as a Cleveland teenager I noticed baseball teams playing on an open field near my home, I saw only men engaging in the sport, and I never realized that women participated. Now I wish that the Fort Wayne Daisies, whose team would have been the nearest club of the All American Girls Professional Baseball League, had traveled to Cleveland to play. If I had seen their games, my view of women's potential might have expanded considerably. A fan named Everard Hall was luckier: he wrote Seymour from Chicago in 1990 that when as a soldier in 1945 he was stationed at Camp Grant, he attended games of the Rockford Peaches, and "they were excellent."

But during the forties and fifties the participation of women in baseball never intruded on my consciousness. When I remember that American women received the vote in 1920 only after a long and hard fight, I realize how unlikely it was that men, who controlled the sports pages, would give a women's baseball league much attention in the media around twenty years later. Women's issues continued to be discounted by men into the nineties, when we all observed, in the newspapers and on television, the spectacle of politicians electing to assume that the hapless Anita Hill lied when she accused Clarence Thomas of sexual harassment and then, dismayingly, the further insult of Thomas's eventual confirmation as a Supreme Court judge. Will women, I wondered, ever be taken seriously? Certainly, their league of the forties was generally considered merely a substitute for the men's professional game, a stopgap for baseball fans to focus on when the big-league teams were depleted because so many players were fighting a war. Support for the women's baseball aspirations frittered away as the men returned and television rose in importance.

Because of my years-long experience of collecting notes demonstrating women's participation in baseball in many ways, these chapters in *Baseball: The People's Game*, which I wrote, covered exhibition play like that of teams calling themselves "Bloomer Girls," some individual women who played on men's teams, school and reformatory players, women's industrial teams, intramural and intercollegiate ball, and the successful campaign of women educators to switch women from baseball to softball — an effort that of course penalized those skilled players who wanted to engage in real baseball.

Many women have enjoyed playing softball, but those who aspired to play baseball against others of high skill were usually prevented from engaging in it by college educators, partly because those educators believed that women should not develop a competitive spirit. It appears that "women's place," in the minds of these educators, was wherever women could do the least to change the status quo. Educators seemed to believe that women should all accept whatever social and personality requirements society imposed on them.

If women had been free to compete in baseball during their school and college years, some might have developed a competitive and even aggressive spirit — characteristics whose acquisition could have helped them enter high-level jobs and professions much earlier and more successfully. Maria Pepe, a CPA who as a twelve year old in the early seventies was banned from the Little League but has since continued participating in organized sports, asserts that being involved in athletic competitions has helped her in the professional world because "the interaction within a sports team is similar to the team spirit [needed] on the job."

Professor Allen Guttman believes that American women's lack of a competitive spirit, missing because of the disapproval of competition on the part of university physical education instructors, surely caused the mediocre performance of the American gymnastics team at the 1936 Olympics. For years afterward, only women considered exceptional, like Babe Didrickson Zaharias, developed into true competitors. She once said, "All my life I've been competing, and competing to win.... It's not enough to just swing at the ball. You've got to loosen your girdle and really let fly."

For girls of the early 1940s and early '50s who had a chance to see the women of the AAGPBL in action, just watching them became a revelation of "what my sex could do," as one pre-teenage girl, Susan Johnson, recalled. Those players, she said,

> showed us women doing something difficult and dangerous, something that took physical courage, intelligence and a fighting spirit. Moreover, the ballplayers were doing this as a team, working hard with other women to achieve something worthwhile....

Thus did the AAGPBL inspire girls to become more than the social norms seemed to allow. The amazing resurgence of women's baseball in the twenty-first century, perhaps stimulated in part by the positive presentation of women players in the film *A League of Their Own*, shows us once more that although women are often reluctant to insist on following their own path (seldom having been encouraged to do so), they eventually realize that desire and determination can lead to success and even respect for their own wishes and their own abilities.

Meyer was enjoying the work being produced for *The People's Game* and wrote flattering comments:

> The new chapter really is splendid.... [December 16, 1974] I have noticed the growing ease and fluency of your prose style.... [May 21, 1976] I read with great enjoyment Chapter 15, Women Touch All the Bases. There is a great deal of fascinating detail in the chapter.... [June 27, 1986] This chapter on women outside the colleges works exceptionally well. It not only covers a vast amount of ground but contains many fascinating incidents. It also gives a full sense of how extensive was women's participation in baseball between the wars.... I feel this is one of the best chapters I have read so far.... [July 9, 1987] Intramural versus Intercollegiate Ball presents a wide-ranging study of women's collegiate athletics in the 1920s and 1930s and fits well with the preceding chapters on women and baseball.... [October 9, 1987] The two chapters on the armed forces flow well and cover the subject in fascinating detail. I am amazed at the amount of information you have found on the subject. [January 26, 1989]

The final section of *Baseball: The People's Game* dealt with the story of early participation by black people in baseball. As before, to obtain background for the participation of this segment of society in sport, I read much about early black history, including specialized books on blacks in industry, the military, education, and recreation. To write these chapters I collected a great deal of material on early blacks' baseball play on their own teams, formed after their exclusion from organized baseball, but because most of this material concerned professionals, it could not be used in a book about the amateurs and still languishes in the Seymour Collection at Cornell. Since I began studying this aspect of baseball history, many doctoral dissertations and several good books on blacks and baseball have been published. I wish I had been able to contribute to those books.

11

Cleanup Hitter

Baseball: The People's Game seemed to fall into sections devoted to the entrance into baseball of large groups of everyday Americans — your brother the soldier, your father the factory worker, your nephew and niece the college students, even your uncle the incarcerated prisoner. It follows their participation in the game up to the time of the second World War.

Seymour, in pondering the book's organization, came up with the idea of viewing baseball as a house with many rooms, each devoted to one segment of the participating population. He saw organized baseball at the top level of the house, with the occupants of the Baseball Hall of Fame rising from them. In the ground floor of the house he envisioned the college players, town teams, industrial players, semipros, military players, and softball participants. He thought of Native American and prisoners as occupants of the basement of this house, with boys' baseball as the foundation of it all. As for women, he saw them in an annex, and blacks, since they built their own structure after being excluded from the main house, as in an outbuilding. He called this arrangement The House of Baseball. After considerable discussion, we agreed on the placement of each group. I thought this metaphor clarified the structure of the book, so I sketched a diagram demonstrating the way this image worked out, and Oxford had an artist draw it professionally for the book's front matter.

In the Preface to *Baseball: The People's Game*, Seymour ungenerously displayed his scorn of academics who waited to enter the field of baseball history until it had been opened for them or until they were so well entrenched in their teaching positions that they had been granted tenure. Their reluctance to endanger their careers was, I thought, understandable. But not to Seymour. He also attacked those few who had made mild criticisms of his work or who had used parts of it without acknowledgement. I could not persuade him to eliminate these remarks, which only revealed unpleasing aspects of his disintegrating personality as it was being undermined by his disease.

As Seymour interpreted baseball for the book's Preface, he saw the structure of the game as completely dependent upon the solidity and vitality of the game's foundation among boys. He believed that baseball for adults, many of whom continued to play (as well as to watch others play) after their childhood experiences, developed solely out of this foundation. As I see it now, he might also have pointed out the theme that I use currently in my presentations to groups who ask me to speak about baseball: that most institutions of American life have demonstrated the same evolving series of responses to the desire of their section of the population to play ball. First refusing to permit baseball, these institutions gradually recognized the possible benefit to their own groups of allowing it to exist, then decided that it might be turned to their own advantage and actually began sponsoring it. This sequence of responses to baseball was repeated in boys' baseball, college ball, military ball, industrial ball, and women's baseball. Even in prisons, where initially the administration would allow nobody to even speak a word, much less to take part in exercise, baseball was gradually permitted and then sponsored for the hoped-for purpose of improving discipline. A similar sequence took place in Native American schools, where children knew nothing of baseball when they entered, so there the instructors introduced the two activities of baseball and band, both because the students need not know any English in order to participate and because the instructors, harboring the ethnocentric views common in those days, believed the two activities could serve the "civilizing" purposes of the institution. Churchmen, at first uninterested in physical activities, later used the lure of baseball teams and free uniforms to attract souls to their congregations. In black baseball, where black people were at first (after the Civil War) part of every institution, including government departments in Washington, they were gradually shut out and forced to grow their own institutions, including those where baseball could thrive.

Through the lens of baseball, we see American society gradually loosening, with some activities at first forbidden, then permitted, and finally supported. Is this a theme that plays out in all aspects of American life? Consider just one example: the way American views of dating have loosened over a century. Preventing young people from meeting casually and depending only upon European-style arranged marriages proved inconvenient in this still-new and developing country, but social leaders could and did greatly constrict the circumstances in which young adults would meet and could lay down narrow rules for their conduct during early courtship. In nineteenth-century middle-class America, potential mates could come together only in certain ways and could get to know each other only under carefully-supervised conditions. These rules gradually loosened so much that now, in the twenty-first century, most adults feel free to decide themselves where they will go to meet possible mates; they have even gone so far as to create social organizations sponsoring meetings that might lead to permanent relationships. Seeing an opportunity to make money, commercial dating organizations formed and took over this process, starting businesses that became clearinghouses for the scheduling of meetings between individuals. Today, online dating is a business earning more than four hundred million dollars a year.

So, as with baseball, dating in America was at first frowned upon, then controlled, and finally sponsored, often by organizations that profited from these meetings — as with the old-time European matchmakers. Have we come full circle in the matter of boy-meets-girl?

As the work on *Baseball: The People's Game* began approaching its final stages in the late 1980s, Seymour started to receive increased recognition for his contribution to scholarship. At the same time, our patterns of work shifted. When Seymour was asked to review a book based on the baseball exhibition "Diamonds Are Forever" for the *Journal of Sport History*, I studied the material and performed the research necessary for evaluating the painters and writers described in the book; then I wrote a detailed report, and Seymour used it to prepare the first draft of a review, which I edited heavily. The *Journal*'s editor published this review in the spring of 1990.

Two authors, recognizing the value of Seymour's name, asked him to write introductory pieces for their books. Ethan Casey, who with Michael Betzold wrote *Queen of Diamonds: The Tiger Stadium Story*, phoned to ask if Seymour would write the Foreword. I studied the book and wrote the Foreword, which Seymour read and approved. John Holway of the Society for American Baseball Research asked Seymour to write the Introduction to SABR's *Run, Rabbit, Run: The Hilarious and Mostly True Tales of Rabbit Maranville*. Seymour had seen Maranville play and knew a lot about him. I read the book, took notes on what Seymour told me he wanted to say about Maranville, then wrote the Introduction.

When the publisher of John Garraty's popular textbook, *The American Nation*, planned a revision, Seymour was asked to review the manuscript of the new version. We both read it; I wrote detailed comments, Seymour annotated them, and I prepared the final report.

James Roberts, president of a group in Washington, D.C., called Radio America, phoned to say he planned a series of radio programs on baseball history, saying that for the help he needed with this series, Seymour is "the obvious choice" and asking for an interview. This idea never came to fruition. But a personal contact with a British writer, Huw Richards, who wrote for the *London Times Higher Education Supplement*, did occur when Richards, who planned to visit the United States, wrote to ask if he could come to Keene and interview Seymour. For his travel to our small town I gave him directions and made a reservation in a small motel nearby. Richards later wrote an insightful article for the *Supplement* on the basis of his interview.

Then Dr. Alvin Hall, who annually arranged a Symposium on Baseball and the American Culture at the Hotel Otesaga in Cooperstown, invited Seymour to become the keynote speaker at the 1990 event. At that time Dr. Hall acted as dean of continuing education for the State University of New York at nearby Oneonta. In these annual meetings, a group of academics who studied the place of baseball in American history and culture were invited to present scholarly papers. Each year this gathering attracted about a hundred academics who attended to speak or listen and comment. Being invited to deliver the keynote address at the Symposium represented a distinct honor.

We both knew Seymour could no longer deliver a speech, and he accepted my suggestion that I do it for him. Although travel was becoming difficult for him, he would attend. We both had ideas for what to include in the speech, so we wrote the first draft together, and then I edited the address heavily.

When I delivered the speech at the meeting, I told the audience to pretend I was Seymour by picturing me as a pipe smoker with a bushy moustache. In this presentation I gave an illustrated lecture on *Baseball: The People's Game*, telling some of our best stories about topics like town and industrial ball. I used transparencies that included the image of "the House of Baseball," the structure that Seymour had devised for the book.

The *Oneonta Daily Star*, in reporting on the meetings, said that Seymour "is credited with paving the way for other scholars to study the sport legitimately" and quoted Dr. Hall as saying that before the advent of Seymour's efforts, "Baseball was too trivial to occupy a serious academic inquiry.... Now scholars who love baseball can combine the two." Dr. Hall thus admitted that the work we had done in baseball history gave permission for entrance into the field to other academics who lacked Seymour's strong will.

Pictured with me on Main Street of Cooperstown, New York, is Dr. Alvin Hall, who directs the annual Symposium on Baseball and the American Culture that I addressed for Harold Seymour in 1990. Dr. Hall also helped arrange the ceremony in Cooperstown on June 8, 1995, when Seymour's ashes were spread on first base at Doubleday Field. (Photograph by Roy E. Mills.)

When Seymour was invited to serve as keynote speaker in June of 1991 for a week-long "Celebration of Baseball" at Cleveland State University (formerly Fenn College, where I had so long ago studied history with him — and where he had once been fired!), I delivered the speech for him again. It was essentially the same one I had presented at the Symposium in Cooperstown, although more focused on Ohio history. In it I retold some of the good stories about early college ball (the ten-cent fine for swearing in an 1859 game), town teams (games featuring a barrel of beer on first base), industrial ball (a rainstorm soaking a team's uniforms and shrinking them embarrassingly), Civil War baseball (Confederates capturing a New York regiment's center fielder and stealing their only baseball), college women's baseball (a Smith girl chased by a gang of boys when she picked up a bat they had left on the sidewalk), and prison ball (a runner on a prison team called out on a close play called the umpire a robber and was told not to get personal!).

After this presentation, the University's magazine recognized Seymour as "baseball's foremost historian and academic chronicler of the game." Seymour had, declared the writer, "taken a pastime and examined it with scrutiny and care. He has elevated the sport to a study, and has justified doing so by validly pointing to the wide range of people and places that baseball has affected."

While we were at Cooperstown in 1990 and staying at the Otesaga, Seymour was approached during a luncheon by Lynn Novick, a producer who worked with the talented Ken Burns in his company, Florentine Films, asking if Seymour would consider a connection with Ken and the film he planned on baseball history. Seymour, who had never joined with others in any baseball project, was reluctant and put her off.

We were both familiar with Ken's work and his reputation, gained from his previous historical films, especially his highly-rated film on the Civil War. I wanted Seymour to be part of Ken's baseball project, partly because I was sure that association with it could result in the appropriate recognition for Seymour's unique contribution to baseball history, even though the invitation for him to participate had arrived so late in his career. I felt that, with my assistance, he could manage it. I was wrong.

Lynn and Ken were not, of course, aware of the condition of Seymour's health, which was by then in steep decline, so Lynn wrote a letter with a formal invitation for Seymour to take part in Ken's project, adding, "We do not think we could do justice to the subject without your participation." At my urging, Seymour accepted an offer to participate in meetings, script reviews, and screenings, at a fee of $500 per day. This consulting job never materialized because by the time Ken reached the point of needing it, Seymour was unable to perform.

But Ken also wanted to videotape an interview with Seymour, and he offered to bring his equipment to our house in order to conduct the taping in our living room. He visited us on June 13, 1990, to talk it over, zooming up to the house in his red convertible (and admitting he'd paid speeding fines in the past!). Ken no doubt failed to realize, from his talk with us, that Seymour's meager responses to his remarks stemmed less from reluctance to cooperate with Ken than it did from his decreasing ability to participate in conversation.

The taping took place at our home on June 25. Ken arrived with Lynn and a cameraman, plus a great deal of videotaping equipment that Ken said was so sensitive that it would pick up even the slightest sound. To obtain the necessary background silence, Ken asked me to turn off the refrigerator, unplug the phone, and ask the neighbor to stop running his lawn mower. After taking care of these matters, I withdrew into my office and closed the door.

Filmmaker Ken Burns, who asked Harold Seymour to consult on his documentary *Baseball*. Ken interviewed Seymour on videotape for that film, but the resulting taped segment proved unusable because of Seymour's illness. Ken's assistant consulted me frequently on research for his film. (Photograph by Pamela Tubridy Baucom, courtesy of Ken Burns.)

Much later I got a note from Ken's researcher, Susanna Steisel — now an assistant producer with Ken's company — to tell me that, although an effort had been made to keep Seymour's interview in Ken's film, the last bit of the interview he taped that day at our home had finally been removed. Because of Seymour's incipient illness, she said, "The energy [level] was just too low to hold up." Seymour's voice and personality failed to come through sufficiently. Film as a media for presenting one's persona is absolutely unforgiving, and this method of displaying Seymour's knowledge simply came too late for him. I persuaded Ken not to discard the film, however, but to send it to Cornell University for the Seymour Collection. I never watched the film; I'm sure it would be too depressing for me to view.

After Seymour's passing I consulted for Ken through Susanna Steisel, his researcher, receiving many phone calls and visits from Susanna requesting help in finding baseball materials and photos. Susanna wrote me later, "Your warm graciousness in opening up your home to me will always be appreciated." She added,

> The research that you and Dr. Seymour provided in your books was invaluable to us over the last four years, and we constantly turned to them for in-depth information and also for the final say-so in any disputes. For that we are most grateful.

As a result of my assistance in this project, Ken listed my name in the credits for his film, and in the book that followed he listed Seymour.

About this time I fielded a phone call from a researcher helping to produce the John Sayles film about the Black Sox, *Eight Men Out*. The researcher needed to know what sort of shouts or catcalls from fans in the stands might be heard during the 1919 games. I looked up the answer in our notes and talked to Seymour about it, then returned the call with our joint suggestions.

Another honor came to Seymour when Drew University, his undergraduate college, decided to induct him into Drew's Athletic Hall of Fame. At long last Drew was publicly acknowledging Seymour's contribution to the early sporting life of the University. Seymour wanted to attend the ceremonies inducting him and others, which were held September 28, 1991, but while we were there he felt unable to walk to the front of the room to receive the plaque, so I got up and accepted it for him. This award recognized Seymour's "stellar achievements as a varsity athlete, team leadership and spirit."

By the middle of the year 1989, as we approached the end of the manuscript's preparation, I was doing all the work. Seymour could no longer contribute, and I wrote the final thirteen chapters myself. I had become the cleanup hitter.

As we neared publication, my resentment began to surface concerning Seymour's lack of appropriate and formal recognition for my participation in the project. From my long experience in publishing, I was able to contrast the way other authors recognized those who made heavy contributions to their books with the way Seymour recognized my contribution to his. I thought of writing teams like that of Charles and Mary Beard, for example, a team we resembled. Mary was an author in her own right but also wrote books in collaboration with her husband, books in which the partners received equal billing on the title page. Other books with multiple authors ranked them according to the weight of their contributions. At Ginn and Company, authors were classified as either the main author or as junior authors.

Moreover, publishers used various ways of listing substantial contributors on the title page of a book, one being insertion of the word "with" preceding the name of a secondary author. As for people who made minor contributions to a project, such as preparing a questionnaire for it, or lending a copy of an article, they were acknowledged by having their names mentioned as part of a short piece written to appear in the front matter, like a Preface or Acknowledgments page. My work was obviously more than minor. I was certainly Seymour's collaborator on all his books; yet my name had never appeared on the title page of any. Instead, I was always relegated to the list of people who kindly sent a bit of information or a picture.

I could accept Seymour's desire not to give me equal billing. But I believed I was certainly entitled to be recognized on the title page as a major contributor, as was the usual practice in recognizing collaborators, since Seymour had produced his books, and especially this book, only with very substantial assistance from me. His recognition of my work seemed increasingly inappropriate and unsatisfactory. Perhaps I was recalling that quotation from Emerson, the New England Transcendentalist whose work appealed to me since my study of it in my college years, in which he affirms, "I must be myself.... I cannot break myself any longer for you...."

When I revealed my dissatisfaction to Seymour, however, he brushed it aside, and my resentment of this treatment began to build. I resolved to prove my case by documenting my work, at least on this book, on which I had worked so extensively, by writing him a formal memo stating my claim.

In this memo, dated June 1, 1989, I requested that the title page read: "Baseball: The People's Game/Harold Seymour, Ph.D.,/With Dorothy Z. Seymour." I continued the memo with the following explanation:

> My name should be included on the title page of this book, for proper recognition of the work I did on it, work that is usually part of the author's responsibility.
>
> In substantiation of my claim, here is a partial list of my work on the book.
>
> **1. Research**. I have done most of the research for this book. I spent many Saturdays in the NYPL and many full days in the BPL as well as in the Fairhope, Newton, and Keene libraries, bringing back stack after stack of informative notes. I spent a summer at Widener in Cambridge, made research trips to three colleges, and did research in historical societies in

Detroit and Keene. I also brought home for study numbers of books and theses ordered through interlibrary loan, studied them, and took notes from them.

My work on the research has been a key factor in the book's development. I have good control of the subject matter and know the sources.

2. Analysis. I sifted, analyzed, and organized all the research, putting it into a form that would make it intelligible and from which the writing could be done. I produced hundreds of pages of outlines interpreting as well as quoting from the research. This analysis took uncounted hours of study.

Without this analytical work, the writing would have been impossible. This kind of study of the material is usually done by the author.

3. Writing. I wrote the final thirteen chapters of the book. You edited them. In other words, at this point we exchanged roles. Meyer likes the chapters. You called some of my work on these chapters "terrific."

Moreover, each chapter took me less than a week to write, partly because I am completely at home with the material, having done the research and analysis myself.

If I had not taken hold of the writing when I did, the manuscript would not now be done.

I have therefore written about a third of the book.

4. Final revision. As I input the final version of the manuscript, I edited as I went along, cutting the unnecessary parts that Meyer wanted removed and improving the manuscript in every possible way.

My insistence on getting a computer for the manuscript was another key factor in the speed with which the work could be completed.

5. Editing. I edited every bit of writing every step of the way, revising as necessary. I sometimes rewrote entire sections as well. The editing work on the book amounted to a task I handled daily.

6. Correspondence. I handled the correspondence related to the research. When a letter needed to be written for information, I wrote it. I handled correspondence for illustrations, too. The wording of these letters took time and thought.

7. Typing. In a manuscript as long as this one, where the chapters sometimes went through seven drafts, typing became a major burden. I estimate that I typed about 8,000 pages, counting my work on the outlines. This took time, energy, and attention.

8. Clerical work. I filed, organized, and kept track of everything. This includes all research notes, documents, bibliography, and illustrations. I have taken care of the copying and mailing. If something is needed, I find it.

9. Illustrations. I am preparing the captions, credit lines, and expense list.

10. Bibliographical note. This piece will be a major task and could take several weeks of work. I will no doubt be doing most of it, since I am so familiar with the materials used.

11. Index. As before, you want me to handle the writing of the index, a tedious task that is the responsibility of the author.

12. Publicity. I am the logical person to handle this work, since obtaining publicity is one of my skills. I expect to spend considerable time planning and carrying out promotion.

Any combination of some of the above responsibilities entitles me to have my name on the title page, as it should have for Volume 2.

Since the book was your idea, you should be considered the Senior Author, but if you are the Senior Author, then I am surely the Junior Author. The attached title page reflects that relationship. [Here I referred to my requested wording of the author line as "With Dorothy Z. Seymour."]

You are concerned with the way your name will appear in the book. I, too, am concerned with the way my name will appear, and in view of all the work I put into the book — devotion is not too strong a word — I do not think it fair for my name to appear only in the acknowledgments, among people who might have sent in an article or cooperated as a librarian. Yet I should be mentioned there. Below is a paragraph about my contribution that I would like to appear in the acknowledgments:

"My wife, Dorothy Z. Seymour, an editor and author, worked closely with me on the preparation of this book. She did most of the research, carried on the correspondence, and did all the typing and clerical work. She analyzed and organized the mass of material collected through research and put it in a form from which the writing could be done. She also edited the writing as it was produced, and she wrote the first drafts of thirteen of the chapters. Moreover, with my participation she performed the final revision of the manuscript as she input it into the computer."

This memo had no effect. Seymour refused to consider my request to place my name on the title page. I made it clear that from then on, I was continuing to work on the project only under protest. That meant nothing, of course, since the main thing was that I was continuing to work. When Seymour prepared the preface, he devoted only one sentence to my assistance. I resigned myself to my usual position. At least for the time being.

We included a long Bibliographical Note in *Baseball: The People's Game*. For a book of more than 600 pages, source notes would have been impractical anyway, and, knowing in advance that Oxford would not publish notes, we used the same acknowledgment technique as before: referring to many sources within the text, especially when they were the result of others' research (for example, inserting the phrase "as Professor Barbara Deckard has pointed out").

The fourteen-page Bibliographical Note for this book covers the many libraries and other repositories that were used; the documents, dissertations, and other manuscripts consulted; and the letters and questionnaires (which I devised) that elicited information from companies, colleges, prison officials, government officials, Native American schools, and Japanese sources. It also describes the interviews, guides, handbooks, pamphlets, and releases that proved useful. It mentions the Japanese translator we hired to give us information from books on Japanese baseball, as well as other translators who gave some help. Then it launches into the many newspapers used, including those sent us by prisons and reformatories; the files of military newspapers that proved valuable (I had particularly enjoyed the sources describing the sports carried on while building the Panama Canal); newspapers on Native American life that gave us enlightening information (I discovered *Wasaja* in a library in Newton, Massachusetts); and newspapers covering black life, like the *New York Age,* that proved informative. Each newspaper devoted to a particular part of American society bore its own special characteristics and gave a special flavor to the story of the way baseball developed in its branch of the population.

The Bibliographical Note continues by describing the countless periodicals I used, including those specializing in subjects like social history, regional history, boys' interests, business and industrial sports, and softball. The final section describes the many types of books used and cites some of the more important ones on such topics as boys' work, public parks, settlements, leisure, church work, delinquency, the American Legion, government programs like the Civilian Conservation Corps, college and town history, company history, foreign sport, Cuba, World War I, biography (I was riveted by the biographies of Native Americans like Ohiyesa and Luther Standing Bear), prison life (Osborne was certainly a fascinating prison innovator and administrator), and of course on women and on American blacks, for which I was especially delighted to unearth, in the Boston Public Library, the book by J.H. Nankivell on the history of his black regiment and its baseball triumphs.

This Bibliographical Note displayed, more than anything, the research that I accomplished and for which Seymour was given the credit.

12

The Change-Up

At the time I was completing *Baseball: The People's Game*, besides working part-time for Stillpoint I was also starting something else: a large project that would be wholly my own. I sensed that *The People's Game* might be the last one on baseball history that I would work on, and I believed that it was time for me to turn instead to a large project that I'd had in the back of my mind for months, if not years.

I wanted to investigate the historical background of my mother's people, the Austrians, and to get a better understanding of the reason they had in the 1930s come under the influence of the German Nazis. I thought of using my mother as the focus for the book. She had told me some stories about her early life, and I could tell that, with her many skills, she could — if she'd had the confidence — have developed herself into a leader in her field. I conceived the work I had in mind not as a history but as a historical novel, because with a character resembling my talented mother as the protagonist, I could develop those talents for her through my writing.

Having long enjoyed reading historical novels, I understood the writing conventions they required, but I also wanted to create my own conventions by writing a different kind of novel, one without the standard low point, climax, and happy ending, one that would portray life as it really is: a series of seemingly unrelated events, some occurring as low points in the protagonist's life and some high, that eventually come together in unexpected ways to clarify life's theme and enlighten us with its meaning. After all, that's the way my own life seemed to be working out.

I began by collecting information on Austrian history and biography in the Boston Public Library while completing the work for *Baseball: The People's Game*. Launching a research project is not unlike engaging in a voyage of discovery to an unmapped land, where the explorer hopes to meet fascinating strangers to learn about and to cultivate. In other words, it's exciting. As I explored this new field I found it satisfying to perform research for my own independent project as well as for what I thought of as Seymour's work — not realizing that his work had become my own as well. For research trips from Keene to Boston I often stayed overnight at the home of friends in Newton, just as for research trips from Chester to New York City I had often stayed with Manhattan friends. That plan gave me two full days of library work at a time.

In my own office I worked sporadically at my new writing idea, keeping it under wraps. Seymour had in the past accepted my detours to engage in short non-baseball projects, realizing that they might bring in some needed income. But this new project, I knew, would not be a short one. And I had the feeling that Seymour would disapprove of my engaging in anything of this magnitude or this different from anything I had yet done.

One day Seymour came into my office unexpectedly and found me writing something that was obviously outside the field of baseball. (Later, I recalled the scholar-historian Barbara Tuchman's telling about stuffing a history book under the sofa cushion when her disapproving husband came unexpectedly into the living room.) In response to Seymour's question, I admitted that I was working on another project, this one a historical novel. His predictable reaction — scoffing, "You can't write a historical novel" — hurt and offended me. I knew I could do the job. And I was determined to accomplish it, although because of my baseball work as well as my writing assignments and editorial jobs, completing it to my satisfaction took me a long time, almost ten years.

When we came to the end of *Baseball: The People's Game*, Oxford University Press, not realizing that I had actually written so much of it, then hired me to edit the manuscript! Through the company's editorial director, Leona Capeless, Oxford had in the recent past hired me to edit other book-length manuscripts. Leona knew of my editorial skills. I decided to accept the job.

This assignment afforded me the opportunity of giving the manu-

12—The Change-Up

script a final and thorough editing while I prepared the front matter and back matter. During July of 1989 I spent ninety hours performing this final edit, and Oxford paid me a thousand dollars. This is the first pay I ever received for work on baseball history.

Baseball: The People's Game was published in 1990. I was confident that it conveyed itself as a solid work of history, but it was also pretty far afield from the first two books in the series. We had not revealed to baseball history aficionados that this new book would veer off the subject of the major leagues to devote an entire volume to the history of early baseball play by everyday Americans. Because Seymour insisted on keeping the switch secret, fans did not expect it and were surprised. As one said to me at a baseball meeting I attended soon after, "Your husband threw us a change-up."

Reviewers, however, reacted with amazed admiration, particularly at the amount of evidence we had collected and presented to document our main point: that during the first decades of the nineteenth century, baseball, at first suspect among those who controlled important American institutions, gradually insinuated itself into those institutions until the managers of those institutions themselves actually took control of it for their own purposes. Through the story of amateur baseball we demonstrated this progression in many aspects of American life.

Jonathan Yardley, in the *Washington Post*, pointed out that the book entered "uncharted territory" in writing about the beginnings of amateur baseball. A Catholic journal called *America* lauded "Seymour's monumental research," saying he had "performed prodigies" into "areas hitherto unexplored." *The Library Journal*, too, admired the "exhaustive research." *Virginia Kirkus Reviews*, which librarians look to for book evaluations, called the book "remarkably well-researched."

Professor Warren Goldstein of New York University wrote in the *Journal of American History* that the book was "unique," for "never before has so much information about baseball outside the major and minor leagues been assembled between two covers. So much, in fact, that a brief review can only gesture at the wealth of material in the book." Goldstein praised the book's "remarkable breadth and richness of detail" and its inclusion of "wonderful stories."

The New York Times, in a review by Roberto Gonzáles Echevarria, described the book as "rich, detailed, and lavishly researched." The scientist Stephen J. Gould of Harvard, who loved baseball and often wrote about it knowledgeably, said in the *New York Review of Books* that *Base-*

ball: The People's Game was a "magisterial compendium," calling Seymour "the leading professional in a small but growing field of sports history." Gould conjured up a picture of Seymour as manipulating "hundreds of thousands of index cards" to organize his ideas; he never knew, nor did anyone at the time, that Seymour organized no notes, or that I performed virtually all the research they admired so much. Gould summarized his view of the three Seymour baseball volumes as "a distinguished series by the doyen of baseball historians."

Much later, Professor George Grella of the University of Rochester summarized the significance of *Baseball: The People's Game* by pointing out that the book "reminds us all that the best, the most authentic baseball does not take place in the sterile confines of some concrete cereal bowl that owners call a stadium but in other venues far from the Major Leagues; out there, all over America, it is truly the people's game as the people actually play it."

Several reviewers mentioned the important theme revealed in the book: that American institutions, beginning their relationship to the game by banning baseball, ended by taking it over for their own purposes. The review in *America*, for example, said that the book "documents ... attempts to [use] baseball as a tool of indoctrination and conformity, to enlist it in the cause of chauvinism, and to justify it by citing its dubious potential for character building." Gonzáles Echevarria thought the book presented "in dramatic fashion, the use of baseball for social purposes" both in prisons and in the armed forces. He called it "a wide-ranging cultural history of the United States from the mid-19th century to the beginning of World War II," focusing on baseball in broad social processes and demonstrating the existence of a "vast unplanned scheme to impose values that would ease the growth of capitalism." I agree with this reviewer's description of *Baseball: The People's Game* as Seymour's "most important book because it raises broader issues about the game and touches the lives of more people."

A writer named Ed Hardy, who reviewed the book in the *Cornell Alumni News*, covered this same point when he wrote,

> What emerges is the richly detailed picture of a pastoral children's game that soon becomes regulated and appropriated by adults. Long seen as a political safety valve and a badge of assimilation, baseball through the early twentieth century was gradually employed in a number of causes from instilling American values to fostering religious conversion.

Warren Goldstein, too, noticed that "much more successfully than in his earlier book, Seymour links developments in baseball to larger social and cultural contexts"; for example, in presenting American Legion baseball, Seymour "makes precisely the kind of connection often overlooked by sports historians."

I wonder now, although I didn't think of it at the time, whether this same takeover by American institutions has occurred, as "a vast unplanned scheme," in other cultural aspects of American life, like its music, its art, its theatre. In thinking about these institutions, despite my limited knowledge of those branches of life, I believe that to some degree the commercial takeover of Americans' original creative efforts, like jazz, may have occurred as well in the field of music, as the entertainment business sought new music on which to make money. So perhaps this gradual encroachment by our institutions is a trend in American life.

I was also gratified to see reviewers mentioning the "entertaining" and "fascinating" stories that the book presents. *Publishers Weekly* said *Baseball: The People's Game* was "delightful to read" and "enlivened by Seymour's many wry asides." Paul W. Gates, the chairman of Seymour's doctoral committee, wrote Seymour a note of congratulation, calling this third volume "a superb book" and telling Seymour that he deserved "the highest commendation for it."

Altlhough the book failed to make the *New York Times* list of best sellers, it did make the list called "And Bear in Mind," made up of titles that comprised "Editors' choices of other recent books of particular interest"—a phrase I always thought carried the implied meaning, "Books of lasting value that *should* have made the list of best bellers."

In working on this volume, I really hit my stride as a researcher-writer and interpreter of history. While preparing *Baseball: The People's Game* I found that I could with great enthusiasm take hold of the subject, which was much more culturally embedded than the subjects of the two previous books.

As I worked on the book, its importance clarified for me: it demonstrates that baseball affected all aspects of American society in tangible ways. It affected children, business and industrial workers, women, college students, servicemen, prisoners, and ethnic minorities. It made an impact on what children read and how Native American schools and "bad boys' schools" dealt with their charges. Moreover, the book presented abundant evidence that the major institutions of our society gradually discovered ways and reasons to take over baseball play completely, promoting it either to make money or to train people in the way they believed Americans should develop or both. The way all this worked out fascinated me.

Colleges, for example, used baseball to drain off excess student energy and to call attention to their institutions. Schools and city recreation departments and even church organizations used it to focus children's attention on socially-acceptable activity. Directors of Indian Schools used it to make their charges seem more like the mass of American young people. Their use of baseball attests to the game's position as a recognized aspect of being a socialized American. Business and industry used it to keep employees satisfied with their lot, since businessmen came to view baseball as a wholesome activity that could keep employees from turning to unionism. The military used baseball to stimulate and channel competitive urges. Female physical education teachers used it to give students exercise and group cohesion while steering them away from tendencies they believed unfeminine and therefore socially unacceptable. The clubs of organized baseball used it to make more money: in order to build future fans, they offered free or cheap seats to women and boys on special occasions.

I was not the only one concluding that American institutions used sport for the purpose of social control. In 1980 Steven Riess's *Touching Base*, in 1981 Dominick Cavallo's *Muscles and Morals*, and in 1985 David Nasaw's *Children of the City* showed that social agencies like the schools deliberately fastened upon sports as a way of molding children and young people in the way their managers thought Americans should be formed.

Baseball: The People's Game is, of course, much closer to social history than are the first two baseball volumes, which are more akin to company histories. In some ways *Baseball: The People's Game* also does what Seymour had envisioned so long ago when he first proposed a college course on sport: it presents American history through baseball. And it does so more directly than did the first two volumes. *Library Journal* recognized that the book is "a cultural history of America viewed through its national pastime."

Baseball: The People's Game reveals the history of everyday American life of the period through the glass of the American national game, telling us as much about our history as an economic or political history tells us about American life, certainly as much as a history of American music of the period does. It shows American life changing through gradual alterations in our parks, schools, colleges, prisons, and the military. In so doing, it shows our ideas about life evolving, by means of changes in the way we looked at the place in our lives that should be occupied by fun, exercise, games, recreation, and entertainment. In this way, *Baseball: The People's Game* is an even more unique work than the earlier two, and I'm proud to have been so closely involved in developing it.

Seymour was finally becoming acknowledged as supremely important in his field. John Thorn, editor of *The National Pastime,* using Seymour's own metaphor, remarked of Seymour that "In the house of baseball historians he sits in the penthouse." When Huw Richards published his interview in *The London Times* he stated that Seymour was recognized as "the father of academic sports history in the US, his reputation founded firmly" on his three books.

But the occupant of the penthouse was declining fast, both physically and mentally. I realized that he must be suffering from Alzheimer's disease.

When the Society for American Baseball Research named *Baseball: The People's Game* as winner of the annual SABR-Macmillan Baseball Research Award and invited Seymour to appear at its next convention, we both knew Seymour could no longer travel or make an acceptance speech. I offered to attend the convention to accept the award on his behalf, especially since the convention took place in Cleveland, my home town. He agreed.

Then *Baseball: The People's Game* won the Casey Award, offered annually by *Spitball: The Literary Baseball Magazine,* as the best baseball book published in 1990, and the editor, Mike Shannon, said the book had won conclusively over all finalists, including George Will's *Men at Work*. Mike invited Seymour to attend the magazine's annual banquet to accept the award. Since that was impossible, I instead hired a local photographer to videotape Seymour thanking the judges who had selected *Baseball: The People's Game* for the award. I wrote the speech — a few paragraphs couched in very short sentences — and printed the sentences in large letters on big cards. I held them up so that he could read them in front of the camera; he could just barely manage that. Then I sent the resulting videotape to Mike, who replied that the tape would be played at the banquet. In 1991 the Hall of Fame at Cooperstown asked for a copy of this videotape for its archives.

Honors kept arriving. A Drew alumnus, Herman Estrin, informed Seymour that he had just been honored by an award naming him as one of the best New Jersey authors. He qualified for the award, Estrin explained, because of having been a New Jersey resident while attending college. It was *Baseball: The People's Game* that had inspired this recognition.

Then the book won the prestigious award for the best book in the field of sport history that was presented annually by the North American Society for Sport History. NASSH consists of a group of more than 200 scholars who study and write about not only baseball but other sports, or about recreation or physical activity. Most members are university instructors, and many of them teach the history of sport, a field that Seymour's work inspired. In bestowing its award, NASSH referred to Seymour as "the father of baseball history." Seymour's peers were thus recognizing him as preeminent.

Perhaps the most unique honor is the one implied when Seymour was asked if he would agree to have his own baseball trading card as part of a proposed new set called "Major League Writers." For this I furnished a copy of a recent photo and the needed information to be included on the card. The company producing the cards, called Little Sun, published a set featuring 23 writers, including Henry Chadwick, the first baseball writer and reporter, along with more recent authors like Mark Harris, Dick Young, Larry Ritter, Roger Kahn, Red Smith, and W.P. Kinsella. Little Sun distributed 5,000 sets of these cards through Ball Four Cards, and the Baseball Hall of Fame and Museum in Cooperstown has a set in its collection.

By then Seymour was listed in encyclopedias recognizing those who had contributed importantly to scholarship. At the editors' request, I furnished information about him for inclusion in *Contemporary Authors*, the *Dictionary of International Biography*, and the *Dictionary of American Scholars*.

Seymour, said Professor Goldstein in his review of *Baseball: The People's Game*, "has reason to be proud of his achievement." But the achiever was reaching a point in his debilitating illness that he hardly realized what his achievement was.

Then in mid-1992, everything stopped.

Alzheimer's is a terrible condition. Although I found that caring for Seymour at this stage of the disease to be almost overwhelming, he

12—The Change-Up

steadily refused to permit me to bring in outside help. Inevitably, a day came when a crisis arose that I couldn't handle. I took him to the hospital, which admitted him while I searched for a nearby facility that could take him in. I found the right one in the McKerley Center of Keene, offering a comfortable and caring environment, and I went there daily, sometimes twice a day, to visit and help care for him. It was located close enough that, if necessary, I could walk to or from the Center.

While he was at McKerley, I announced through the SABR newsletter that because of poor health Seymour was receiving therapy, and I invited fans to write him. A flood of mail came in, mostly appreciative letters from readers who were fans of the three Seymour books but also from other authors. In my daily visits to the Center I took these letters with me and read them to him, hoping that, as well as giving him pleasure, they would keep his mental faculties functioning.

A cross-section of these appreciative letters, many of them from people we had never heard of, demonstrates that many fans were enjoying the books, both in the facts that they conveyed and in the way they were written. Ken Carrano of Illinois wrote, "What most impresses me about your books is not the accuracy of the information but the ease with which it is presented. Your love of the game of baseball leaps off every page and takes the reader on a wonderful ride." Scott McClellan of Georgia said he greatly enjoyed the series, particularly *Baseball: The People's Game*. Stephen Murdock of Massachusetts admitted that at first he was disappointed to discover that the third book wasn't about the majors, but "it turned out to be my favorite of the three, a wonderful book." He added, "A hundred years from now someone will draw pleasure from your work." Joe Naiman of California praised the work as "the most comprehensive series" of any baseball histories, asserting that "No serious baseball library is complete without it."

Those who were themselves engaged in writing about baseball were among the most appreciative. Dan Gutman of New Jersey, then writing a baseball book for children, stated, "I admire your work very much." Professor Richard L. Miller wrote that, in teaching a course at the University of Cincinnati on Baseball and American Culture, he always points out that Seymour is "the best researcher that baseball has ever known." Lowell Blaisdell of Texas, a retired history professor who had produced several baseball articles, singled out Seymour as "clearly the single best baseball historian."

Some wrote to discuss their own baseball research. Irving Stein of Illinois thanked Seymour for recommending that he contact William C. Brown Publishing Company of Wisconsin about his manuscript on Buck Weaver, a manuscript that became the book *The Ginger Kid*. The head of the Brown publishing company in turn wrote thanking Seymour for having referred Stein to him and praising Seymour's "groundbreaking work."

Kevin Seymour (no relation) of North Carolina declared that Seymour was an inspiration to his joining SABR and announced that he was pursuing several baseball projects of his own. Neil Isaacs of Maryland wrote to say that he wanted to include Seymour in a book he was writing about batboys for major-league teams.

An unusual comment came from Stephen Murphy, a science professor at Queens University in Ontario, Canada. Murphy, although interested in baseball, was nearing the completion of his doctorate not in history but in biology. His admiration of the Seymour books resided in the way they used logical analysis. He stated that he used the Seymour books in his teaching, recommending them to his science students "as one way to learn to analyse evidence in a critical fashion."

Some people well known in the field took the opportunity of getting in touch with Seymour at this time. John Holway wrote thanking Seymour for writing "a great preface" for his book on Rabbit Maranville. Professor Eugene Murdock wrote of his gratitude for Seymour's kind words in reviewing his biography of Ban Johnson. Leverett T. Smith, Professor of English at North Carolina Wesleyan, congratulated Seymour on *Baseball: The People's Game*. And Richard Topp, then president of SABR, asked if he could drop by for "a hot stove conversation." In a story about Seymour in the *Boston Globe*, the reporter quoted Topp as calling Seymour "a super, super heavyweight. He's like a god to us in baseball research terms."

Seymour's boyhood friend from Brooklyn, Herb Wittkin, who had played on the early teams Seymour coached in the 1920s and '30s, wrote admiringly of Seymour's intrepid spirit: "You were a pioneer in an area only a visionary would dare enter.... Now, of course, everyone has jumped on the bandwagon."

I believe that these missives cheered Seymour somewhat, but after his admission to McKerley his condition continued to worsen, and a physician finally confirmed that he was suffering from Alzheimer's disease.

12—The Change-Up

Then, in consulting with the Social Security Division of the government, I discovered that, because Seymour had specified that the income from the Cornell trust be sent in checks made out to him, I could not cash those checks to cover living expenses, and that, moreover, the state of New Hampshire would within a few months appropriate this money, because as soon as our bank account was depleted by the expenses of his care at the McKerley Center, the state would, through Medicaid, begin taking all our income, and I would lose my home this way as well.

Frightened, I discovered that I must persuade the Cornell Trust Department that it was Seymour's dementia that had caused him to specify that the income from our money in the Trust be directed to him alone. I asked that checks now be made out to me, so that I could continue paying for his care. My Social Security adviser pointed out that in order to remain in our home I also had to change the listing of its title from joint ownership to ownership by me. I managed both these matters in July of 1992.

I knew it was time as well to inform Oxford of my role in the preparation of the books, since otherwise I would be unable to cash any royalty checks. Sheldon Meyer, his long-time editor, in reply to my revelation, wrote me that he was "astounded by the news that you had actually written a good part of Volume III and received no credit for it. I don't know whether there is anything we can do to rectify the situation at this late date. It is certainly an injustice to you." He added that both he and Leona Capeless, the editorial director, with whom I had worked closely, "thank you deeply for your large contribution to Volume III." He added that the three volumes "represent one of the proudest accomplishments of my years at Oxford. It was my great privilege and pleasure to be involved in the publication of this seminal work."

Sheldon, not realizing that the complete collection had been promised to Cornell, also inquired about what I planned to do with the research completed for the fourth volume, adding, "It should provide at least a valuable research tool for other scholars, and perhaps some scholar in the future might be interested in continuing Seymour's work. I don't really have anything in mind regarding this, but this is a valuable archive that should be available in some form." Later, Sheldon asked me if I planned to complete the fourth volume myself. I said no.

Seymour's life lasted only a couple of months longer, and then, in September, it was over.

Then it was up to me to carry out his wishes. I sent out the release I had promised him to write, telling of his passing and explaining his importance to the world of baseball history.

President Rhodes of Cornell wrote me a kind letter of condolence, adding,

> Dr. Seymour's distinguished career and splendid books on baseball brought great credit to Cornell and a new understanding of the importance of sports in American history. His pioneering work brought pleasure to his readers and expanded the possibilities of historical research for other doctoral students. He will be long remembered for his devotion to scholarship, to baseball, and to Cornell.

Cornell's Dean of the College of Arts and Sciences, Don M. Randel, wrote,

> A historian myself, I am particularly appreciative when colleagues open new doors for serious study, as your husband did with the subject of baseball. He is a near-mythical figure in the field of sports history, and his story will be an inspiration to all students honored with the Harold Seymour Graduate Fellowship in American History.

An obituary in the *New York Times* of September 29, 1992, was headed "Harold Seymour, 82, A Pioneer/In the Field of Baseball History," and explained that many regarded his three-volume history as "the seminal work in establishing baseball as a subject for serious scholarly inquiry." It added that before entering a nursing home "he had been at work, with his wife's assistance, on a fourth volume."

A more interpretive assessment appears in *Baseball: An Encyclopedia of Popular Culture*, where the description of Seymour's main accomplishments are sandwiched between portrayals of Tom Seaver and Red Smith. Seymour, says the obit,

> made baseball respectable for the historian and contributed enormously to our understanding of the history of the game. Each person who studies baseball as an important dimension of American society owes an extraordinary debt to this pioneer.... [His work] demonstrated a depth of historical research previously unknown in books about baseball. Making exhaustive use of source materials, Seymour wrote the first truly detailed, accurate, and substantiated history of the origins and rise of the game. [Moreover,] his love of the game [gained as a participant] never left him, and the fan remained always within the scholar.

After preparing the release about Seymour's passing, my next job was to organize our entire baseball collection for accession by the Cornell University library.

My feelings about releasing the materials I had collected and lived with for so long were mixed. I told myself that forty-three years in baseball was long enough, more than long enough, and that it was time for me to turn away from it in favor of writing and research that were exclusively my own. I retained memberships in both SABR and NASSH, but for the first few years after Seymour's passing I sent to Cornell all the baseball journals, books, and other sports materials I received through these organizations. I told my friends I never wanted to write about baseball again. After all, writing baseball history had not been my idea initially. I had moved into it sideways, so to speak, because it was blocking my way to other work I wanted to do.

Yet I had grown so close to baseball history as to make myself a specialist in the field. I had to admit that I found it fascinating, particularly the way it disclosed much about what had happened in this country that no other study had revealed for me. Although I believed that the baseball part of my life was over, I knew that baseball history would always mean a lot to me.

But it was time to release the material: the many books, magazines, rolls of microfilm, articles, clippings, pamphlets, photocopies, computer disks, audiotapes and videotapes, pictures, newsletters, dissertations, guides, journals, speeches, legal materials, Congressional hearings, interview records, and all sorts of other printed and manuscript materials. Also the file drawers full of correspondence records. And above all, the boxes and boxes of notes we took — mostly, I myself took — over the years, notes for the books written and for those still unwritten. The bibliographical boxes alone seemed formidable and included not only a box of miscellaneous sources used, like bulletins, college magazines, indexes, pamphlets, speeches, yearbooks, and ephemera but also a color-coded file of items considered but not used.

I contacted Cornell to plan the transfer of the collection, then began sorting and packing it for pickup. Setting aside items I judged too personal for the collection and mailing those to Seymour's son, I organized my files, the note boxes, and everything on my shelves that related to sports history. Dr. Herbert Finch, Cornell's archivist at the time, explained that the materials, although remaining as a unit, would become part of the Rare and Manuscript Collections of the University Library.

As soon as they were accessioned, they would become available for the use of scholars in the field of baseball history.

It was at this time that I began revealing my large part in the preparation of all the baseball books. When Herbert Finch understood my collaborative role, he wrote me that "we think it [the Seymour Collection at Cornell] should have both your names on it to recognize the contribution both of you made to its completeness and usability."

Professor Sherman Cochran, Chairman of Cornell's Department of History, wrote me,

> My wife and I are pleased to hear that you and your husband have worked together on historical research just as Jan and I have done. The two of us are joined by everyone in the History Department in conveying to you the pride that we have taken in your husband's and your own successes in historical studies.

In May, Herbert Finch arrived in Keene personally with a large van and packed the baseball collection, driving it to Cornell himself for accessioning. Then it was gone.

In the last year of Seymour's life, two men important in baseball realized that he deserved national recognition for his achievements. They were Thomas R. Heitz, director of the National Baseball Library in Cooperstown, and Lloyd Johnson, then director of the Society for American Baseball

My office in Keene, New Hampshire, featured stacks of baseball research materials on shelves as well as in files. This material was eventually contributed to Cornell University and became part of the Seymour Collection at Cornell's Kroch Library. (Photograph by Harold Seymour.)

12—The Change-Up

Research (SABR). "Dr. Seymour," said Tom in July of 1992, "is without question the prototype and ultimate role model for baseball history practitioners." Tom, on learning of Seymour's poor health and residence in a nursing home, wrote him kindly, "your books and writings continue to be used here on a daily basis, and we could not do without them."

Pursuing the idea of formal recognition, Tom told me he had been discussing with Lloyd Johnson — who was also Tom's former colleague at the library of the Hall of Fame — about a plan to establish an annual SABR award in Seymour's name for his "significant contribution through research and writing to our understanding of the game's past."

Tom continued,

> My great regret is that this effort is made so late in Dr. Seymour's career. Dr. Seymour has been a beacon and an inspiration to many scholars and researchers in and out of the academic world for many years. To many he was an almost mythical figure, whose legendary writings about our National Pastime formed the bedrock upon which later scholarship was fashioned.
>
> I was privileged to meet the man in person. Having met Dr. Seymour, [I realized that] his books (which I have used almost daily since arriving here ten years ago) took on a new dimension. One can appreciate the care and labor that went into those pages all the more after meeting the person who produced them.

At the time Tom wrote this letter, he had no idea, despite my constant presence with Seymour at the library during our research there, of the large contribution to the Seymour books that I had made, a contribution that, when he and SABR became aware of it, caused them to change the proposed name of the Award to The Dr. Harold and Dorothy Seymour Award.

I was about to become deeply involved in the history of baseball once more.

Ironically, Tom's formal proposal to the SABR Board of Directors for establishment of the Award is dated the very day of Seymour's passing, September 25, 1992. The Award, said the proposal, was to be named in honor of Dr. Harold and Dorothy Seymour, "whose lifetime contributions to baseball's historical scholarship are unparalleled." A bronze medallion would be struck, said Tom, with a suitable baseball design, to be awarded annually "in order to encourage baseball historians, both professional and amateur, to attain the highest standards of historical scholarship, as exemplified by the published works of Dr. Harold Seymour, and to honor those whose works reflect these standards." Tom said that those who received the medal would be honored at annual SABR meetings and invited to make a special presentation of their work.

Tom's proposal also established rules for a book's consideration as winner of the award. Recipients, it said, should demonstrate exceptional scholarship, superior writing skills, and the full range of conceptual, theoretical, investigative, and analytical skills employed by accomplished historians. Those who had broken new research ground would get the priority. Recipients, Tom thought, need not be trained historians, but their work must reflect "baseball historical scholarship and analysis."

SABR accepted this proposal. But, as Tom, had predicted, it took a year for the proposal to move into the phase of actually preparing the medallion. Morris Eckhouse, SABR's president in 1993, enlisted the talents of Cleveland illustrator Jeff Suntala, who was also a SABR member, to design the medal. I was asked to send photos of both of us in profile, answer questions about Seymour's life and participation in the game, and comment on the artist's initial sketches.

After I approved the final design, Morris assigned the preparation of the medal to a company in Providence, Rhode Island. The completed medal, a heavy and impressive-looking bronze object that is three and three-quarters inches in diameter and a half-inch thick, is designed for display on a small wooden stand. Its obverse side presents our profiles and our names, with the outlines of a baseball diamond in the background. On the reverse is the SABR logo with crossed bats and a baseball resting in a glove, appearing on a field of an open book.

Each presentation of the Seymour Medal is made in conjunction with a beautiful hinged wooden box. Inside is a wide green ribbon designed for lifting the medal out of its nest.

SABR also adopted formal rules for the awarding of the Medal. The group wanted to be sure to cover all exigencies: Should good writing count, for example? Would documents relating to baseball history be considered? Could a multi-volume work receive the Award? Must the Award be given every year? Who could nominate an author for the Award? Must the nominee be a member of SABR? Who would judge the books? SABR's rules covered it all:

> The Seymour Medal honors the author(s) of the best book of previous history or biography completed during the preceding calendar year.

Showing the obverse side of the Dr. Harold and Dorothy Seymour Medal, just after the Kansas City ceremony at the SABR Convention in which I was awarded the first medal. From a story in *The Province*, Vancouver, B.C., Canada, June 18, 1996. (Photograph by Peter Blashill, courtesy of Kate Bird, librarian of *The Province*.)

Eligible works must be the product of original research or analysis and must significantly advance our knowledge of baseball. They must be characterized by understanding, factual accuracy, profound insight and distinguished writing.

A collection of primary documents may be considered for the medal if the editorial contribution to the work includes substantial research, a substantial introduction, and substantial notes accompanying the text. Single volumes of multi-volume works are eligible. Multi-volume works as a whole are also eligible if at least one of the volumes was published during the preceding calendar year and if the author has not received a medal for any of the works separately.

No more than one Seymour Medal shall be given each year. If, in the judgment of the awards committee, a worthy candidate cannot be found, the medal shall not be awarded. There is no limit to the number of times an individual may win the award, but it must be awarded each time for a wholly new work.

Nominations on behalf of others or self-nominations are equally acceptable. Nominees need not be members of SABR to be eligible for the award.

The nominating petition is intended for the confidential use and information of the awards committee only.

In addition to submitting a nominating petition, each nominator must see to it that copies of the nominated book be sent to the committee. A list of judges will be provided upon nomination.

Nominations for the next award must be received at the address shown below no later than midnight of January 31. Please complete a nominating petition and return it to: The Seymour Medal, PO Box 93183, Cleveland, OH 44101

My recognition by SABR as an equal partner in the Seymour legacy was one of the most satisfying events in my life. At last researchers and writers in the field to which I had devoted so much of my adult life recognized my contribution to this work.

But I was already deep into other intriguing projects that for a time distracted me from baseball history.

13

Who's on First?

My editorial work for publishers, as well as for some individual writers like Lowell Kammer, Alvan Levenson, and Meredith Young-Sowers, was only part of my work outside baseball. I worked in the Stillpoint office and also at home for that publishing company, evaluating stacks of manuscripts, editing those selected for publication, and working closely with Stillpoint authors to develop their books. I edited the books of Caroline Myss, who twice made the *New York Times* best-seller list after a double appearance on *The Oprah Winfrey Show*. I also published features in the local newspapers, particularly one on a theme that would become more significant to me later: vegetarianism. I wrote as well about writing and editing, for journals like *ComputorEdge, Broomstick, Writers' Journal, Editors' Forum,* and *Canadian Author & Bookman*. But my new and absorbing interest became my historical novel about the Austrian Nazis of the 1930s. I wanted to make another trip to Austria, this one on my own.

I had already traveled alone to Europe. A short trip to Ireland in the fall of 1987 for a medical procedure had come about because I'd had two operations in Ireland and trusted the medical system there. During my first Christmas alone (1992) I flew to New York for a week's vacation. Later that winter I spent a week in the Caribbean. Now I planned a more ambitious foray: a research trip to Austria. I had made some Austrian connections that I believed would assist me in my research.

John Weitz, born in Germany and a one-time spy for the OSS (Office of Strategic Services, predecessor of the CIA, Central Intelligence Agency) had, before becoming a New York fashion designer, written a valuable biography of Joachim von Ribbentrop. Through him I obtained

13—Who's on First?

Interviewing the Countess Harriett Walderdorff at her hotel, Der Goldene Hirsch, in Salzburg, Austria, October 1995. The Countess gave me introductions to several other members of the Austrian aristocracy so that I could obtain information as part of the research for my historical novels. (Photograph by Roy E. Mills.)

introductions to the Countess Harriett Walderdorff, owner of Der Goldene Hirsch, a small and elegant hotel in the oldest part of Salzburg, where I had stayed once before, and to the Princess Marianne zu Sayn-Wittgenstein-Sayn, as well as her brother the Baron Mayr von Melnhof. Through them in turn I would eventually make contact with the Countess Eleanore Dr. Thun-Hohenstein, with Kurt von Schuschnigg (son of the 1930s Austrian chancellor), with the Archduke Heinrich von Habsburg-Lothringen (great-nephew of the Archduke Ferdinand whose assassination in 1914 sparked the events that led to World War I), and with Prince Heinrich von Starhemberg, son of the man who became a main character in the Austrian section of the book, Prince Ernst Rüdiger von Starhemberg, vice-chancellor of Austria in the thirties.

For this trip I treated myself to luxury, traveling via the *Queen Elizabeth II* (no fleas or roaches), and hiring a car and driver to get me to the residences of people outside Salzburg, to the historic little castle known as Schloss Fuschl, and to the beautiful town of Hallstatt, which was the important archival site of the ancient Kelts in Austria. These venues, and others I had experienced on earlier European trips, would become integral to the book and the sequel that followed. During my trip to Austria I didn't think about baseball history. Yet it was my training and experience with Harold Seymour in historical research, gained through my absorption in baseball history, that enabled me to pursue this work successfully.

A more momentous trip for my future took place during the Christmas holiday period of 1993, when I enjoyed a cruise through the Caribbean on a ship that was formerly *The France,* a vessel on which I had once traveled from Europe to the States. The ship had been purchased by the Norwegian Line, which bestowed on it the new name *The Norway.* On this cruise I met a Canadian, Roy Mills, a retired officer of the Royal Canadian Air Force, whom I would eventually marry. Roy's solicitous support of my interests, both in baseball history and in my other research and writing, have made for a different kind of personal relationship than the one I had experienced with Harold Seymour.

Before the Seymour Medal reached the stage when it could be awarded, Tom Heitz, director of the library of the Cooperstown Hall of Fame, arranged another honor. I had queried Tom about the possibility of having Seymour's ashes delivered to Cooperstown and used as the focus for some kind of ceremony at the Hall of Fame. Tom carried through on this, planning an event that would take place during the 1995 sessions of the annual Cooperstown Symposium on American Culture, an occasion for which I had once delivered the keynote address.

Tom decided to request permission from the village fathers to distribute Seymour's ashes on first base at Cooperstown's Doubleday Field, where General Abner Doubleday probably never played but where two major-league teams annually present an exhibition game during Induction Day ceremonies. Doubleday Field is a small-town park with wooden benches and no lights. With Dr. Alvin Hall, the Symposium's director, Tom designed a twilight ceremony for June of 1995 that scholars attending the Symposium could attend. He asked me to furnish him with background material on which he could base his eulogy, along with selections from Seymour's writings that could be read aloud during the ceremony by Symposium participants whom Dr. Hall would select.

Tom clearly recognized Seymour's importance in the field of baseball history, calling the Seymour books "scholarly landmarks" and pointing out that those attending the Symposium were "the academic children, so to speak, of Dr. Seymour's breakthrough work, which did much to legitimize baseball as a subject of scholarship."

So it was that a group of scholars gathered in one section of the stands on a soft June evening to pay tribute to the first scholar of baseball in an occasion that often moved into the humorous. Tom opened by presenting the eulogy. Then Dr. Hall read one of the more amusing selections from Seymour's article, "Big-League Batboy," about what it was like dealing with Manager Wilbert Robinson of the Brooklyn Dodgers and his "colorful incompetents,"

Tom Heitz, librarian of the Baseball Hall of Fame, delivers the eulogy for Harold Seymour at Doubleday Field, Cooperstown, New York, on June 8, 1995, a memorial occasion for Harold Seymour. (Photograph by Roy E. Mills.)

and about the consequent increase in the batboy's knowledge — of profanity. Dr. Richard Gaughran, professor of English at James Madison University, read a few paragraphs from *Baseball: The Early Years* revealing the major league owners' unsuccessful attempt in the 1880s to agree on limiting player salaries — a topic highly applicable to events then occurring in major-league baseball.

Richard's rendition was followed by a selection from *Baseball: The Golden Age* read by Dr. Thomas Altherr, professor of American Studies at Metropolitan State College. It brought a smile to the faces of many when it revealed that players of an earlier era who contracted what were known as "the social diseases" generally had their illnesses reported in the press as "malaria."

This reading was followed by a selection from *Baseball: The People's Game* presented by Dr. Linda Mapes of Broome Community College. It told the story given me in Keene, New Hampshire, by the woman who helped dig up cactus in a field so that she and her high-school friends could have "a glorious time" playing baseball. Dr. Hall then presented me with a suitable memento of the occasion: a handmade wooden lap desk bearing a painting of Doubleday Field.

I responded briefly to these tributes, and then many members of the audience trooped onto the field with flashlights to watch Christopher Jennison, a friend, baseball writer, and New York editor, spread Seymour's ashes around first base, the position he played in college. It seemed appropriate that Dr. Hall should then ask us to sing not some dirge-like hymn but "Take Me Out to the Ball Game." Hall closed the proceedings by commenting that he had often listened, at the library of the Hall of Fame, to the famous Abbot and Costello humor routine called "Who's on First?" Now, said Dr. Hall, he *knew* who was on first! We left the park smiling.

Three of Seymour's former students attended this ceremony, one traveling all the way from Texas. Another person in attendance that evening was Dr. George Grella, professor of English at the University of Rochester. He had never met Seymour personally, but the ceremony touched him so much that he often talked about the occasion to friends, who urged him to write about the experience. The resulting piece, "Harold Seymour, 1910–1992," a lyrical interpretation of the event, was published in *The National Pastime*, a SABR journal.

In this piece Grella told of the gathering of scholars in a quiet, almost holy place that was "just the right backdrop for the contemplation of eternity" during an occasion "intended as a solemn final tribute to an important pioneer who blazed the way for innumerable followers" and whose work displayed "a thorough grounding in basic research, a meticulous regard for fact, and a refreshingly disinterested point of view." Grella added that "Doubleday Field is obviously the real field of dreams ... the universal home town of the American imagination. It's the only proper place for a passionate fan and distinguished scholar of the game to repose." Those of us who were there that evening will, whenever we think of Doubleday Field, always think of Seymour on first base.

My connection with baseball did not sever even then, as I assumed it would. Again I was honored by the world of baseball when in 1996

SABR presented me with the first Seymour Medal in Kansas City, Missouri, during the organization's 1996 national convention. Bob Feller, the Hall of Fame pitcher who is closely associated with Cleveland baseball history, kindly attended the ceremony. I treasure my award and keep it on display in my office. It leaves there only when I bring it along to show during speeches I make before baseball audiences.

At Kansas City, SABR also presented its first Seymour Medal ever given to the author of the best book of baseball history or biography published in the previous year: to David Zang, an instructor in the new field of sports studies at Towson University, who wrote the exemplary biography, *Fleet Walker's Divided Heart,* for publication by the University of Nebraska Press. Because David was unable to attend, a representative of his publisher accepted for him. It was a proud occasion for me to have my name on the award given to such talented researchers and writers as David Zang. I admired his book and was pleased that the SABR committee selected it for the initial award to a writer in the Seymour tradition of good baseball history.

At that time I had married Roy Mills and was living in Canada. A Canadian newspaper, the *Vancouver Province*, published a story about my work on the Seymour books and my SABR Medal, headlining the

Chris Jennison, editor and baseball author, spreads the ashes of Harold Seymour on first base of Doubleday Field during the memorial ceremony held at Cooperstown on June 8, 1995. (Photograph by Roy E. Mills.)

piece "Diamonds Are Forever" and calling me "no run of the Mills historian." In the story I'm quoted as admitting that I'm not a baseball fan or a games person: "if anyone ever threw a ball at me, I'd probably drop it." To most reporters this situation is a great anomaly, since in the pre–Seymour era only people who loved baseball as a sport or an entertainment had ever written about it. Until that time, nobody had ever viewed it disinterestedly, the way a historian must.

Besides David Zang, the first finalists for the Seymour Medal also produced distinguished books, three of them biographies: Charles Alexander on Rogers Hornsby (that dimpled ball player), David Falkner on Jackie Robinson (who didn't realize he wasn't the first black in the majors), and Henry W. Thomas on Walter Johnson. The other outstanding books named by the committee as finalists were William Humber's story of Canadian baseball and David Nemec's book on the American Association.

Subsequent scholars recognized by the SABR committee produced biographies of other figures worth studying like Judge Kenesaw Mountain Landis, the early labor leader John Montgomery Ward, famous players like Billy Sunday and Denton "Cy" Young, and eccentrics who made their mark in baseball, like Charles "Victory" Faust.

Bob Feller, superb Cleveland Indians pitcher, with me at SABR's 1996 Kansas City Convention, where I was awarded the initial Dr. Harold and Dorothy Seymour Medal. Having grown up in Cleveland, of course I watched Bob pitch at Cleveland Stadium. (Photograph by Roy E. Mills.)

All these books exemplified the road that the writing of baseball history had moved since the advent of the Seymour books: the production of valuable monographs and biographies exploring subjects that we had opened up by means of the Seymour series. Seymour had envisioned this result and mentioned it in a preface. I often recall that Lee Allen believed, as he commented in his *New York Times* review of *Baseball: The Early Years*, that when the "definitive history" of baseball was finally written (perhaps implying that it would be written by one person), the result would come in the form of a huge, multi-volume project. This was of course a naive view of the way historical writing is produced.

There is no "definitive" baseball history. What came instead is what happens with any historical field: many volumes, yes, but all written by different historians attempting to fill in different blanks left by previous works and also to reinterpret or correct the coverage of earlier authors. As well, they contributed the expected chronological extension of those topics.

As a result, today we have excellent books on such topics as the development of baseball literature, studies of the race, class, and gender of American players, studies of the relationship of religion to baseball, economic analyses of club and league business, histories of black baseball in cities, solid club histories, studies of the relationship of ball parks to their cities, and even the history of prisoner-of-war baseball during World War II. This rich lode of informative books represents the natural and logical progression of baseball as a part of historiography. The progression occurred because many historians were finding the courage to enter the field of baseball history, although even today, more than forty years after Oxford University Press published the

With the three Seymour books and the Seymour Medal, just after the SABR Convention in Kansas City, June 1996, where I was honored to receive the first medal ever awarded. (Photograph by Peter Blashill in *The Province*, Vancouver, B.C., Canada, June 18, 1996. Courtesy of Kate Bird, librarian, *The Province*.)

Professor David Zang of Towson University, who in 1996 became the first author to earn a Seymour Medal. His book is *Fleet Walker's Divided Heart* (University of Nebraska Press, 1995). (Photograph by Kanji Takeno, Towson University; courtesy of David Zang.)

first scholarly book on the history of the American national game, mention of baseball as a subject of historical study still raises eyebrows.

Researchers other than formally-trained historians are contributing to our knowledge of baseball history. As in the tradition of English "amateurs" who make themselves into specialists, some Americans without degrees in history have become experts in certain baseball topics, and some SABR chapters even publish their own newsletters or participate in internet chat lines informing others of their discoveries and presenting their ideas for future research. Members of SABR who love baseball research have shown great resourcefulness in tracking down, for example, the origins of baseball before the Knickerbockers and some details relating to the Black Sox Scandal. A librarian discovered an 1823 newspaper reference to a baseball game in Manhattan. A history professor found hints that baseball may have been played during the War of 1812. A systems engineer found a reference to something called *das eng-lische Base-ball* (English baseball) in a 1796 book written by the Saxon physical education pioneer Johann Guts Muths. And non-historians as well as historians, diligent in their pursuit of baseball topics, have even won the Seymour Medal.

SABR awarded the second Seymour Medal to Arthur Hittner, an attorney, in 1997 for a solid biography of Honus Wagner, the third in 1998 to Patrick Harrigan, a college professor of history, for a club history of the Detroit Tigers, and the fourth in 1999 to Bruce Markusen, a Cooperstown researcher, for his book on Finley's Oakland team. Dr. William Marshall, who won the Medal in 2000 for *Baseball's Pivotal Era: 1945–1951,* is a librarian and archivist.

By that time SABR had decided to hold its Seymour Award presentations separately from the annual conventions, hosting them each spring as weekend gatherings in Cleveland. I took advantage of these occasions to return to my home town, to perform research in the Cleveland Public Library, to congratulate the Award winners, and to enjoy the presentations of scholarly papers at what was now termed the annual Seymour Medal Conference.

With me is Dr. William Marshall, author of *Baseball's Pivotal Era: 1945–1951* (University Press of Kentucky, 1999), just after the award ceremony of the Seymour Medal Conference in Cleveland in May of 2000, in which Dr. Marshall received the medal for his book. He is director of Special Collections and Archives for the University of Kentucky Libraries. (Photograph by Barry K. Evans of Chicago.)

Women scholars, like men, were studying baseball history. Jean Ardell, a writing instructor at the University of Southern California deeply interested in baseball, was at work on a book about women and baseball as early as 1994, when she wrote me for information about my contribution to the Seymour volumes. She contacted me because she had noticed references to me in the prefaces to the books and asked pointed questions about my research and writing. We talked several times about this, and she decided to devote space to me in her book.

Sports history remained in my mind. During my 1994–1998 residence in Canada with Roy Mills I became interested in curling, a sport entirely new to me and very different in flavor from American baseball, especially from the American professional game. When the editors of the new *International Encyclopedia of Women and Sports* searched for contributors to their project, I volunteered to write a piece for them on the history of women's curling, since the article on women's baseball had already been spoken for by Gai Ingham Berlage, who had written a good book on the subject. While conducting the research I noticed that although adult curling developed differently, its inception as a game for gentlemen is remarkably similar to that of American baseball. In working on the article I found that I could use my new husband, Roy Mills, an accomplished curler, as one of my sources of information. Macmillan published its valuable three-volume reference work on women's sport in 2001. From a curling club in Calgary I obtained a delightful photograph of a 1920 team of women with their curling equipment; dressed in street clothes, tams, scarves, and coats — some with furs — they are smiling and mugging for the camera, obviously pleased with their participation. The editors of the *Encyclopedia* used this photo as part of their advertising for the series.

At the same time, through a remark made on the internet by a Danish research director, Dr. Jørn Møller, I heard of another sports matter: a fascinating tale about the European Union preventing Danish children from playing hopscotch. How could the Union keep children from playing this game, I wondered, and why would it? Inquiring about the matter from Jørn, I learned the story: for safety reasons, the Union banned children's play with anything made of glass, although Danish children had for generations engaged in hopscotch with heavy, round, virtually-unbreakable glass objects thrown into the squares of the pattern they jumped into and out of. These objects were engraved with beautiful designs, especially those derived from the Hans Christian Andersen fairy tales, and the children were much attached to their hopscotch stones, which had suddenly become illegal. Jørn Møller and a colleague began a national campaign to reinstate them. While I was performing my research into the events, the children and their backers won, thus beating the entire European Union. What a story!

On top of this, in researching the game of hopscotch I discovered its ancient origins and its connection with prehistoric labyrinths, thus deepening my understanding of a topic I was developing for my historical novel, *The Sceptre*, which hinged in part on this symbol. Its sequel, *The Labyrinth*, would depend upon it even more. Moreover, I had discovered, in the stacks of the library of the University of Victoria, British Columbia, old books hinting that not only hopscotch but also the game of baseball had descended from the practice of early fertility rites performed within this prehistoric pattern, the labyrinth. The origin of baseball may thus be much more ancient and more basic to human experience than were the Mayan ball-tossing games it has been linked with. Doesn't this bear thinking about? The possible connection of baseball with early fertility rites is certainly the stuff of which historical novels are made, and I took advantage of this intriguing suggestion when I wrote *The Labyrinth*.

In trying to get the resulting hopscotch article published, I collected at least a dozen rejections from magazine editors, one of them a handwritten note on *New Yorker* stationery from the respected baseball writer Roger Angell, praising it as an "offbeat piece" with a "fresh subject," but I was used to rejections that included praise; many writers are. Roger is, of course, one of the many who knew nothing of my baseball connection.

The Tampa Review: Literary Journal of the University of Tampa accepted the hopscotch article with the stipulation that I cut out a large chunk. I did so, and the *Review* then published the remainder in 1999 as "Hopscotch Wars." I took the rejected section of my manuscript (it contained some of the juiciest material) and wrote it up as "Banned in Denmark" for *Commonweal*, which also published a new piece revisiting the black English controversy that had, back in the seventies, given the magazine a classic article (the topic had flared up again in the American press). For the *St. James Encyclopedia of Popular Culture*, published in 1999, I wrote the entry about the history of hopscotch, briefly explaining its ancient origins.

The Sceptre (Patrician Publications, 1998), my historical novel of the 1930s Austrian Nazis, which librarians and other readers (including writers) have described as "riveting." (Cover reproduction courtesy of Xlibris Corporation, Philadelphia, Pennsylvania. The artist is Joy Smith of Sidney, B.C., Canada.)

More important for my future work in baseball was the renewal of my contact with Ethan Casey. I had first corresponded with Ethan back in the eighties, when he asked Harold Seymour to write a foreword for his book with Michael Betzold about the city of Detroit and its ball park. Now Ethan learned that I had written that foreword myself. In contributing to *Blue Ear*, Ethan's online literary magazine, I developed a working relationship with Ethan. I sent him a piece on European museums that I had written for him following a research trip I'd taken with Roy Mills, during which I visited a dozen museums in six countries, along with two national libraries and countless bookstores, coming home with a stack of books two feet high, two notebooks full of notes, and a bagful of clippings, folders, and miscellaneous items. Ethan liked the article resulting from this research tour, and his editor serialized it, giving it the quirky title, "From E for Excrement to V for Vagina: Museum-Hopping through Europe." Research I conducted at those museums and libraries contributed signally to my preparation of *The Labyrinth*.

Ethan was one of those urging me to write a baseball book. I demurred, feeling reluctant to return to that subject and being much occupied with *The Sceptre, The Labyrinth,* and other smaller projects, especially a group of articles I wrote

Ethan Casey, author and editor, who suggested that I write an article for his literary magazine, *BlueEar.com*, about my participation with Harold Seymour in the writing of the first scholarly history of baseball. The article revealed to fans and other baseball historians my extensive work on the Seymour books for Oxford University Press. (Photograph courtesy of Ethan Casey.)

about self-publishing for an online magazine called *BookArts*. Writing and speaking about new options available in self-publishing, an important development for mid-list authors like me who had wearied of seeking commercial publishers in a newly-tightened market, had become part of my activity.

Research for *The Sceptre* and *The Labyrinth* proved more wide-ranging than I expected. I found that, to understand what I had discovered about the Keltic base of the Austrian population, I needed to study the Keltic background of Europe during prehistory. This study opened for me a subject that felt highly personal: the evidence, discussed by Riane Eisler in *The Chalice and the Blade* and by others, that in ancient times women held an equal position in society, and that men only later challenged this arrangement. At some point in early history, then, men decided to subordinate the interests of women to their own. For *The Sceptre*, and later for its sequel, *The Labyrinth*, I imagined how and why the transformation of social structure from equality of the genders to the domination of one by the other could have happened, and I described the possible events of this change in ways that thrilled readers. My understanding of my own position in society, as well as the position of women in general, thus expanded as the result of my research into prehistory.

The Labyrinth (Patrician Publications, 2003), sequel to my historical novel *The Sceptre*. Readers call the story "thrilling." (Cover art is by Jary Sell of Naples, Florida. Reproduction courtesy of Xlibris Corporation, Philadelphia, Pennsylvania.)

Research remained central to my writing. Readers of *The Sceptre* and *The Labyrinth* marveled at the amount of research these books displayed — in the same way readers of *Baseball: The People's Game*, and to

Top: When performing research abroad, I gravitate not only toward museums but also toward bookstores, like this one in Zürich, Switzerland, shown in a snapshot taken in October of 1995. There I purchased books on Austrian history for background on my historical novels, *The Sceptre* and *The Labyrinth*. *Bottom:* My office in Naples, Florida, where the collection of research materials on baseball and other fields is increasing. I am holding one of my historical novels, *The Sceptre*, just after its publication in 1999. (Photographs by Roy E. Mills.)

some extent the earlier two baseball volumes, marveled at the amount of research on which they were obviously based.

It's research that builds the rich texture of a book, whether history or historical fiction. A book's construction must of course rest upon a unique idea or theme conceived by the author, but the research that supports that idea is what creates a story that a reader will find worth pursuing. A book, once its idea is conceptualized, can be defined basically as the felicitous rearrangement of supporting material collected from a myriad of other published and unpublished thinkers, all reinterpreted through the lens of a writer with an idea that represents a fresh point of view. The trick of being a good writer of either history or historical fiction is to find the right material that supports the book's unique theme and to organize it in an entirely new way. The main problem with carrying out this plan is that the unique theme of a book doesn't always reveal itself immediately; it becomes clear only after a great deal of the research is already completed.

Readers often ask me which I prefer to write, history or historical fiction. The latter, of course. History and historical fiction both "bring the past to life," as Louis Menand puts it in describing Edmund Wilson's 1940 book about Lenin, *To the Finland Station*; but writing historical fiction offers more play for creativity, and the author of fiction is afforded much more leeway about what to include. For history, an author must consider everything that might apply to the theme and then pursue methods designed to uncover it: methods like topical research, peripheral research, background research, biographical research, and of course grouping, organizing, and analyzing the results. For historical fiction, the author can pick and choose those discovered facts that might relate to the life of a character that the author creates and sets in motion. Both kinds of writing are fun.

More than that, I like to write in other forms: essays, recipes, news stories, releases, humorous articles, poetry (only some of mine has been published), scholarly writing, travel pieces, letters, children's stories, editorial reports for publishers and for the writers I mentor — whatever seems required in order to express the idea or the purpose I have in mind.

One purpose I had long stored in the back of my mind was making clear to the world of baseball how I contributed to the Seymour books. After all, just asserting that I am myself a baseball historian is merely "talking a good game"; supporting my declaration seemed necessary. An appropriate vehicle for that purpose arrived when Ethan Casey requested an article about the subject for his web-based magazine, *Blue Ear*. Ethan edited the resulting piece, "A Woman's Work," and in 2000 he and Royce Webb co-published it, Ethan in his magazine, and Royce in his, *SportsJones*.

Reactions to the publication of "A Woman's Work" ranged from "astonishing," "compelling," "terrific," "fascinating," "important," "a brave thing to do, and the right thing," all the way to "disturbing." I suppose that to some fans it seemed iconoclastic and irreverent: the "prodigious researcher" Harold Seymour had a sort of secret clone after all. Some remarked on the restraint and dignity, or the lack of bitterness, with which I commented upon my role in the production of the books; others contributed additional examples of uncredited wives performing their husbands' literary work. Most applauded the revelation of my role in preparing the Seymour books, and several commented that the article should profoundly affect young women by encouraging them to pursue their own private dreams. I hope it will. "A Woman's Work" has been reprinted at least six times in various journals, and I would like it to continue attracting readers.

By this time SABR members had begun to grasp the depth of my contribution to the field of baseball history. SABR asked me to speak at its upcoming national convention, its thirtieth. Because the event was held just across the Florida peninsula from our new home in Florida, Roy and I drove there so that I could present a description of the Seymour Collection at Cornell University and explain how researchers could utilize it themselves. In making this presentation I perforce mentioned my own role in the preparation of the Seymour books, and SABR furnished copies of "A Woman's Work" in pamphlet form for use as handouts. Positive reactions again prevailed, and more people suggested I write a book about baseball. My response to the suggestion continued to be negative.

14

Throw Like a Girl

Nothing has given me more gratification than the results of my work on women's baseball history. Five solid chapters in *Baseball: The People's Game* devoted to the early history of women in baseball resulted from this engrossing research. Beginning with the first glimmerings of American interest in exercise for women, these chapters carry the story of women in baseball through their early gym days in baggy bloomers through their attempts to play ball in dresses and up to their success in hooking up with men's teams in the twenties.

The title of the first of these chapters, "Who Ever Heard of a Girls' Baseball Club?" comes from an 1886 book published in an era when women were expected to be "ladies," with all the restrained behavior that the word implies. Women tired of societal restrictions, however, and some even wanted to play baseball. The women's game almost reached its fullest expression in colleges — until women educators sabotaged it. So individual women who liked to play found the ball passed to them, and more of them became proficient players than most Americans realize, playing with professional men's teams if they could get accepted there.

Realizing that the five chapters on women's baseball in *Baseball: The People's Game* resulted primarily from my work on the subject, the Women's Committee of the Society for American Baseball Research, headed by Dr. Leslie Heaphy of Kent State University, listed me among the twenty-five most important women in baseball. I felt honored to see my name appear among names like Effa Manley and Helene Britten, who ran baseball clubs; Alta Weiss, a proficient player who pitched for men's teams in the 1900s; Amanda Clement, a respected umpire of the same period; Margaret Gisolo, who as a girl showed that she could play as well as boys; Jackie Mitchell, the first woman to sign a professional contract; and Babe Didrickson Zaharias, probably the top sportswoman of all.

Then the Women's Committee joined with Justine Siegal (then Justine Warren), head of the Women's Baseball League, in announcing that I was the first woman to be inducted into the Women's Hall of Fame that the League was establishing. Justine herself had been the first woman to play in Cleveland's "Men's" League. She invited me to become the keynote speaker at the first Women's Baseball League Conference in Cleveland in February of 2001.

During the course of this Conference I delighted in meeting a group of women ball players of today, along with their umpires and coaches as well as backers, people like Tom Giffen, Patrick McCauley, and Jim Glennie. Meeting Audrey Daniels, a player in the famous All American Girls' Professional Baseball League of the forties and early fifties, was a thrill. The AAFPBL presented an unusual opportunity for young women at the time, but fulfilling its promise also meant unusual young women had to respond to it and convince their parents to allow them to join it. Audrey Daniels was one of them.

My keynote presentation at the banquet ranged over the early history of women in baseball, their difficulties and successes, then centered upon my own experience in baseball history. I told the audience that I finally decided I must leave teaching and make the radical shift into the field of publishing, so that I could work with words in ways that would develop myself and my own large writing projects instead of limiting myself to my husband's work on baseball history. "Success came to me in my desired line of work," I pointed out, "because I finally developed the confidence I needed to plunge into the work I wanted to do." Explaining why I wrote my first historical novel, *The Sceptre*, I revealed that I based its heroine on my mother, who lacked the confidence in her own skills that could have made her a star in her field, so in *The Sceptre* I developed them for her. "Confidence," I pointed out, "comes from knowing you have developed the skills required to perform the job. When you have the skills, you can find the determination to succeed in your desired field, whether others think that's an appropriate field for you or not." I finished by telling the audience of my favorite inspirational slogan: *Behind every successful woman is ... herself.* "So if you plan to be successful, get behind yourself, and push."

The importance of this slogan came late to the surface of my consciousness, but by that time I finally realized that I am the child (intellectually) of Elizabeth Cady Stanton in believing, like her, in "the necessity for self-dependence." And if Stanton is my intellectual mother, Ralph Waldo Emerson fills the place of my intellectual father, for I never forgot my college reading of his famous essay, "Self-Reliance." At the heart of Emerson's theme in this essay lies his pithy phrase "Trust thyself." It's what we must all do.

At the end of my speech Justine presented me with a beautiful red-painted and inscribed baseball bat as well as a baseball signed by the champion Toronto Blue Jays. I cherish the photo taken of the two of us with these thoughtful awards. It delighted me to be able to encourage these talented young people in pursing their untraditional role in life.

In the fall of 2002 Tom Giffen of Roy Hobbs Baseball invited me to participate in the ceremonies to honor the winning teams in the national women's baseball championship. In the week preceding the championship game, 162 teams from all over the continent competed, in various venues in and around Fort Myers, Florida, under the auspices of the Amateur Athletic Union, to reach the finals of the AAU Women's National Championships. That's pretty close to two thousand good players. Does the baseball public even suspect that this many good female players can be found?

> There was a time [remarked Sally Scott Maran in *Smithsonian*] when the term "female athlete" was an oxymoron. Muscles and sweat were not feminine, and few parents encouraged their daughters to compete in "unladylike" activities. But as women won more rights, attitudes began to change.

It's occasions like the championship series I saw in the fall of 2002 that make attitudes change.

The skill demonstrated in the final championship game I witnessed was a revelation to me and to others who hadn't seen top-level women players in action. In fact, watching them almost made me into a baseball fan. The women in this league, from age sixteen and up into their forties, play standard American League rules on a standard-size diamond. In the game I saw, they displayed thorough knowledge of what used to

Justine Siegal (then Justine Warren), president of the Women's Baseball League, awards me an engraved baseball bat and autographed baseball in Cleveland, February 2001, as the first person elected to the Hall of Fame of the Women's Baseball League. I was the keynote speaker at this first conference of the league. (Photograph by Patrick McCauley, courtesy of Justine Siegal.)

be called "inside baseball," and I noticed no evidence of careless play or lack of knowledge of the rules. The pitchers threw hard, fast, and with a smooth motion; catchers returned the ball with the typical "throw from the ear"; fielders thrilled us with double plays worthy of male pro players; hitters batted with skill and ease.

Anyone in the audience who still thought "He throws like a girl" was an insult must have rethought that metaphor after seeing those women at work. Scoffers should know as well that the Tucker Center for Research on Girls and Women in Sport at the University of Minnesota has produced a videotape to encourage women in sport; celebrating the skill of women, it's called "Throw Like a Girl."

After the championship game I saw, the players were hot and sweaty

14—Throw Like a Girl

Awarding silver medals to the members of the Chicago Storm, runners-up of the AAU National Women's Baseball Series, at Lee County Stadium in Fort Myers, Florida, November 10, 2002. Standing behind me, in white baseball cap, is Dolores ("Dolly") Brumfield White, former player with the All American Girls Professional Baseball League, who is now the league's president. (Photograph by Jack Zerby, Naples, Florida.)

but happy. A Florida team, the Ocala Lightning, won the championship, beating the Chicago Storm in a twelve-inning thriller 5–4. At Tom's invitation, I awarded silver medals to the Chicago team while Dolores ("Dolly") Brumfield White, a member of the famous women's league of the forties and fifties, presented gold medals to the champions. Dolly, who entered pro women's baseball at age fourteen, played for the Fort Wayne Daisies. Now she's the director of the AAGPBL, which is searching for sponsors for a Girls' Little League so that girls who want to play ball can do so with and against other girls instead of trying to get onto boys' teams.

Many men believe that girls want to play baseball with and against boys and that women want to play with and against men. Not at all. Women join men's teams only if there's no other way to play on a skilled level. Women players realize, and are quick to point out to those who ask, that their relative size and strength make them different enough from men physically so that playing against each other gives them the right competition. "Can female athletes ever match the records of male athletes?" asks a science reporter in the *New York Times*. That's not what we're all about, women baseball players would retort; we want to compete against each other.

If women of a hundred years ago had found opportunities and encouragement instead of blocked doors and ridicule, they, too, might have started A League of Their Own. A showcase like the championship series I saw in Florida may in time lead to even greater prominence for women in the national game. At least the days are over when young college women played "under sheltering trees" on their "retired grounds" in an effort to keep their parents from hearing about their baseball participation. At the game I attended, the mother of Catcher Katie Bason sat right behind me, cheering her daughter on. But women have not forgotten the days of yore, either: clothing companies have started manufacturing old-time women's uniforms so that women, like men, can engage in "vintage" baseball games.

The Women's Committee of SABR, continuing its goal of highlighting the importance of women's baseball, plans a book on the subject. Dr. Leslie Heaphy, who was herself a Seymour Award finalist in 2003 for a book on the Negro Leagues, asked me to write a chapter about Elizabeth Murphy for the Committee's book on women in baseball. Elizabeth was a serious New England player who participated in skilled semipro games on men's teams of the twenties and thirties. The purpose of the Committee's project is to examine the role of women in the history of American baseball. This historical role is worth examining.

Back in the eighties, when I was preparing the five chapters on early women players for *Baseball: The People's Game*, information on good female players was fragmentary. Today, good books by such scholars as Gai Ingham Berlage and Barbara Gregorich have made clear the true abilities of many female baseball players of the past. Women of the present continue to make strides in baseball. Ila Borders, a pitcher and the first woman ever to earn a baseball scholarship, as well as the first woman to win a men's college game, followed these successes by playing three full seasons of pro baseball in the (unaffiliated) Northern League. But Ila didn't come through these years without experiencing the same scorn as heaped on earlier women players. "I've been spit on, had beer thrown on me, and been sworn at, and while in college I was hit eleven times out of eleven at-bats." What Ila prefers to recall, however, is the ovations she received for successful performances.

Men often assume women's goal as players to be the advancement of feminism. Many serious women players desire to play baseball, yes, but not to make some feminist point. On the contrary; their stated goal is the same as that of serious male players. "I wasn't out to prove women's rights or anything," declared Ila. "I love baseball. Ask a guy if he's doing it to prove men's rights. He'll say he's doing it because he loves the game." Ila loves the game.

What we all want out of life is to engage in the work we love. The work I love is writing — various kinds of writing, not only baseball writing but also something as different from it as cookbook writing. Like many women, I enjoy cooking and creating new recipes. My work in the field of vegetarianism came about because of a personal health problem: after an operation in the mid-seventies, I found myself unable to digest meat. Casting around for something delicious enough to use as a meat substitute, I finally found a soy product that I could develop into meaty-tasting entrees that resembled those I used to enjoy before being cut off from this standard part of most American diets.

Again using research techniques I had developed over the years largely through research into baseball history, I found many recipes that I judged adaptable into entrees that even my guests would enjoy. Moreover, when I served them these meals, guests assumed that the entrees included meat! At some point it occurred to me that the hundred recipes I had created for myself could make a publishable book that would help other people besides me.

As with *The Sceptre*, I wasted a good deal of time querying publishers about their interest in this book. But the field of publishing had changed since the eighties, when I published several nonfiction books. In the nineties, conglomerates were picking up publishing houses and changing their goal from a search for good books to a search for a few blockbusters, or ones they believed could be shaped into blockbusters, thus shutting out most mid-list books like mine. So I self-published for the second time, producing *Meatless Meat: A Book of Recipes for Meat Substitutes* through my own publishing house, Patrician Publications, which I had established in order to bring out *The Sceptre*.

Then another publishing project thrust itself upon me. One day a stranger wrote me about something she had found on *amazon.com*: a dozen requests posted there from readers, all of them women, who were desperate to find and own copies of a little children's book I had written back in 1965. This book, *Ann Likes Red*, had without my realizing it become a classic, and women who grew up with it in the sixties and seventies had for years been searching for rare old copies of the book, paying as much as a hundred dollars for them at used-book shops and web sites.

Meatless Meat: A Book of Recipes for Meat Substitutes (Patrician Publications, 2001), my vegetarian cookbook, with a hundred original recipes based on the use of a dried soy product to stand in for the meat. The book is popular with vegetarians who miss the taste of meat. (Reproduction courtesy of Xlibris Corporation, Philadelphia, Pennsylvania. Cover photograph by Brian Myers of Naples, Florida.)

Astonishingly, these people wanted *Ann Likes Red* not only to share with their own little children but also because they loved it so much that they wanted to hold it in their own hands once more. That's how closely we become attached to our favorite childhood books. It may be significant that Ann, the protagonist of this story, is an independent little girl who knows what she likes, and, when given a choice, selects clothing in her favorite color, so the entire outfit ends up being red: dress, belt, hat, and sandals. The women who grew up with this book admired Ann's independence. "She knows what she wants, and she goes after it," as one of Ann's many fans puts it admiringly.

Ann Likes Red did something else for these women when they were children: it taught them to read. Dozens of women have told me that when they were three (or four or five or six) they learned to read by means of this book. If a story truly appeals to our inner desires, even if it's told with only sixteen words in just twenty-two pages, it has the power to draw us into it and teach us something new.

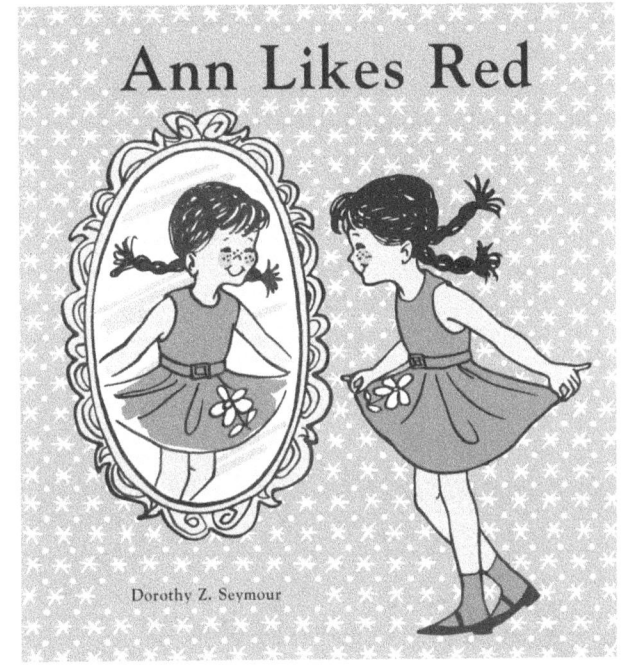

Ann Likes Red, my classic children's book of 1965, the story of an independent child who knows what she likes. The book was republished in 2001 by Purple House Press to satisfy public demand for its return. (Cover reproduction courtesy of Purple House Press, Cynthiana, Kentucky, and publisher Jill Morgan.)

I discovered that a reprint publisher named Jill Morgan was waiting in the wings to sign me to a contract for reprinting the book in order to satisfy the new demand. The only trouble with this development was that I couldn't sign Jill's contract: I didn't own the rights to the book, having sold all ten of my little stories outright for a hundred dollars each, in those long-ago days when I knew nothing about the world of publishing and the way publishers might exploit writers. Grosset, I realized (recalling an interview with the company's editor after publication), had sold these little books internationally by the thousands and made a great deal of money for the company while my interests as author were left by the wayside.

Investigating the status of the rights to those stories, I learned that the copyrights had become available, so I bought back my words by paying the United States Copyright Office for all ten of the books, then signed with Purple House Press to republish *Ann Likes Red*. This move brought me hundreds of letters of appreciation from fans I never knew existed, along with requests for copies of some of the other children's books, particularly *Ballerina Bess*, which I learned boasted almost as many fans as did *Ann Likes Red*. So I republished that book myself, and later I also republished others from the original set of ten.

But the baseball side of my life was not forgotten, and its position among my interests began shifting. A knowledgeable friend and fellow author, Dr. Charmaine Wellington, had already started helping me build a web site to display my various writing interests when I received a message from a talented professional web designer, Ralph Wallace of Chicago, a fan of the Seymour histories who had learned of my work on those volumes. He generously volunteered to design, mount, and maintain a truly professional-looking web site for me at no cost, simply because of his admiration for the Seymour books. So Ralph took over from Charmaine, completing the job.

Ballerina Bess, another popular children's book of mine, published originally in 1965. I republished it through my own company, Patrician Publications, in 2002. Others from this set of ten have also been brought back because of popular demand. (Cover reproduction courtesy of Trafford Publishing, Victoria, B.C., Canada.)

Soon Ralph suggested that we prepare a second web site devoted entirely to the Seymour books. I knew Ralph's suggestion represented a project I should engage in. To collect appropriate material, I traveled to Cornell University at Ithaca, New York, and spent several days researching in the Seymour Collection there, returning with many notes and photocopies that became the sources of articles I wrote for the new site. Together, Ralph and I developed so many ideas for *www.HaroldSeymour.com* that it eventually became an elaborate and almost book-length project. I wrote the material; Ralph made apt suggestions for its further development and found attractive ways to mount it.

Ralph Wallace of Chicago, who suggested, designed, and mounted my two web sites gratis, out of respect for the Seymour histories of baseball. Ralph, besides being a talented web technician, is also president of College Sporting News and publisher of two on-line sports magazines. (Photograph courtesy of Ralph Wallace.)

I saw the site as a way to assist baseball researchers as well as a method of featuring and explaining the uniqueness of the Seymour books. Supplementing descriptions and reviews of these books was information I presented about Seymour's background in baseball. That meant including events of his early life, like his baseball play on the famous Brooklyn Parade Grounds, where so many professional players got their start in competitive baseball. As part of this section, I published reminiscences about the Parade Grounds written for me by men who had played ball there in the twenties and thirties. And I revealed Seymour's success as a "bird dog" in obtaining tryouts for two of his players, Bill Lohrman and Harry Eisenstat, when he wrote directly to Branch Rickey, who built his famous Cardinals farm system because of his awareness that minor-league clubs could serve as feeders for a big-league team. Through Rickey, Lohrman received a tryout with George "Specs" Toporcer, then managing the Rochester Red Wings, and eventually made a solid career in major-league baseball while Seymour developed a long friendship with Toporcer.

I bolstered the assistance I was giving researchers on the new web site not only by listing the books that each year won SABR's Seymour Medal and those that made the finals for the Award, but also by soliciting scholars to write reviews of those books being honored through their selection as worthy of consideration for the Medal. In this way, many well-known baseball historians helped me build the web site. I added a section called "Ongoing Research," where I could post research queries that scholars asked me to include. Ralph thought of other baseball services I could include, like lists of historical baseball museums. And he kept urging me to write a baseball book. Again I demurred.

Following the example of other authors, I began publishing a free monthly e-mail newsletter for fans of my various books, including my baseball fans. The baseball section of these newsletters eventually became so extensive that I finally broke off the baseball material from *The DJM Fan Club Newsletter* (DJM representing my initials) and began publishing a separate one about baseball history, *The HSC Baseball History Newsletter*, where HSC stood for Ralph's abbreviation of the web site, *HaroldSeymour.com*. More than five hundred subscribers receive newsletters each month with the aid of software that Ralph designed. In the baseball history newsletters I comment on baseball events and report on my sports activities and writing. At first I was casting around for material that I wanted to include in the newsletters, but before long baseball people began asking if I would include information that would promote their own baseball interests. It surprised me that, when Jim Bouton self-published another of his controversial books—one that his publisher wanted to censor—he wrote me to ask if I would mention this book in my newsletter.

Oxford had permitted two of the three Seymour baseball history books to go out of print, but with the advent of print-on-demand publishing (a development that had helped so many self-publishers, like me), all three books became available again, in hardcover and paperback.

Oxford also granted Easton Press the right to republish the three Seymour volumes as part of a collector's set called "The Baseball Hall of Fame Leather-Bound Library." In presenting this set, Easton published twenty-seven classic baseball books in a deluxe edition, producing them with gilded page-ends, fine leather covers bearing 22-karat gold designs, silk bookmarks, and illustrated endpapers. Others in the set of twenty-seven books include works by Roger Angell, Mark Harris, and Ring Lardner—good company, indeed! This edition of the three Seymour books is available only through Easton's book club.

I contributed my leather-bound set to the library of Cleveland State University, the former Fenn College, where I met Harold Seymour when he was a professor in the 1940s and where I was his student. This contribution seemed like an appropriate addition to the College library. It commemorates those long-ago days when I was not only relishing my luck in being able to study English at a college level, I was learning to understand what it meant to perform scholarly research with Harold Seymour in the history of baseball.

When after being selected for inclusion in *Who's Who in America* I was also chosen in 2003 for listing in *Who's Who of American Women*, I felt both honors deeply.

15

Extra Innings

In 1998, long after Seymour and I completed our work on early baseball, I read an article in *The New Yorker* about rare publications that the New York Public Library had recently sold by the pound. It detailed the objections of some collectors, who declared that these discarded materials had great value. In the course of the story the author, Mark Singer, mentioned "the now dispersed A.G. Spalding Collection of historical baseball artifacts." Now dispersed!? What a throwaway line! How could this be? Had the marvelous and unique Spalding Collection been trashed, like so many other pieces Singer described? I read further.

Singer's story revealed that the Library of Congress had bought, for six thousand five hundred dollars, a single item from this collection, none other than an 1859 copy of *The Base Ball Player's Pocket Companion*, which is believed to be the first published work devoted exclusively to baseball. This is the delightful little book I used when I sketched early baseball equipment while we were preparing Harold Seymour's dissertation for Cornell University. If the *Pocket Companion* had been sold, where was the rest of all of this valuable material? And why had it been split up?

With the help of a Cornell librarian I refreshed my memory of this unique set of materials by obtaining a complete listing of items in the Spalding Collection. Its twenty-two linear feet of materials, I learned, includes the Henry Chadwick scrapbooks and diaries, the Harry Wright Scrapbooks and correspondence, the A.G. Spalding scrapbooks, and the Knickerbocker Baseball Club materials. After pondering this valuable list I wrote Paul LeClerc, president of the library, and asked what had happened to the great Spalding Collection on which so much of our early work on baseball history had been based. What exactly did "dispersed" mean, and why had the collection been disposed of?

A reply came from William D. Walker, senior vice president, who assured me that "virtually all of the several hundred volumes in the collection" had been either microfilmed or given individual conservation treatment or both, and that after this attention they were retained in the Manuscript and Archives Division. Pamphlets, however, were microfilmed and then sold. So *A Base Ball Player's Pocket Companion* was considered a "pamphlet" and "dispersed."

Regrettably, in my opinion. Nothing can substitute for handling the original of any piece of history. Future researchers in the wonderful New York Public will no longer be able to get the feeling of viewing this piece of original literature as people more than a hundred and fifty years ago could view it. Microfilm is often irritatingly smudged and even renders some research items illegible.

I often think what a misnomer "microfilm reader" is for a machine built to hold the film version of printed matter and make it accessible; it's the person, not the machine, that is the reader — or at least the person attempting to do the reading. The machine displays what are often dim, hazy images of partial pages; clicking on an entire page, for the purpose of browsing, makes the page illegible because the resulting type size is too small to be read. Trying to read microfilmed sources usually turns out to be frustrating; yet it's often the only way to use them, so those of us who do a lot of research resign ourselves to frustration. I realize now that much of my difficulty in using microfilm is due to the poor quality paper of the original sources and blurred printing as well as poorly-maintained machines. Still, using a microfilm reader is far from my favorite method of performing research.

Nowadays, when I enter a library to use some of its microfilm, the librarian supervising the machines approaches me with my ordered film and asks gently, "Do you know how to use this machine?" I smile inwardly, remembering my fifty-plus years of turning handles on microfilm machines. I'm sure I appear to be an unlikely user. How could I pass as a student? (What grey-haired woman would need to write a term paper for History 101?) I'm reminded of J.G. Taylor Spink's surprise at my appearance in the newsroom of *The Sporting News,* and I suppose the librarian is thinking the same thing that the writers in Spink's newsroom were thinking: What in the world is *she* doing here?

Checking microfilm of the *New York Times* during research in the Olin Library of Cornell University in 2001. (Author's collection.)

"Yes," I respond, "but remind me how to operate it, in case this one is different from others I've used." Actually, the operation of all the microfilm readers of today, except for their being a bit more mechanized, hardly differs from the operation of the ones I began using more than fifty years ago. Using the newer ones as opposed to those of long ago is similar to activating a sewing machine by pressing a button instead of by pumping pedals with one's feet, as required on the early Singer models. The newest microfilm machines do offer the added feature of allowing users to make a photocopy of a page, but often that page is so dim as to copy poorly anyway, so that's a feature I seldom use.

Two years after the warning line in Mark Singer's short *New Yorker* piece, Nicholson Baker published a long alarmist article in the same magazine revealing how libraries all over the country are actually destroying *(destroying!)* original newspapers because of the expense of storing and preserving them. Baker argued persuasively that the paper isn't disintegrating as fast as librarians' patience with efforts to find space for those volumes. In the back of my mind lurked a vague fear of experiencing an era like the one during which the great library of Alexandria was destroyed in a raid, and because "a single building ... was crucial to the advancement of an entire civilization," world knowledge suffered greatly after that one building's loss.

I also began to realize what a dinosaur I am: I lived through the era in which viewing originals was common and microfilming was only beginning. Probably, those of us who were privileged to touch pieces of history simply didn't appreciate the opportunity as we should have. When the Baker article appeared in *The New Yorker*, the prominent historian and researcher Arthur Schlesinger, Jr., wrote to the editor,

> Microfilm is the bane of the scholar's existence, and dismally far from a replacement of the real thing. Bound volumes of newspapers convey the feeling, force, and flavor of the past in a way that microfilm can never do. More power to Baker in his crusade to rescue the raw material for our nation's history.

Technology has for a long time failed to serve the preservation of history as it might. The internet of course makes accessible to readers a huge amount of collected and reorganized information, and I'm thrilled with the internet as an aid to researchers and writers, but all of us know that much of what is available on the internet is untrustworthy because it is not fact-based. Opinion has value, but it should be labeled as such.

In the field of baseball research, however, informational offerings on the internet are improving, thanks in part to dedicated researchers, many of them members of SABR. A few newspapers are becoming digitized now, although some charge for their online use (whatever happened to the great tradition of free libraries in this country?). Some magazines and scholarly journals are making their archives available on line, so research into baseball history may become a whole new ball game. One of the new aids to sport historians is a network of sport librarians like David Kelly of the Library of Congress, who are committed to facilitating sport research.

Microfilm, as irritating as it can be, is still the preferred means of preserving not only the meaning that the words convey but also the looks of the conveyance. The best news in this regard is that the National Endowment for the Humanities has started funding efforts to preserve thousands of old newspapers, especially "brittle books and serials," like the ones that disintegrated when I tried to turn the page, scattering little yellowed crumbs of paper over my clothes. But participants in the new program who handle these old newspapers are finding many problems, like evidence of the lack of pest control. Workers have had to be furnished not only with smocks and gloves but also masks, in order to deal with unpleasant discoveries like "BG" (bat guano)! Participants in this program are also investigating electronic methods of preservation. For the sake of posterity as well as current researchers like me, I hope their efforts eventually improve conditions for scholars.

For writers, computer technology will never replace the value of paper-based manipulation of knowledge, however. I agree with Malcolm Gladwell in asserting, as part of his thoughtful article, "The Social Life of Paper," that paper offers advantages over the computer screen in performing certain kinds of cognitive tasks needed for writing history, like scanning, sorting, organizing, and of course analyzing. Although I compose directly on the computer, my desk and table always contain piles of papers related to various projects in different stages of development. And although I often get my most original insights when away from my office (and often in the middle of the night), studying and arranging these papers on my desk is conducive to other aspects of writing, like analysis. When as a child I "played office" by organizing papers bearing interrelated ideas, I was teaching myself to analyze — a task vital to the higher-level thinking required in writing history.

I'm not the only researcher looking back at the early eras of research. Baseball research of the past is being re-evaluated, and properly so. Periodically, historians who are revisionists take a fresh look at past work, reappraise it in the light of what followed, and begin to fit the new research into the old. In this way we receive reinterpretations of the past that can present it more accurately than could those who opened the field for study.

In 2003, Dr. Steven Riess, a respected baseball historian at Northeast Illinois University, published a retrospective article about Seymour's work, calling him "the father of modern baseball history" and explaining his unique contribution. Riess's article provided excellent summaries of all three books and evaluated them in the light of the baseball research and writing that followed them over the years since their publication.

In this article Riess asserted that Seymour "established an extremely high standard for research and analysis," although he omitted to point out that I performed much of that research and analysis. Riess did, however, mention in a footnote that for the third Seymour book, *Baseball: The People's Game,* "much of the research and writing for this volume was actually done by his wife Dorothy Seymour, now Dorothy S. Mills."

I hope that the explication in this book clarifies my contribution to the Seymour volumes by establishing that my work in baseball did not begin with the research and writing of *Baseball: The People's Game,* and that I have been performing baseball research, analysis, and writing since at least 1949, long before Cornell accepted the dissertation on which the first book in the series was based. I consider myself a pioneer in the field, perhaps not quite on the same level as Harold Seymour, since I did not initiate the lifelong project in which I have been engaged, but a pioneer nonetheless, delving into untapped sources and discovering long-forgotten facts on which three good books of history could be based, books I helped to shape and write. Preparing these books helped shape me as a writer, too.

Today I'm as heavily involved in writing and editing baseball history as I ever was. These are extra innings for me, beyond the time I spent on the Seymour books. My work in this field has gradually returned to the level it reached when I was contributing to the Seymour projects, but now it's completely self-generated, and it has to share my time with my other work in various fields. I still work a sixty-hour week, and I still contribute to baseball scholarship, but in different forms — and with the aid of others who contribute their own work to mine.

My sports library shows signs of regrowth, and my office is crowded with journals and other baseball material produced since I contributed the Seymour Collection to Cornell. The bookshelves full of Seymour Award books and others in the field of sport history stand near shelves of references I need for writing historical fiction. My files contain not only baseball materials but information relating to my other work, not just historical fiction, children's literature, and vegetarian cooking but also help for other writers, some of whom I mentor.

Nowadays, just as Harold Seymour was, I'm asked to review baseball books for respected journals like the *International Journal of the His-*

tory of Sport. Journal editors also request that I review baseball poetry and prose. Researchers not only in the United States but abroad query me about baseball materials and research problems. I speak at baseball conferences and advise researchers where to get materials. I'm invited to serve as consultant for baseball projects as well as for radio and television programs on baseball. I have finally reached the level of being considered a person with special knowledge about baseball history. Sometimes when the Seymour books are listed in bibliographies, although I'm not usually cited as the co-author, I may be called "editor." I'm pleased to be mentioned no matter in what way.

Since contributing the Seymour Collection to Cornell I have visited there three times, twice for extensive periods of research. The Collection, which welcomes serious scholars, is suitably housed in a building with careful control of humidity and temperature in order to preserve the materials archived there.

The Harold and Dorothy Seymour Collection is available at Level B of the Carl A. Kroch Library, one of Cornell University's seventeen libraries, as part of the library's Rare and Manuscript Collection. The building is accessed by first walking through the main floor of the Olin Library and taking the elevator at the rear of that building. Olin is a lending library; Kroch does not lend its materials.

The Kroch Library consists of three levels. When you enter the elevator of the library, you discover that it will take you not up but down! The building is constructed entirely underground, because Olin is at the top of a rise, so anything connected with it must be at a lower level. The only evidence of the Kroch Library's existence that can be observed at ground level is the emergence to the surface of four skylights that rise from a landscaped courtyard. These skylights center upon the building's atrium, where mirrors magnify the light from above even on cloudy days. This innovative facility, a fascinating place to do research, opened in August of 1992, only a month before Seymour's passing.

Who was Carl A. Kroch? I wondered, upon learning that the Seymour Collection would be part of a library named after him. Kroch, I discovered, was the son of an Austrian immigrant, a highly-literate and cultured bookstore owner who loved books and, according to information from Cornell, assembled exceptional collections of rare books for his own pleasure. Moreover, says Cornell's description, "Perhaps more than any other individual, Carl Kroch has shaped modern bookselling

15 — Extra Innings

With some of the 71 boxes of archived research material of the Harold and Dorothy Seymour Collection at the Carl A. Kroch Library, Cornell University. This collection resulted from our forty-three years of collaboration on baseball history. I used the collection myself for research in 2001 and again in 2003. (Author's collection.)

in the United States." Kroch, a Cornell graduate, gave the University ten million dollars to help build the library that the University, in gratitude, named after him. The Kroch Library houses Cornell's special collections in the humanities and social sciences. I'm proud to know that the Seymour Papers are archived in the same building as those of author E.B. White (stepfather of the baseball writer Roger Angell) and those of James Joyce (whose wife Nora makes a cameo appearance in one of my historical novels), along with the papers of important founders of the University.

The Kroch Library is open Monday through Friday from nine to five and is serviced by a staff supervised by Dr. Elaine Engst, director of the Rare and Manuscript Division. Restrictions upon using the col-

With Dr. Elaine Engst, curator of the Rare and Manuscript Collections of the Kroch Library at Cornell, where the Seymour Collection is located. Dr. Engst, an archivist, welcomes scholars who want to consult the materials in the collection. (Author's collection.)

lection include those common at rare book and manuscript divisions of libraries everywhere: scholars must write or phone in advance to explain what sort of work they are doing and to reserve a seat in the reading room, no pens are allowed for note-taking, and only one box of material at a time is furnished to researchers.

The Library has printed a "Finder's Guide" to the Seymour Collection, an aid to locating the various types of material filed in the 71 boxes of material. Most of these boxes are much larger than the file boxes in which I kept the notes collected for the books; their size best suits the manuscript-size correspondence that comes from my file drawers. The Finder's Guide is now available online as "Guide to the Harold and Dorothy Seymour Papers, 1830–1998, Collection Number 4809, Division of Rare and Manuscript Collections, Cornell University," at *http://rmc.library.cornell.edu/*. The compiler is Mary Warren, who has also worked on other collections for the University. Besides the manuscript materials in the 71 big file boxes, the Seymour Collection also includes 15 boxes of books and other published materials, none of them yet listed in the Finder's Guide.

I've found that researching at Cornell in the summer is preferable, since the University is perched on the top and sides of a high hill, and its walkways can be slippery in winter. But going through this Collection at the Kroch Library, like examining any original source material, is exciting any time of the year: the raw material of history can be held in the reader's own hands. The Collection contains information available nowhere else. Handling original manuscript material

Top: Examining items in a file of the Seymour Collection at the Kroch Library during summer of 2000. *Bottom:* Using the Kroch Library's Finding Aid for the Harold and Dorothy Seymour Collection. This finding aid is now available online as well as in the library at Cornell. (Author's collection.)

is often its own reward, even if no particular project is contemplated; it enables us to get the feel and the look of the past. Several scholars have already visited and used the collection, and more of them arrive each year.

Interestingly, SABR, too, is thinking of its own papers, and in the year 2000 its leaders wisely arranged with the Western Reserve Historical Society of Cleveland to serve as the repository for its archives. The Historical Society, a prestigious organization, is located at University Circle, suitably near several buildings of Case–Western Reserve University, an alma mater of mine, and within walking distance of the famous Cleveland Art Museum, where as a child I took Saturday morning art lessons, as well as the recently remodeled Severance Hall, where I first heard good symphony music played by a fine orchestra. The Historical Society, too, welcomes researchers.

And SABR itself is changing. Women are engaging in baseball research and joining this group and NASSH, which boasts women scholars among its membership. Dr. Susan Bandy has added to her web site on Women in Sport, *http://raw.rutgers.edu/womenandsports/*, a section that will list the names and interests of women scholars who are working in this field of research. Today SABR even has a woman president.

Harold Seymour's name continues to be recognized. In 2003 the Naples, Florida, chapter of SABR was given the new name "the Harold Seymour Chapter." That same year, the library of the National Baseball Hall of Fame and Museum in Cooperstown, where Seymour and I performed so much research over a period of many years, created a bibliography of all the dissertations published on baseball history, named it after Seymour, and prepared it for mounting on the Hall of Fame web site, *www.baseballhalloffame.org*, where it will be available to fans and scholars.

I cherish the memories of my contribution to baseball history, which developed me in ways I could never have foreseen. It moved my writing into a channel that it might not have traveled without my introduction to scholarly research and analysis. It opened my mind to new ideas and new ways of viewing life. Since I started writing, the field of research has changed for the better: wives still help their husbands with work initiated by the male member of the team, but now husbands also help wives with projects that the women envision.

My own work life is often seen as divided into three separate careers:

for sixteen years I was a full-time teacher; then, from 1967 and into the eighties I was a full-time editor. Finally, beginning with the eighties, I became, and still am, a full-time author. Actually, however, the three careers ran concurrently, like life sentences for serious crimes, because while I taught full time I was also editing constantly and producing considerable writing; while I edited full time I was also lecturing and producing articles; and as a full-time author I continue to edit and lecture. So during my lifetime the balance of my activities shifted, first emphasizing teaching, then editing, and finally writing — the activity I longed to specialize in since my grade-school days. I've finally reached my goal.

I have no desire to become known as the world's top expert in baseball history; I have too many other writing interests in fields outside baseball. But I do take great satisfaction in having helped to open the field and keep it developing as one of the ways to understand America. Lou Brock says baseball is the background music to American life. I think it's closer to the foreground than that: it's the music to which we dance.

Baseball history has been central to my life, which, as Winston Churchill once remarked wryly of his own, is already long and has not been entirely uneventful. I have often threatened to return, after my passing, as a *Spalding Guide*. In fact, I think I'm beginning to resemble one already: loaded with information and opinions about long-forgotten events important to only some people, three-quarters of a century out of date and yet still not completely without value, and perhaps worth more now than the original cost of ten cents.

I smile as I read the following encomium from the 1889 *Spalding Guide*:

> ...if any one can present to us a sport or pastime, a race or a contest, which can in all its essentials of stirring excitement, displays of manly courage, nerve and endurance, and its unwearying scenes of skillful play and alternations of success equal our national game of ball, we should like to see it.

By golly (I'm thinking), that isn't far from the truth. Perhaps I'm becoming a fan after all.

What returns to me often now is that day nearly sixty years ago when as a Cleveland teenager I walked down my street filled with the excite-

With my husband, Roy Mills, at an autographing session in February of 1999 at the B. Dalton store in Naples, Florida, for one of my historical novels, *The Sceptre*. When making presentations of these novels or autographing them, I always wear one of my Austrian costumes. (Author's collection.)

ment of studying English at college while the sounds of a baseball game being reported on the radio insinuated themselves into my consciousness. Nothing could typify my life more.

And the game hasn't been called yet.

Bibliographical Note

In the tradition of the three Seymour volumes, I am ending this book not with a list of sources but with a note describing the sources I used and where I obtained them.

Main Sources

The major source of information for this book was the Harold and Dorothy Seymour Collection at Cornell University, consisting of the materials used to prepare the books that Harold Seymour and I wrote together as well as the dissertation on which his Cornell doctorate is based. I have explained, in the text of this book, where the Collection is located and how it may be accessed.

For my research into the Collection, I examined material that I had myself produced, some of it more than fifty years ago, including notes and outlines I wrote and letters I sent and received. The Collection includes communications like those from well-known persons referred to in this book, like J.G. Taylor Spink and A. Bartlett Giamattti. It also includes letters from not-so-famous people, like those Seymour coached on baseball teams as early as the 1920s. Some of these letters were written when the players were boys, back in the 1930s; some were sent to me after Seymour's death, in the 1990s.

Besides the Seymour Collection at Cornell, I used my own office files, here in Naples, Florida, on baseball, sports, and memorabilia, along with files relating to the books and articles I published under my own names — Dorothy Z. Seymour or Dorothy Jane Mills.

Of course, in preparing this book I referred often to copies of the three Seymour books published by Oxford University Press. They are *Baseball: The Early Years* (1960), *Baseball: The Golden Age* (1971), and *Baseball: The People's Game* (1990). Also invaluable was the Seymour dissertation, "The Rise of Major League Baseball to 1891," written for Cornell University and presented for the degree of Doctor of Philosophy, a degree that was awarded in June of 1956. Copies of the dissertation are available from UMI (University Microfilms) Dissertation Services, which is now using ProQuest Company to produce paperbound versions of the microfilm master copy. The original dissertation, bound in two volumes, is at Cornell. I own a copy of the UMI version, which is bound in one volume 632 pages long.

I also used back issues of my free email newsletters, *The DJM Fan Club Newsletter* and *The HSC Baseball History Newsletter*, published monthly from 2000 to the present through TOTK.com Sports Publications. Printouts are in my files, but back issues can be accessed through the archives at my web sites, *www.DorothyJaneMills.com* and *www.HaroldSeymour.com*.

Helpful in preparing this book was the extensive work I did on my two web sites, especially the latter. The sites themselves are based partly on material in the Seymour Collection, along with information from my personal files and my memory.

Other Collections

This book refers often to research that Seymour and I conducted in various libraries and historical societies, and in most cases I've mentioned where these collections of materials are located. Here are a few more locations: The Pythian Baseball Club Papers, 1867–1870, are in the Gardiner Collection of the Historical Society of Pennsylvania and consist of fifteen folders of manuscript.

The Detroit Public Library holds the Ernie Harwell Collection.

The Chicago Historical Society owns the Alfred J. Scully Baseball Collection.

I have examined these collections as well as all the others mentioned in the Bibliographical Notes of the three Seymour books and the Seymour dissertation.

Book Reviews

I have quoted here from many reviews of the three Seymour books, identifying their sources. I'll mention details of a few:

"The Umpire Strikes Back," by Huw Richards, published in the education supplement of the *London Times* of July 26, 1991, reviews all three of the Seymour volumes. "I Hear America Swinging," by Roberto Gonzáles Echevarria, in the book review section of the *New York Times* April 1, 1990, reviews the third volume, as does "The Virtues of Nakedness," by Stephen Jay Gould, in *The New York Review of Books*, October 11, 1990.

Lee Allen's review of *Baseball: The Early Years* was published in the *New York Times* on April 10, 1960.

The review of the third Seymour volume in the publication called *America* appeared on August 18, 1990.

The mention of this third volume in the *New York Times* list called "And Bear in Mind" appeared on April 8, 1990.

Thomas Lask's review of *Baseball: The Golden Age* was published in the *New York Times* of August 4, 1971.

My own review for the *Journal of Sport History* of the baseball exhibition called "Diamonds Are Forever" was published in the Spring of 1990.

My review of Richard Ben Cramer's *Joe DiMaggio: The Hero's Life* (Simon and Schuster, 2000) is in *The International Journal of the History of Sport* for December 2002.

The first review of *Fear Not to Sow Because of the Birds* cited here is by Staci Milbouer in the Nashua, New Hampshire, *Sunday Telegraph*, February 12, 1989. The second review quoted here is by James A. Rousmaniere Jr., editor of the Keene, New Hampshire, *Sentinel*, published in his own newspaper on December 7, 1988.

Steven Riess's retrospective article about the three Seymour books is in the Spring 2002 issue of *The Journal of Sports History*.

Interviews

The *Boston Globe* interview with Seymour that I mentioned in connection with his dislike of research appeared on November 18, 1990.

The article in the *Newburgh Evening News* accompanying a picture that showed Seymour and me working together is based on the reporter's interview with Seymour. It appeared on July 24, 1964.

The interview with me in the *Vancouver* (B.C., Canada) *Province* headlined "Diamonds Are Forever" appeared on June 18, 1996.

Personal Information

The article about the work-study program for Fenn College students is "Dream Becomes Reality: Work-Study Program Gives Practical Training to 300 Fenn College Students," in the *Cleveland News* of September 10, 1947.

My article, "A Woman's Work," written for *Blue Ear, www.BlueEar.com*, appeared there and at *www.SportsJones.com*, in 2000, and is still available through the archives of those on-line journals as well as through my baseball history web site and in various other journals published in hard copy.

Correspondence of Sheldon Meyer to Harold Seymour is in the Harold and Dorothy Seymour Collection at Cornell; Sheldon's correspondence with me is in my own files, including his letter to me of June 29, 1992, expressing surprise and dismay at the news that I wrote a good part of the third volume and received no credit for it.

Edward J. Rielly's *Baseball: An Encyclopedia of Popular Culture* (ABC-Clio) came out in 2000; his obituary of Harold Seymour appeared on p. 273.

The original letter of J.G. Taylor Spink of *The Sporting News* to "Prof. Harold Seymour" on September 14, 1949, is in the Seymour Collection, and a copy is in my files.

Harold Seymour's story of meeting two professors at a history convention who could hardly believe that Oxford published his book on baseball history was reported by Michael Burke in *Leisure Weekly* (Keene, New Hampshire), May 28, 1987.

My article for a Keene newspaper on vegetarianism is "The Great American Meatout," *New Hampshire Leisure Weekly*, March 1991.

Gary Kowalski's letter to me about my editorial contributions to his books, dated October 14, 1991, is in my files.

Ralph Waldo Emerson's quotation, "I must be myself," is from a John Updike article, "Big Dead White Male," in *The New Yorker*, August 4, 2003.

Information about the special bibliography of dissertations and theses being named for Harold Seymour is in a letter, in my files, from James L. Gates, Jr., Librarian of the National Baseball Hall of Fame and Museum, Inc., dated August 11, 2003.

The original of my memo to Harold Seymour on June 1, 1989, requesting that my name be listed on the title page of *Baseball: The People's Game,* is in my files.

From Magazines and Journals

John Montgomery Ward's *Lippincott's Magazine* article, "Is the Base Ball Player a Chattel?" appeared in August of 1887. He also wrote a shorter piece for that magazine in August of 1886 and another in *Cosmopolitan* in October of 1888.

Louis Menand's comment about history comes from his article "The Historical Romance" in *The New Yorker,* March 24, 2003.

From Miscellaneous Sources

The souvenir postcard from the Bodleian Library illustrating medieval ball-playing remains in my files.

Information on the exploits of famous players at League Park, near Dunham School, comes mainly from a pamphlet called *League Park,* printed in 1978 by Cleveland's Osborn Engineering Company and distributed in 1992 by SABR, as well as from the article, "League Park," in *The Encyclopedia of Cleveland History* at *http://ech.cwsru.edu/.*

A copy of the transcript of Howard K. Smith's program, "What Has Baseball Got That the Others Haven't?" (American Broadcasting-Paramount Theatres, April 11, 1962) is in my files. An original is in the Seymour Collection at Cornell University.

Information about Sheldon Meyer's career comes from a profile of Sheldon at *http://www.princeton.edu/.*

Information on Carl A. Kroch and the library named for him at Cornell University comes mainly from a pamphlet, "The Carl A. Kroch Library; Cornell University," produced by Cornell in 1992, a copy of which is in my files.

Lou Brock's comment about the position of baseball in American life comes from a news story by Alan Schwarz, "In the Spirit of Koufax," in the *New York Times* of September 9, 2001.

George Gmelch's quotation concerning the difficulty of teaching about baseball is from Jeffrey Selingo's article, "Notes from Academe," in *The Chronicle of Higher Education*, July 18, 2003.

I am grateful to Charles Korr for finding the column by Leonard Koppett in *Sporting News,* May 8, 1983, that the sports writer published after attending a conference of sport scholars, a meeting that Korr said, in an email message to the Sport History Listserv, June 27, 2003, was "Koppett's introduction to the academic study of sports."

About Women

I've mentioned several magazine and newspaper articles about women. Sally Scott Maran's *Smithsonian* article, "Women Athletes Put on Their Game Face," was published in June 2001.

Letters from Jean Hastings Ardell are in my personal files. Jean has written extensively about Ila Borders. My information on Ila's accomplishments are from Jean's article, "Ila Borders Retires" in *www.MsWBL.com*, the site for the Women's Baseball League, an organization conducted by Justine Siegal, formerly of Cleveland and now living in Toronto, Ontario, Canada.

The information on Mary Garber of Winston-Salem came mainly from *www.womenssportsfoundation.org*.

The quotation from a science reporter for the *New York Times* is from Gina Kolata, "A Strength Not Yet Tested, Not Yet Known," on June 15, 2003.

Allen Guttmann's statement about the 1936 Olympics is on page 200 of his book, *Women's Sports: A History* (Columbia, 1991).

Babe Didrickson Zaharias is quoted about competitiveness on page 455 of Elaine T. Partnow's compendium, *The Quotable Woman* (Checkmark, 2001).

Maria Pepe, who believes athletic competition for women helps them succeed in their jobs, is quoted in "Alumni Profile: Maria Pepe," *FDU Magazine*, Fall/Winter 1998, a Fairleigh Dickinson University publication at *http://www.fdu.edu/newspubs/magazine/fw98/alumniprofilepepe.html*.

The videotape called "Throw Like a Girl: A Revolution in Women's Sports," was produced by The Tucker Center for Research on Girls & Women in Sport at the University of Minnesota in Minneapolis.

Everard Hall's letter to Harold Seymour of September 4, 1990, mentioning the women's team he saw in 1945, is in the Seymour Collection at Cornell, with a copy in my files.

The article called "Where Woman's Place Is Not" comes from the *New York Times* of May 22, 1957.

Documentation of women reporters' permission to enter the clubhouse with other reporters is covered in Susan Fornoff's audiotape, *Lady in the Locker Room: Uncovering the Oakland Athletics*, produced in 1993 by High Top Sports Productions, Los Angeles, and published by Sagamore Publishing, Champaign, Illinois.

The figure of $400 million being earned by online dating services comes from the *New York Times* of June 29, 2003.

About the Black Sox Scandal

The note recording Seymour's memory of his visit to Joe Jackson in Greenville, South Carolina, is in the Seymour Collection; the circumstances of the visit are as Seymour described them to me.

The book that details the impact of the Black Sox on the American consciousness is Daniel A. Nathan's *Saying It's So: A Cultural History of the Black Sox Scandal* (Urbana: University of Illinois Press, 2003). I reviewed this book for a journal called *Sport in History* (formerly *The Sports Historian*), which, like the publications of NASSH, promotes the serious study of sport in society; it's published in Leicester, England. My review is, at this writing, still in press.

About Black Players

My comment on the number of doctoral dissertations that have been written on black baseball is based on "Bibliography of [Master's] Theses & [Doctoral] Dissertations on Negro League Baseball" at *http://my.execpc.com*, a list that includes more than two dozen titles that demonstrate interest beginning in 1961 and continuing through the nineties.

About Research

For the Love of Libraries, by Diane Asséo Griliches, is a set of library photographs on large postcards published in 1998 by Pomegranate in Rohnert Park, California. The photographs are from her book *Library:*

The Drama Within, published in 1996 by the University of New Mexico Press.

Mark Singer's short *New Yorker* piece on the New York Public Library, "Missed Opportunities Dept.," appeared in "The Talk of the Town" on January 12, 1998. Nicholson Baker's long article, "Deadline: The Author's Desperate Bid to Save America's Past," appeared under the lead-in "A Reporter at Large" in the same magazine on July 24, 2000, and Arthur Schlesinger's comment on Baker's article was published in "The Mail" on August 12, 2000.

The letter in my files from William D. Walker of the New York Public Library to me is dated February 18, 1998.

Nicholson Baker is also the author of a celebrated (and vilified) article not referred to here, one detailing the related subject of libraries that are throwing away their catalog cards; it's called "Discards" and is published under the lead-in "Annals of Scholarship" in *The New Yorker* of April 4, 1994. That article informed me that changes I'd observed in the NYPL catalog system were occurring everywhere. Those interested in the subject may enjoy Baker's related book, *Double Fold: Libraries and the Assault on Paper* (2001), as well as a book by William Blades called *Enemies of Books* (Dover, undated).

The quotation about the destruction of the library at Alexandria comes from an article with that title by J. Harold Ellens in *Odyssey*, July/August, 2003.

Information on the funding by the National Endowment for the Humanities of a United States Newspaper Preservation Program is from two internet summaries of a "Symposium on Access to and Preservation of Global Newspapers" that was held May 27–28, 1997, in Washington, D.C. The two summaries are by Linda Naru and Walter Cybulski. Naru's is at *http://arl.cni.org/collect/symp/* and Cybulski's, which mentions "unpleasant surprises" like bat guano, is called "Toward a Solution of the Newspaper Preservation Conundrum: The United States Newspaper Program and the New York State Newspaper Project" and can be seen at *http://wwwcrl.uchicago.edu/ icon/597/cybulski.htm*.

Index

Numbers in **bold** refer to photographs; HS refers to Harold Seymour

AAU Women's National Championships 201
AAUP [American Association of University Professors] *Bulletin* 58
Abbot and Costello routine, "Who's on First?" 186
Abraham G. Mills Papers 26, 41, 42; *see also* Mills, Abraham G.
Adelman, Mel 77
Al Roon's (club) 78
Albert Spalding (sporting goods company) 39; *see also* Spalding, A.G.
Alcott, William A. 130
Alexander, Charles: biography of Grover Cleveland 119; biography of Rogers Hornsby 188; biography of Ty Cobb 119
Algren, Nelson, on Chicago 108
All-American Women's Professional Baseball League (AAWPBL) 149–151, 200, 203
Allen, Frederick Lewis 108, 129
Allen, Lee **55**, 69, 75, 108, 189
Altherr, Thomas 185
Alumni Achievement Award (Drew University) 80
Alzheimer's disease 172, 174
Amateur Journal 126
amazon.com 206
America (journal) 167, 168
American Association 26, 43, 44, 46, 47, 63
American Association of University Women 82
American Baseball Guild 115
American Biographical Encyclopedia 119
American Chronicle 37
American Council of Learned Societies 80
American Dialect Society 36
American Historical Association (AHA) 32, 55, 76
American Historical Review 72
American League 49, 57, 93, 100, 105, 201
American Legion 127, 164
American Magazine 108
American Mercury 108
Amherst College 128
Andersen, Hans Christian 192
Anderson, Marian 13–14
Angell, Roger 193, 210, 219; *The Summer Game* 84
Ann Likes Red 206–208, **207**
Annals of Iowa 62
Annapolis 129
Anson, Adrian "Cap" 14, 67; *A Ball Player's Career* 31
Anti-Suffragists 96
Anzeiger des Westens 48
Appel, Marty 117
Ardell, Jean 65, 191
"Are We Learning to Think?" *Topper* 17
Army and Navy Journal 126
Asinof, Eliot 78; *Eight Men Out* 100; *see also* Sayles, John
Atheneum (library) 137
Athletic Hall of Fame, Drew University 160
Atkins, Larry 73
Atkins, Marcy 73

Index

Axelson, Gustaf, *"Commy"* 31

B & B (Bohme & Blinkmann) 12
Baker, Nicholson 214–215
Baldwin-Wallace College 27
"Ball, Bat, and Bar," *Cleveland-Marshall Law Review* 57
Ball, Bat, and Bishop 28
Ball Players' Chronicle 36
Ballerina Bess **208**
Baltimore Federal League Club (Baltfeds) 99–100
Baltimore Sun 70, 71
Bandy, Susan 222
Bang, Ed 10
"Banned in Denmark," *Commonweal* 193
Barkham, John 70
Barnes, Donald Grove 21, 72
Barnhart, Clarence 119
The Base Ball Player's Pocket Companion 36, 212–213
The Base Ball Tribune 31
Baseball: The Early Years: organization of 62; **63**; reviews of 69–72; standing in field of history 77–78; theme of 62, 67–68; topics in 62–64
Baseball: An Encyclopedia of Popular Culture 176
Baseball: The Golden Age: organization of 92–106; **93**; reviews of 109–112; theme of 28, 107; topics in 92–106, 107
Baseball: The Modern Era (unpublished) 74
Baseball: The People's Game **123**; organization of 126, 153; reviews of 167–169; theme of 122, 153–155, 169–171; topics in 126–135
Baseball guidebooks (Beadle, De Witt, Reach, Spalding, Spink) 31, 36, 37, 39, 42, 43, 223
Baseball Hall of Fame, Cooperstown, New York 105, 153, 171, 222; *see also* Library of the Baseball Hall of Fame and Museum, Cooperstown
Baseball Magazine 32, 39, 110
Baseball Reliquary's "Shrine of the Eternals" 94
"Baseball's First Professional Manager" 32
Bates, Sanford 133
Beard, Charles and Mary 160
Beecher, Catharine 148
Benedict, Ruth, *The Chrysanthemum and the Sword* 85
Bennett, Lerone 134

Benswanger, William E. 71
Berlage, Gai Ingham 192, 204
Betts, John R. 59, 124
Betzold, Michael *see* Casey, Ethan
"Big-League Batboy," *Sports Heritage Magazine* 140, 185
"Black Children, Black Speech," *Commonweal* 90, 119
Black Sox Scandal 63, 76, 100–103, 190
Blaisdell, Lowell 173
Bligh, Edwin 75
Blinkmann, Harry 12
Bodleian Library 73
Bohme, Arno 12
Bohn, William, *I Remember America* 107
Book Arts 195
"Books Before Baseball," *The National Pastime* 140–141
Boorstin, Daniel 129
Borders, Ila 205
Bossard, Emil 11
Boston Forum (television program) 86
Boston Globe 110, 111, 174
Boston Public Library (BPL) 87, 91, 98, 126, 128, 136, 141, 164, 166
Boston University 87
Bouton, Jim 94, 210; *Ball Four* 84
Brashler, William, *Josh Gibson* 84, 124
Bretz, Julian 14
Brissie, Lou 17
Britten, Helene 199
Brock, Lou 223
Brockway, Zebulon 133
Brooklyn Bums Newsletter 140
Brooklyn Dodgers 15, 106, 115, 140, 185
Broome Community College 186
Broomstick 182
Brotherhood (players' union) 48, 64
Brown Brothers (picture agency) 98
Buckeye International 128
Buffalo Bisons Baseball Club 54
Burns, Ken 158–160, **159**
Business Week 109
"Buyer Beware" (radio program) 19

"Call Me Doctor!" *Educational Record* 58
Camp Grant (Chicago) 150
Campanella, Roy, *Campy's Corner* (radio program) 84–85
Canadian Author & Bookman 182
Cantwell, Robert 109
Capeless, Leona 166, 175
Carl A. Kroch Library, Cornell University 218–222; *see also* Kroch, Carl A.

Index

Carney, Gene 103
Carrano, Ken 173
Case Institute of Technology 10; *see also* Case–Western Reserve University
Case–Western Reserve University 10, 222; *see also* Western Reserve University
Casey, Ethan of *Blue Ear* **194**, 197; and Michael Betzold, *Queen of Diamonds: The Tiger Stadium Story* 155–156, 194
Casey Award 171
The Cauldron 7
Cavallo, Dominick, *Muscles and Morals* 170
"Celebration of Baseball," Cleveland State University 157–158
Celler Hearings 45
Central Intelligence Agency (CIA) 182
Central Park 130
Chadwick, Henry 35, 38, 39, 172; *The American Game of Base Ball* 31
Chambers's Encyclopedia 119
Chandler, Albert "Happy" 79, 114
Charles C. Thomas, Publisher 145
Chase, Hal 104
Chattanooga News-Free Press 70
Chattanooga Times 111
Chicago Cubs 95
Chicago Defender 76
Chicago Historical Society 76, 100
Chicago Library 27
Chicago Sentinel 70–71
Chicago Storm (ball club) 203
Chicago Sun-Times 109
Chicago Tribune 27, 39, 40, 42, 71, 76, 100
Chicago White Sox 76
Churchill, Winston 223
Cincinnati Baseball Club 25, 40, 42, 44, 47, 50–51, 75, 96–97; Collection 43, 46
Cincinnati Enquirer 26, 40, 43, 47, 55, 71, 75
Cincinnati Red Stockings 25, 37
Civil War 36, 37, 131, 132, 134, 157
Civilian Conservation Corps 164
Clement, Amanda 200
Cleveland Art Museum 11, 222
Cleveland Better Business Bureau 18–19, 21, 22, 54
Cleveland Buckeyes 20
Cleveland Indians 5, 11, 13
Cleveland Law Library 104
Cleveland Leader 22, 39, 42, 43

The Cleveland News 8–10, 11, 53, 109, 149
Cleveland Plain Dealer 10, 22, 43, 109
Cleveland Press 10, 11, 22
Cleveland Public Library (CPL) 22, **23**, 24, 35, 38, 40, 43, 45, 47
Cleveland Public Schools 20–21, 22
Cleveland Stadium 21
Cleveland State University 78, 157, 210–211; *see also* Fenn College
Cleveland State University Library 32, 211; *see also* Mills, Dorothy, and research
"The Cliché Expert Testifies on Baseball," *The New Yorker* 36
Clymer, Ted 89
Cobb, Ty 21, 104, 105
Cobb-Speaker Scandal 104
Cobbledick, Gordon 10
Coca-Cola 96, 108
Cochran, Sherman 178
Coen, Miss 117
Coleman, Zella 75
Collier's 60, 108
Collins, Eddie 21 101–102
Collinwood Spotlight 7
Columbo, Detective 76
Comiskey, Charles 103
Commissioner of Baseball 71, 100, 114, 117, 141
ComputerEdge 182
Congregational Christian Historical Society 137
Contemporary Authors 172
Cooperstown, New York 34, 137, 156, 158; *see also* Library of the Hall of Fame and Museum
Cooperstown Symposiums on Baseball and American Culture 77, 156–157, 184
Cornell Alumni News 142, 168–169
Cornell University 13, 15, 16, 21, 51, 52–53, 142–143, 159, 175, 212, 217; *see also* Seymour, Harold, and Cornell University; Mills, Dorothy, and Cornell University
Cox, George B. 93
Craig, Peter, "Monopsony in Manpower," *Yale Law Journal* 46
Cramer, Richard Ben 106
The Crisis 134
Curling 38, 62, 192

Daniels, Audrey 200
D.A.R. (Daughters of the American Revolution) 13–14

Index

Dartmouth College 128
Deckard, Barbara 163
DeMott, Ben 78
Denver Post Tournament 132
Detroit Club 44, 190
Detroit News Call-Bulletin 70
"Diamonds Are Forever" article in *Vancouver Province* 187–188; review of book on baseball exhibition, *Journal of Sport History* 155
Dictionary of American Biography 119
Dictionary of American Scholars 121, 172
Dictionary of International Biography 172
DiMaggio, Joe 106, 114
Doby, Larry 115
Doubleday, Abner 28, 34, 70, 184
Doubleday Field, Cooperstown 184–186
Drew University 15, 28, 73, 80, 140, 141, 160, 172; *see also* Seymour, Harold, and Drew University
Dunham Elementary School 20–21

Eagle Club 35
Easton Press 210
Ebbets Field, Brooklyn 15, 96
Eckhouse, Morris 180
Editors' Forum 182
Education Digest 90–91
Eisenstat, Harry 209
Eisler, Riane, *The Chalice and the Blade* 195
Elementary English 91
Elementary School Journal 91
Emerson, Ralph Waldo 161, 201; "Self-Reliance" 201
Engst, Elaine 219
Estrin, Herman 172
Euclid Beach Park, Cleveland 131
European Union 192
Everybody's Magazine 108
Excelsior Club 35

The Facts (newsletter) 18–19, 54
Falkner, David, biography of Jackie Robinson 188
Fallon, William 100
Faust, Charles "Victory" 188
Fear Not to Sow Because of the Birds **146**; *see also* Keene, Paul
Federal League 98–99, 104
Feller, Bob 20
Fenn College (Cleveland State University) 5, 7, 16, 17, 27, 148
Fenway Park, Boston 65

Fijux, Madame 35
Fimrite, Ron 110
Finch, Herbert 177–178
Finch College, New York 57, 73, 78
"Finder's Guide" (to Seymour Collection), Carl A. Kroch Library 220–221
Flanagan, Ed 16
Flood, Curt 138
Florentine Films 158
Ford, Franklin 111
Fort Wayne Daisies 150, 203
The France 116, 184
Frick, Ford 71–72, 80
"From E for Excrement to V for Vagina: Museum-Hopping through Europe," *Blue Ear* 194
Fultz, Davy, and Fraternity (players' union) 98, 104

Gandil, Chick 110
Garber, Mary 66
Gardella, Danny 78
Garraty, John 156
Gates, Paul W. 13, 14, 52–53, 169, **194**; *see also* Seymour, Harold, and Cornell University; Seymour, Harold, and Paul W. Gates
Gaughran, Richard 185
Giamatti, A. Bartlett 141
Gietschier, Steve 14
Giffen, Patrick 200
The Ginger Kid 174
Ginn and Company 89, 123, 134, 136, 137, 160
Gisolo, Margaret 200
Gladwell, Malcolm, "The Social Life of Paper" 216
Glennie, Jim 200
Globe Pequot Press 146
Gmelch, George 77
Der Goldene Hirsch (hotel) 183
Goldstein, Warren 167, 169, 172
Gonzáles Echevarria, Roberto 167
Gould, Stephen J. 167
Grade Teacher 90
Graney, Jack 5
Gregorich, Barbara 204
Grella, George 168, 186; "Harold Seymour 1910–1992," *The National Pastime* 186
Griffith, Clark 119
Griliches, Diane 30–31
Groff, Patrick, *Word Recognition: The Why and the How* 144–145

Grosset and Dunlap 82, 207
Grosshandler, Stanley 117
Gutman, Dan 173
Guts Muths, Johann 190
Guttman, Allen 151

Hageman, Bert 104
Hall, Alvin 156, 184–186
Hall, Everard 150
Halle Brothers Company 11–12
Halsey, W.F. 129
Hardwick, Herbert, on Effa Manley 84
Harold and Dorothy Seymour Collection, Cornell University 16, 54, 86, 103, 152, 159, 178, 198, 218–222
Harold "Cy" Seymour Sports Lectureship 142
Harold Seymour Annuity Trust Fund 141–142
Harold Seymour Chapter of SABR 222
Harold Seymour Graduate Fellowship Endowment in American History 141
Harper's 58
Harrigan, Patrick 190
Harris, Bucky, *Playing the Game: From Mine Boy to Manager* 31
Harris, Mark 172, 210
Haskell's Indian Junior College 137
Heaphy, Leslie 199
Hearst, William Randolph 27
Heitz, Thomas R. 178–180, 184–**185**
Henderson, E.B. 134
Henderson, Robert W. 28, 70–71
Herrmann, August "Garry" 26, 75, 93
Herrmann Collection, Cooperstown 76, 93, 96, 104
Hill, Anita 150
Historical and Philosophical Society, University of Cincinnati 25, 42
The Historical Society of Western Pennsylvania 124
Hittner, Arthur 190
Hofstadter, Richard 129
Holmes, Oliver Wendell 130
Holway, John 156, 174
Honig, Donald, *Baseball When the Grass Was Green* 84
Hopscotch 192–193
"Hopscotch Wars," *The Tampa Review: Literary Journal of the University of Tampa* 193
Hornsby, Rogers 80, 104, 188
House of David 132
"How Baseball Began," *The New-York Historical Society Quarterly* 125

Howard University *see* Moorland-Spingarn Institute
Hulbert, William 39
Humber, William, on Canadian baseball 188
Hunter, C.M. "Pinky" 5

"I'll Furnish the War: The Story of Yellow Journalism" *Topper* 27
Independent (magazine) 108
Independent (newspaper) 109
Indian Boys' and Girls' Club News 126
Initial Teaching Alphabet (I.T.A.) 81, 117
Instructor 91
International Association of Professional Baseball Players 40
International Baseball Federation 132
International Encyclopedia of Women and Sports 191–102
International Journal of the History of Sport 217–218
International Reading Association 89, 119
Ireland 21; *see also* Moving

Jack & Heinz 132
Jackson, Joe 101–102
James Madison University 185
Japanese Baseball Commissioner 85
Jefferson Encyclopedia 119
Jennings, Hugh 128
Jennison, Christopher 186, **187**
Jewish Exponent 72
John G. White Collection, Cleveland Public Library (CPL) 22
Johnson, Ban 93, 105, 111, 174
Johnson, James Weldon 134
Johnson, Lloyd 178
Johnson, Walter 21
Joss, Addie 20
Journal of American History 114, 124, 167
Journal of Reading 91
Journal of the New-York Historical Society 71
Journal of the Reading Specialist 90
Joyce, James and Nora 219

Kachline, Clifford 112, 117
Kahn, E.J., in *The New Yorker* 108
Kahn, Roger 172
Kammer, Lowell 182
Kanda, Junji 85
Kansas City Monarchs 132
Kansas City Times 53
Kansas Historical Quarterly 62

Keene, Paul, *Fear Not to Sow Because of the Birds* 145–146
Keene (NH) Library 139
The Keene Sentinel 144
Keene State College 149
Kefauver Hearings 45
Keio University 85
Kelly, David 215
Kennedy, Ted 119
Kent State University 199
Kieran, John 66
Kinsella, W.P. 172
Kolko, Gabriel, *The Triumph of Conservatism* 129
Koppett, Leonard 77, 111–112; *A Thinking Man's Guide to Baseball* 84
Kowalski, Gary 144
Kroch, Carl A. 218–219
Kuhn, Bowie 117
Kunz, Dagmar 17

The Labyrinth 193, 194, **195**, 196
Landis, Kenesaw Mountain 99, 102–103, 104, 111, 188
Lanigan, Ernie 26
Lankard, Frank 28
Lardner, Ring 97, 210; *A Busher's Letters* 97; *You Know Me Al* 97
Larrabee, Elizabeth 149
Larrabee and Meyersohn, *Mass Leisure* 107
Lask, Thomas 110, 111
Lawes, Lewis 133
League Alliance 40
A League of Their Own 151
League Park 20–21
Lebovitz, Hal **9**–10
LeClerc, Paul 212
Lehigh University 82
Let's Read 119
Leuchtenburg, William 108
Leuf, A.E.P., *Hygiene for Base Ball Players* 49
Levenson, Alvan 182
Lewis, Franklin "Whitey" 10
The Library Journal 167, 170
Library of Congress 133, 212, 215
Library of the Baseball Hall of Fame and Museum, Cooperstown 26, 41–42, 69, 74–76, 98, 112, **113**, 117, 148, 178, 186
Life 108
Link, Arthur 108
Linotype 7, 8
Literary Digest 60

Little, Brown and Company 136, 143
Little League 127, 151
London Guardian 109
The London Times 171
London Times Higher Educational Supplement 156
Lord's Cricket Grounds, London, England 74
Louisville Times (Kentucky) 72
Louisiana State University 125
Lucas, Henry V. 44, 45
Lucas, John, and Ronald Smith, *Saga of American Sport* 124
Luhrs, Victor, *The Great Baseball Mystery* 100
Luther Standing Bear 164

MacArthur, Douglas 129
Mack, Connie 97
Macmillan reference work on women's sport 192
Madigan, Joe 53
Magee, Lee 104
"Major League Writers" (baseball card set) 172
Manley, Effa 199; *see also* Hardwick, Herbert
Mann, Leslie 132
Mann, Thomas 6
Mapes, Linda 186
Maran, Sally Scott, in *Smithsonian* 201
Marcham, Frederick 14
Markuson, Bruce 190
Marshall, William **191**; *Baseball's Pivotal Era: 1945–1951* 191
Maryland Historical Magazine 62
Masaoka-Ishikawa (importers) 85
Massachusetts Historical Society 141
Mather College of Western Reserve University 17
Mathews, Mitford 36
Mays, Carl 100
McAuley, Ed 10
McCauley, Patrick 200
McClellan, Scott 173
McClure's 108
McGraw, John 97, 128
McKerley Center of Keene 173–175
McKnight, Denny 43, 44
McPhee, Bid 51
Mears Collection (of CPL) 47
Meatless Meat: A Book of Recipes for Meat Substitutes **206**
Memorial School 6

Mencken, H.L. 36, 47
Metropolitan Baseball Club (Staten Island) 47
Metropolitan State College 185
Mexican League 78, 114
Meyer, Sheldon 56–57, 59, 64, 66, 86, 91, 152, 175; *see also* Seymour, Harold, and Oxford University Press
Military Academy at West Point 129
Miller, Marvin 114–115
Miller, Richard L. 173
Millman, Dan 144
Mills, Abraham G. 42, 44; *see also* Abraham G. Mills Papers
Mills, Dorothy Jane Zander (Dorothy Z. Seymour): and Alvin Hall 157; articles 17, 87, 89–91, 191–194, 197–198; awarding medals to women's team 204; and baseball 5, 10–11, 13; on baseball history 189–190, 222; and baseball research 22–32, 60, 87; and Bob Feller 188; book reviews 217–218; book with Paul Keene 145–146; children's books 81–83, 117, 206–208; and *Cleveland News* 8–11, 53, 109; in college 5–10, 6, 12; and Cornell University 198, 212; and curling 191–192; early assistance for Harold Seymour 13, 18–19, 23–24; and editing 7, 9, 88–89, 116, 119, 123–124, 136, 143–144, 166–182; education books 143, 146–147; and Elaine Engst 220; father 8; and Fenn College (Cleveland State University) 5–10, 12–18, 27, 210; first computer in Keene office 145; and Halle Brothers Company, 11–12; meets Harold Seymour 12–13; with Harriett Walderdorff 183; in high school 6–7; historical fiction 102, 165–166, 182–184, 192–196; and hopscotch 192–193; independent research 28–32, 37, 40–41, 45, 47, 49, 50, 59–61, 85–86, 88, 91, 95, 96, 98, 104, 107, 108, 125–126, 129–135, 136–139, 148–149, 196–197; in Irish office 118; joint interviews with HS 78–79; joint research trips with HS 24–25, 58, 59, 64–65, 74–76, 112–113, 148; joint work with HS on articles 57–58; joint work with HS on *Baseball: The Early Years* 59–66, 68, 155–156; joint work with HS on *Baseball: The Golden Age* 74–76, 79–80, 84–88, 91–108; joint work with HS on *Baseball: The Modern Era* (unpublished) 112–115, 137–138; joint work with HS on *Baseball: The People's Game* 10, 115, 124–137, 163–164; joint work with HS on Better Business Bureau publications 18–19; joint work with HS on book reviews and forewords 114, 124–125, 155–156; joint work with HS on dissertation 19–24, 33–51; joint work with HS on speeches, 156–158; joint work with HS on University of Buffalo publications 54; joint work with HS to obtain publisher 5, 54–57; and journalism 6–11, 17–18; with Justine Siegal 202; leaves teaching 87; on libraries 212–216; library work 22, 126; marries HS 17; marries Roy Mills 184, 187; and Mather College of Western Reserve University (Case-Western Reserve University) 17–18, 20–21; meets HS 13; meets Roy Mills 184; and mother 143, 165; in Naples office 196; her newsletters 210; office in Keene 178; organizes material 45, 47, 62–64; and Oxford University Press, 166–167, 175; prepares outlines 88, 97, 101, 138–139; her promotional work 118, 121, 156; recognition for 175, 179, 181, 186–188, 218, 198; releases baseball collection to Cornell 176–178; on research 32, 60–62, 196, 212–216; her resentment at lack of recognition 160–164; her role in the Seymour books 217; with Roy Mills 224; on self-publishing 194–195, 205–206; with Seymour Collection at Cornell 219, 221; with Seymour Medal 181; and teaching 17–18, 20–22, 54, 59, 80–81; with three Seymour books and Medal 189; trips alone 26, 183–184; trips with HS 73–74, 76–77, 116, 138; and vegetarian cooking 105–106; websites 97, 208–210; and Western Reserve University (Case-Western Reserve University) 20–21; with William Marshall 191; and women's baseball 199–205; work with Ken Burns 157–160; work on women's baseball 147–152; writing 119, 123, 144–147, 191–193, 194, 197; on writing 205; in Zürich at bookstore 196
Mills, Roy 184, 187, 191, 192, 198
Mills College of Education 80
Milwaukee Journal 53
Missouri Historical Society 27
Missouri Historical Society Bulletin 62

"Modern Scholars in Ancient Garb"
  (pamphlet) 87
Mohican Club 35
Møller, Jørn 192
Moorland-Spingarn Institute of Howard
  University 128
Moreland, George, *Balldom* 31
Morgan, Jill 207
Morris, Lloyd, on New York 108
Moss, Dick 114
Mount Holyoke 147–148
Moving: Asheville, NC 123; Buffalo, NY 54; Chester, NY 80; Cleveland, OH 20, 21; Fairhope, AL 121; Ireland 116–117; Keene, NH 138; Mars Hill, NC 122; New Rochelle, NY 57; New York, NY 69; Newton, MA 123–124; West Newbury, MA 86
Munsey's 108
Murdock, Eugene 105, 124; biography of Ban Johnson 174
Murdock, Stephen 173
Murphy, Charles 95
Murphy, Elizabeth 149
Murphy, Robert (his players' union) 115
Myss, Caroline 144, 182

Naiman, Joe 173
Nankivell, J.H. 164
Nasaw, David, *Children of the City* 170
National Agreement 45, 92
National Association of Amateur Base Ball Players 134
National Association of Base Ball Players 37
National Baseball Federation 132
The National Chronicle 31
National Commission 26, 42, 75, 92, 93
National Endowment for the Humanities 216
National League 38–39, 40, 41, 42, 43, 44, 45, 45, 48, 49, 50, 63, 94
National Museum, Dublin 138
The National Pastime 171
National Recreation Association 134
Naval Academy Archives 129
Nebel, Long John, his all-night talk show 84
Nebraska Indians 133
Negro American League 20–21
Nemec, David, on the American Association 188
New England Base Ballist 31, 37
New Haven College 28

New York Age 164
New York Clipper 31, 36, 37, 39, 43
New York Giants 115
New York Herald 31
New-York Historical Society 57; *see also* "How Baseball Began"
New York History Journal 110
New York Knickerbocker Club 35, 62, 190, 212
New York Mercury 31, 43
New York Public Library (NYPL) 13, 28, 29–31, 32, 35, 36, 38, 39, 50, 57, 59, 60, 67, 85, 95, 98, 212–213
New York Review of Books 167
New York Telegram and Sun 70
New York Times 31, 42, 60, 61, 65, 66, 69, 100, 110, 117, 119, 167, 169, 182, 189, 204
New York University 167
New York World 31
New York Yankees 104, 114
New Yorker 193, 212, 214
Newark News 70
Newburgh Evening News 82
Newsletters 210
Newsweek 58
Newton (MA) libraries 137
North American Society for Sport History (NASSH) 172, 222
North Carolina Wesleyan University 174
North Shore Community College 86–87, 113
Northeastern Illinois University 216–217
Northern League 205
Northwestern League 40
The Norway 184
Novick, Lynn 158

Obojski, Robert, book on the minors 84
Ocala Lightning (ball club) 203
O'Donnell, Doris 10, 11, **65**, 149
Office of Strategic Services (OSS) 182
Official Base Ball Record (newspaper) 42
Ohio Historical Review 72
Ohio Historical Society Journal 32
Ohiyesa 164
Olin Library, Cornell University 32
Olmsted, Frederick Law 130
Olympic Games 34, 151
Oneonta Daily Star 157
The Oprah Winfrey Show 182
Orange County Community College 80, 86
Osborne, Thomas 133, 164

Index

Outing 60
Outlook 108
Overbeck, Harry 43
Overfield, Joseph 111
Oxford Companion to Sports and Games 119
Oxford University Press, New York 55, 67, 68, 69, 71, 77, 84, 189–190, 210; Oxford University Press, England 73; *see also* Meyer, Sheldon

Paige, Satchel 132
Palmer, Harry, *Athletic Sports in America* 31
Parade Grounds of Prospect Park (Brooklyn) 15, 97, 106, 140, 209
Parma Heights School System 22
Patrician Publications 206
Payne, Palmer 86
Peck and Snyder (sporting goods company) 39
Pelham School System 59
Pennsylvania Historical Society 134
Pepe, Maria 151
Pepper, George Wharton, on Philadelphia 108
Perry, Scott 100
"The Perspective of History," *Topper* 17
Petee, Charles 56
Peterson, Robert, *Only the Ball Was White* 84
Peverelly, Charles, *American Sports and Pastimes* 31
Pipeline to Business and Industry 54
Pitman, James 81, 82
Pitman Publishing Company 81
Pittsburgh Pirates 71
Pittsburgh Press 71
Players' League 48, 49, 64
Players' National League Official Guide 48
Playground and Recreation Association 136
Plaza de Toros, Madrid 74
Porter's Spirit of the Times 26, 36
Povich, Shirley 110
Prentice-Hall 55
Presbyterian College 16
Preston, Howard 10, 109
Publishers Weekly 109, 111, 169
Pulliam, Harry 93
Pythian Club 134
Pytlak, Frank 132

Queen Elizabeth II 116, 183
Queens University, Ontario 174

Quinn, J.A.R. "Bob" 26

Radcliffe College 148
Radio America 156
Randall, Randolph 7, 13
Randel, Don M. 176
Rare Book and Manuscript Collections of Cornell University Library 62, 177
Reader's Guide to Periodical Literature 96
The Reading Teacher 90
Recreation Magazine (Playground) 126
Rhodes, Frank H.T. 142, 176
Rice, Grantland 10
Richards, Huw 156
Richter, Francis C., *History and Records of Baseball* 31
Rickey, Branch 105, 209
Riess, Steven 101, 216; *Touching Base* 170
"The Rise of Major-League Baseball to 1891" (dissertation) 19, 33, 54, 56
Ritter, Larry 172; *The Glory of Their Times* 107
Robbins, John, *Diet for a New America* 144
Roberts, James 156
Robinson, Jackie 49–50, 66, 70, 114, 188; his radio program 84
Robinson, Wilbert 106, 140, 185
Robinson, William "Yank" 43
Robison, Frank DeHaas 20
Rochester Red Wings 79, 209
Rockford Peaches 150
Rogosin, Donn, *Invisible Men* 84
Rose, Pete 104
Rothstein, Arnold 100, 103
The Rotterdam 116
Roy Hobbs Baseball 201
Royal Canadian Air Force 184
Run, Rabbit, Run: The Hilarious and Mostly True Tales of Rabbit Maranville 156, 174
Ruth, Babe 20, 105, 106, 111, 119

Saint Bonaventure College 128
St. James Encyclopedia of Popular Culture 193
"St. Louis and the Union Baseball War," *Missouri Historical Review* 57
St. Louis Cardinals 209
St. Louis Globe-Democrat 27, 43
St. Louis Historical Society 57
St. Louis Republican 27, 43
San Francisco Chronicle 72
Saturday Evening Post 108
Saturday Review Syndicate 70

Sayles, John, *Eight Men Out* 160
The Sceptre **193**, 194–196, 200, 205, 206
Schlagball 74
Schlesinger, Arthur, Jr. 215
Schloss Fuschl 183
Schomburg Library 128
Schwab, Charles 59
Scoil Ursula (the Ursuline School), County Sligo 117
Scott, Foresman 119
Scribner's (bookstore) 73
Scribner's *The Armchair Book of Baseball* 125
Scully, Gerald, *The Business of Major League Baseball* 84
Scully Collection, Chicago Historical Society 100
Seattle Post-Intelligencer Book World 109
Seaver, Tom 176
Segar, Charlie 80
Severance Hall 222
Seymour, Harold: articles 17–18, 27, 57–58, 87–119; awarded doctorate 53; book reviews and forewords 124–125, 154, 155–156; books republished 210–211; and Brooklyn 15; and Cleveland Better Business Bureau 18, 21–22; Cooperstown **94**; and Cornell University 15–16, 141–143; death 175–176; depression and illness 108, 120, 125, 139–140, 143–154, 172–174; desire to display degree 58; desire to include notes 58–59; dissertation topics 34–51; doctoral dissertation 13–14, 19, 51–53; with Dorothy **82**; and Drew University 15, 80, 141, 160; early life 15–17; and Fenn College (Cleveland State University) 12–13, 16–17; and Finch College 57, 73, 78, 80, 180; first marriage 17–18; on future of baseball history 188–189; interviews 78; on journalism 17–18; lack of interest in research 59–60; love for baseball 107; marries Dorothy 17; meets Dorothy 12–13; and Mills College of Education 80; at Monroe, NY **14**; and North Shore Community College 86–87; nostalgia 140–141; and oral exam for doctorate 52; and Orange County Community College 80, 86; passing 176; and Presbyterian College 16–17; radio and television appearances 19, 54, 66–67, 84–85, 86, 109; receives contract for *Baseball: The Early Years* 57; receives contract for *Baseball: The Golden Age* 86; receives contract for *Baseball: The Modern Era* (unpublished) 74; receives contract for *Baseball: The People's Game* 122; recognition for 84, 121, 125, 141, 155–157, 160, 171–176, 178–181, 184–186, 200–202, 212; reviews of all three Seymour books 216–217; speeches 28, 156–158; stops work on *Baseball: The People's Game* 160; and teaching 15–16; and University of Buffalo 54; work with John Sayles 160; work with Ken Burns 158–160; writing style 58, 105, 109, 121–122, 135, 223
Seymour, James Bentley "Cy" 15
Seymour, Kevin 174
Seymour Medal (The Dr. Harold and Dorothy Seymour Award) 124, 179–181, 184, 187, 190–191, 209–210
Seznec, Alain 142–143
Shafer, Boyd 32
Shannon, Mike 171
Shea, Bill 115
Shealy, Norman 144
Shively, Harold 86
Shuy, Roger 89
Siegal, Justine (Justine Warren) 200–201
Sinclair, Upton 6
Singer, Mark 212, 214
Sinnen, Anne 12
Sisler, George 100
Sister Perpetua 117
"64,000 Question" (television program) 54
Smith, Howard K. 66–67
Smith, Leverett 174; *The American Dream and the National Game* 84
Smith, Red 172, 176
Smith, Robert: biography of Babe Ruth 84; book on baseball 31
Smith College 147–148
Social Club 35
Social Security Administration 119–120, 175
Society for American Baseball Research (SABR) 102, 112, 117–118, 140, 156, 173, 174, 178–181, 186, 187–188, 190–191, 198, 215, 222
Sommer, Francis 22, **23**
Southern Workman 134
Spalding, Albert G. 34, 40, 48; *America's National Game* 39
Spalding Collection, New York Public Library 28, 39, 60, 212

Spanish-American War 27
Speaker, Tris 21, 104
Spink, Alfred H., *The National Game* 31
Spink, C.C. Johnson 24, 80, 121
Spink, J.G. Taylor 24, **25**, 64, 113, 213
Spirit of the Times 39
Spitball: The Literary Baseball Magazine 171
Sporting Life 42, 43, 45
The Sporting News 14, 22, 24, 25, 26, 27, 39, 42, 48, 57, 59, 65, 67, 80, 100, 111, 112, 113, 117, 122, 213
Sports Illustrated 109, 110, 111
Sports Illustrated Book Club 112
Stanton, Elizabeth Cady 148, 201
Stars and Stripes 99
Steffens, Lincoln 92
Stein, Irving 174
Steisel, Susanna 159
Stengel, Casey 66
Sterling, Jack, radio program 84
Stevens, Harry 96
Stillpoint Publishing Company 143–144, 165, 182
Suffragettes 96
Sunday, Billy 188, biography of 188
Sunday Oregonian 70
Suntala, Jeff 180
"Surf Baths and Dumbbells," *Baseball Digest* 58
Sussman, Gerald 109

Taft, Howard 100
"Take Me Out to the Ball Game" 186
Takewambait Club 35
Taylor, Frederick 131
"Teaching History Through the Medium of American Sports History" (proposal) 87
Thomas, Clarence 150
Thomas, Henry W., biography of Walter Johnson 188
Thompson, Chuck 66
Thorn, John 125, 171
Thun-Hohenstein, Eleanore 183
Time 58
Times Literary Supplement (London, England) 109
Toad Charts, Paper Faces, and Other Ideas for Visual Comprehension 146–**147**
Toledo Club 49
Topkis, Jay 62
Toporcer, George "Specs" 79–80, 98, 108, 209

Topp, Richard 174
Toronto Blue Jays 201
Tuchman, Barbara 166
Tucker Center for Research on Girls and Women in Sport, University of Minnesota 202
Turner, Lorenzo Dow 134
Tuskegee Institute 128
Twelve Who Made the Game (unpublished) 116

Uniform Players' Contract 51
Union Association 17, 44, 45, 63
Union College 77
"Unions Fail in Organized Baseball," *Industrial Bulletin* 57–58
Unitarian Universalist Association 137
United States Copyright Office 208
U.S. Navy 129
U.S.S. *Powhatan* 129
University of Buffalo 54, 87
University of Chicago 134
University of Cincinnati 130, 173
University of Rochester 168, 186
University of Victoria Library, British Columbia 32
Utter, Gus 8–9

Vassar College 148
Veeck, Bill 10, 100, 115; autobiography 84
Viau, Leon 47
Virginia Kirkus Service 111, 167
Voigt, David Q. 32, 114
Von der Ahe, Chris 43
von Habsburg-Lothringen, Heinrich 183
von Melnhof, Mayr 183
von Ribbentrop, Joachim 182
von Schuschnigg, Kurt 183
von Starhemberg, Ernst Rüdiger 183
von Starhemberg, Heinrich 183

Wagenheim, Karl, biography of Babe Ruth 84
Wagner, Honus 190
Waite, L.C. 40
Walderdorff, Harriett 183
Waldorf-Astoria 96
Walker, Moses Fleetwood "Fleet" 49, 70, 84, 134
Walker, Stanley, *City Editor* 108
Walker, William D. 213
Wallace, Ralph 208–**209**
Walnut Acres (company) 145

Wambsganss, Bill 20
Ward, John Montgomery 188; in *Lippincott's Magazine* 42, 48
Warwick School System 80–82
Wasaja 164
Waseda University 85
Washington, D.C., Army Times 71
Washington Post 110, 167
Weaver, Buck 174
Webb, Royce, *SportsJones* 197
Weiss, Alta 149, 199–200
Weitz, John 182
Wellesley College 147–148
Wellington, Charmaine 144, 208
West Point Military Academy 129
Western Reserve Historical Society 222
Western Reserve University 10, 21, 66, 72; *see also* Case-Western Reserve University
Western Union 96
White, Dolores "Dolly" Brumfield 203
White, E.B. 219
White Motor Company 128
Whiting, Robert, *The Chrysanthemum and the Bat* 85
Who's Who in America 211
Who's Who of American Women 211
Widener Library of Harvard University 137
Wiebe, Robert, *The Search for Order* 129
Wiley, Bell I.: *Billy Yank* 37; *Johnny Reb* 37
Will, George, *Men at Work* 171
William C. Brown Publishing Company 175
Wilson, Edmund, *To the Finland Station* 197

Wilson, Sloan, *The Man in the Gray Flannel Suit* 54
Winston-Salem Journal 66
Wish, Harvey 66
Wittke, Carl 72
Wittkin, Herb 174
"A Woman's Work" (article), *Blue Ear* 197–198
Women in baseball 139, 147–152, 199–205
Women in journalism 11, 65–66
Women's Baseball League 200
Women's Committee of SABR 199
Women's Hall of Fame 200
Woodward, Stanley, *Sports Page* 108
World Series 95, 100
World War I 99, 114, 164
World War II 132
Wright, Harry 28, 32, 37; correspondence 28, 38, 39, 41, 43, 60
Writers' Journal 182

Yankee Stadium 78
Yardley, Jonathan 110, 167
YMCA 134
Young, Denton "Cy," biography of 188
Young, Dick 172
Young, Sherman Plato 28, 73
Young Children 91
Young-Sowers, Meredith 144, 182

Zaharias, Mildred "Babe" Didrickson 151
Zang, David 187–188, **190**; *Fleet Walker's Divided Heart* 187
Zinn, Howard 129
zu Sayn-Wittgenstein-Sayn, Marianne 183

www.ingramcontent.com/pod-product-compliance
Ingram Content Group UK Ltd.
Pitfield, Milton Keynes, MK11 3LW, UK
UKHW041936140426
5217IPUK00014B/515